THE QUARTET

CARE LIVES OF I
HOMEI

6-10-2010
Nazareth house chapel.

JOHN MICHAEL MURPHY

Crooked Scythe Press

Copyright

Published by Crooked Scythe Press
22 The Demesne
North Seaton Village
Ashington
Northumberland
NE639TW

ISBN: 978-0-9955328-1-6

Printed by CreateSpace

Cover Photo: The Quartet in 1934 Copyright © Crooked Scythe Press

About the Author

Michael Murphy was born in Newcastle upon Tyne in 1947 and is married and has 7 children. He received his academic education and professional teaching and social work training at the Universities of York, Leeds, Durham, Dundee and Northumbria.

He has worked as a Head of History Department and Head of Faculty in Secondary Schools and as a Senior Child Caseworker and the Senior Child Protection Manager for a large Northern English City. This latter role and that as the Chair of a Catholic Diocesan Safeguarding Commission, involved extensive experience of managing institutional abuse investigations.

Now retired he pursues his abiding interest in genealogy and family history and especially the issues of identity and memory.

Dedication

This book is dedicated to my wife, Margaret,
who 'put in a shift' in preparing this book for publication.

Acknowledgements

The following persons have been of particular assistance in obtaining or supplying documents and other information used in compiling this book.

Michael Porter

Sister John, Nazareth House, Sligo

The rest of the Nazareth Sisters' Congregation at Sligo (especially Sisters Bernadine, Margaret and Gertrude)

The Sisters of Mercy

Margaret McGowan-Judge

Imelda Fitzsimons (nee McGowan)

Introduction

This book attempts to understand what it was like to live and work in an Irish Catholic boys' home in the 1920's and 1930's. Individual biographies of four of the 'Homeboys', the 'Quartet' shown in the book cover photograph, are interwoven into the central narrative.[1] The life of the sole survivor, 94 year old Michael Laurence Porter, forms the central thread of the book.

The full life histories of the Quartet are completed in the second volume: The Quartet: After-Care Lives of Irish Catholic Homeboys.

Preface

In 2011 a terminally ill, 59 year old woman, Valerie Porter, asked to see me at the home she shared with her 90 year old father, Michael, in Newbiggin by the Sea, Northumberland. The request surprised me because my contact with the family hitherto had been verbal sparring with Michael outside church after Sunday Mass about our shared interests in sport, history and Ireland.

Valerie told me of her fears about her father's ability to cope alone after her death and especially about his lack of social contact. She was also grieved that the family line would die out as Michael had no great grandchildren. My response, assuring her that I would visit regularly and 'keep an eye on' her father and would write an account of his life, seemed to greatly ease her and she died peacefully a few days later.

When I agreed to document Michael's life I knew what his daughter did not: that he had spent his entire childhood in institutional care in Ireland. Some years previously he had unburdened himself of this information to me in the privacy of my home when I had helped him with his genealogy researches. He had never told his wife or any of his 3 children about his care past, carefully steering discussions away from this topic. I had repeatedly advised and encouraged him to tell his family about his care past, even offering to do this for him-but he could not bring himself to do this, telling me that I could inform them about this after his death.

Why had Michael told me, a relative stranger, about his care life, and not those closest to him? One reason may have been that which David Thomson observed: 'It is easier to speak of misery to someone emotionally detached'.[2] A much more important factor was his knowledge of my professional background of several decades experience in child care and child safeguarding. This included managing well over a hundred investigations into institutional abuse as the Senior Child Protection Manager for a large northern city and the Chair of a northern English Catholic Diocesan Safeguarding Commission. I had also conducted a national survey of sexual abuse by clergy and religious in the

vii

Catholic Church in England and Wales.[3] Throughout the book I draw from this professional childcare experience in discussing and commenting upon events.

Prior to retraining in Social Work I had been an historian, teaching in English secondary schools as Head of History and Head of Humanities Faculty. Both professional experiences, historical and social scientific, are interwoven into the book's narrative, and both can be heard in the author's 'voice'.

Without professional childcare experience I would have been most reluctant to write an account of Michael Porter's life. Exploring the long-hidden and denied experiences with a 90 year old was always likely to stir up traumatic feelings. It would have been irresponsible to have done so without the time, energy, experience and emotional resilience to deal with these feelings: well-intentioned efforts without relevant experience can unintentionally produce damaging consequences.

The adult formerly in care can tend to see their experiences as unique and may lack a context to help them make sense of what happened to them. In the process of exploring his past with Michael I introduced many anonymous case studies from my child care work to enable him to compare his experiences with these.[4] [5] This previous group-work with children in care had resulted in the child participants significantly altering their self-perception that each was uniquely disadvantaged. Indeed, by the end of the group work process, each of them had felt that they were relatively fortunate. Michael avidly drank in the accounts of others who had experienced care.

The following extract outlines the 3 core concerns that I included in a letter on Michael's behalf to the Sisters of Nazareth who had cared for him in Sligo:

- 'Lack of family life, family information and contact when in care
- Lack of love
- Lack of information and communication'.

Although the available records were sparse the Sisters and Sister John in particular, added their own verbal and additional material, and greatly helped me locate other critical information about former residents. This led to contact with two of the daughters of William McGowan, Margaret McGowan Judge and Imelda Fitzsimons, who supplied me with a vast amount of correspondence between their father and another member of the Quartet, Paddy Baker, together with their own oral recollections. Margaret and Imelda's repository was sufficiently comprehensive to enable me to widen the focus of the book to include full-life biographies of all four Quartet members.

As the research widened and more and more primary material was uncovered about his fellow 'Homeboys', especially the Quartet members, Michael underwent a fundamental alteration in his understanding of, and attitude to, his care life, his carers, and his family of origin. This, however, took time. It took some three to four years of intense discussions and examination of new information before Michael reframed his understanding of his whole life experiences.

Despite the amount of research conducted for this book I am conscious of its imperfections; aware too that further documentation may cause modifications of perspective. As other authors put it so well:

'We are, nevertheless, keenly aware how necessary it is for us to add a note of diffidence. We dare not hope that we have discovered every early reference ...... nor that those who follow will find no gaps or inaccuracies; we can only hope that however patently they have been caused by our lack of diligence or of erudition, they will be brought to our attention with gentleness'.[6]

The lives of the poor tend to leave fewer records for analysis than those of the more affluent or famous. A guiding principle in the research of the Quartet's lives has been to afford the lives of the 'commoner' as much care, diligence and seriousness as would be given to the most notable in society.

This first volume of the Quartet's lives book is arranged chronologically and many of the chapters can be read independently. A theme throughout the book is memory and adult recollection of childhood events. The book seeks to:

- understand life in a Catholic children's home in Ireland in the 1920's and 1930's
- locate this care in context
- describe the lives of the boys in the immediate period after they left care, and to
- reflect on what happened and why.

Ireland: Significant Places in the Quartet's Childhood

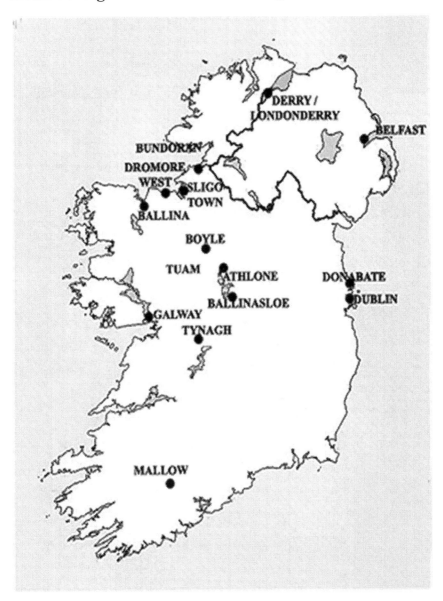

Table of Contents

PART 1

NAZARETH HOUSE, SLIGO: CHILDHOOD (1925-1936)

Chapter1.1: A Parcel is Delivered

1.1.1. The Quartet

The four boys shown below were Brass Quartet prize winners at the 1934 Sligo Feis Ceoil[7] where they represented Nazareth House Boys' Home.

| William Patrick McGowan Born 1921 in County Sligo | Patrick Joseph Baker Born 1923 in County Sligo | Michael Laurence Porter Born 1921 in County Galway | William Walsh Born in 1920 in County Galway |

Illustration 1: The Quartet in 1934

The boys all hailed from poor, Irish, Catholic families. They were otherwise unconnected with each other until each of them was taken into care at Nazareth House between 1925-1928.

1.1.2. From Galway to Sligo

Michael Laurence Porter was taken into care at the age of four in August 1926. His move to Sligo town, to a Catholic boys' home, took him nearly a hundred miles from his family in County Galway.

Michael was placed so far away from his family because of the lack of suitable care places nearer home. In 1910 the Poor Sisters of Nazareth had taken over *Merville*[8], the childhood home of the poet W. B. Yeats,[9] for their two care homes. One of these homes was to accommodate boys drawn from one of the five counties in the Province of Connacht. The other home housed elderly men and women in need of care in their declining years. The resulting 'Homes' were then renamed 'Nazareth House'.[10]

So many aspects of the new place were distinctively different from Michael's Galway home. The newly built boys' home was vast in size. There were a large number of boys accommodated there, including attention-demanding babies. There was the unfamiliar sight of the nuns who staffed the home. These Sisters were clad in dark all-enveloping habits. Their faces were partly hidden by veil and coif. Yet Michael, now a man in his 95th year and possessing an excellent long-term memory, cannot remember anything about such a momentous event in his young life.

From the day of his arrival in Sligo Michael never spent a night outside the Home until he left Nazareth House in 1937. After being handed over to the care of the Sisters he was placed in the nursery, remaining there with the other young boys, some of them babies, until he reached 7 years of age.

1.1.3. Records

Michael's blank memory of the details of coming into care, who brought or accompanied him, or by what form of transport he travelled, is also a feature in the home records. In later years the St. Vincent de Paul Society, a Catholic Charitable Organisation, provided a transport and escort system for children coming to Nazareth House in Sligo.[11] As this system had not begun in 1926, the most likely explanation was that the child was brought by his Parish Priest, Father Bowes, by car.

The Nazareth House Admissions Register lists the boy, Michael Laurence Porter, as the 289th boy admitted to the Home since it had been opened in 1910. He was brought to Nazareth House on Monday 23rd August, 1926. The following barebones information was recorded on his entry to care:

Name: Michael Laurence Porter
Date of Birth: 30/09/1921
Baptised: St. Laurence's Church, Tynagh, Loughrea, Co. Galway
Father's Name: Laurence Porter
Occupation: Labourer
Father: Living at Tynagh

Mother's Name: Margaret Coen
Grandmother: Annie Conway, Killeen, Ballyshall, Tynagh[12]

There is no signed consent on file from parent, guardian or other competent family member entrusting Michael to the care of the Sisters of Nazareth. Despite this absence it is likely that his care admission was 'voluntary' as there is no Court Order committing him to care and Nazareth House was not an Industrial School.

In December 1927 Reverend Mother had written from Sligo to Michael's Parish Priest requesting that he send her the copy of Michael's Baptismal Certificate, promised but not sent 17 months earlier when Michael had been admitted. The certificate was needed to enable Michael to make his first Holy Communion. The reply from Father Bernard M. Bowes, Parish Priest of St. Laurence's Church, Tynagh, County Galway included the information:

I wish to thank you most sincerely for taking this little boy, ... and it was great charity - besides educating him you have saved his life, as had he been left here, I believe he would have contracted consumption. The Nuns of Ballinasloe kindly took his little sister.[13]

The priest made no enquiry about Michael nor gave any additional information about his family in Galway. The one and a half page letter is mainly concerned with apologies, thanking the Sisters and asking to be remembered to the priest's friends in Sligo.

The sparse (and yet inaccurate) details above[14] are virtually all that was recorded by the Nazareth Order and Catholic Church about a child entrusted to care for eleven and a half years of his childhood.[15] The whole admission process feels rather like a parcel being delivered.

1.1.4. Memories and Nightmares

Although Michael could remember nothing of his life at Nazareth House from the ages of four to about ten years he did retain two 'memories' of his life before care. These took the form of regularly occurring nightmares during the first half of his life in care.

His first nightmare found him wandering with an older child, a girl, in boggy countryside. She then pushed him into a stream. He panicked and was drowning until the girl eventually pulled him out. She then took the dripping, shivering boy off somewhere; he never found out where.[16] Michael always believed this to be merely a nightmare, not a memory of an actual event.

His second regular nightmare saw him standing outside the kitchen window at home, looking towards the house. He saw men carrying a large wooden box out of the front door, slowly moving away from him. He knew that his mother was in the box and he screamed as the box containing his mother edged away from him down the long pathway to the front gate. No-one seemed to notice him; no-one consoled him. This memory always ended at this point with nothing before it or after. No matter how hard he tried to recall other images or people he could not do so. Nor could he conjure up his mother's face. His only concrete memory of his first 11 years or so of life was of a wooden box containing his mother leaving him forever. That memory of the house, the shape and size of it, and the garden and path, remained absolutely clear in his mind; so clear that he could have drawn the scene.

The emotions he felt at seeing the box were seared in his memory: despair, loss, confusion, and anger; above all a sense of powerlessness to stop her leaving him. Many a night at Nazareth House saw him disturbed and awakened by this most vivid and concrete recollection. His abiding memory of his childhood is his sense of having no-one to belong to and being entirely alone in the world.[17]

1.1.5. Misperception of Being an Orphan

Michael Porter came to the false belief that he was an orphan, indeed a person without any relatives, totally alone in the world from the time he entered until after he left Nazareth House. He believed this *despite* two mentions of 'family' to him during his career in care.[18] No-one who cared for him during his childhood and young adulthood actively contradicted this false belief; nor was the fact that he had a sister ever mentioned to him. He had retained no memory of her or any other family member. Consequently, although he was not an orphan, he came to believe that he was entirely alone in the world with no living relative, nor anyone who cared for or about him.

1.1.6. Memory

The two memory nightmares were in fact real events in Michael's life. The deeply remembered box incident had occurred when Michael was not quite three years old. Yet the major trauma of his removal into care when he was 4 years old troubled his memory not at all. How selective and idiosyncratic adult recollection of childhood events can be is explored throughout the book.[19]

1.1.7. Michael Porter's Family Background

Father Bowes's letter had indicated 'child rescue', as the reason why Michael and his sister Sadie (Mary Bridget) were taken into care in 1926: the rescue was from risk of death from tuberculosis. An examination of Michael's family circumstances and background suggests a cluster of other, related factors that offer a fuller picture of why he 'was let go' from his family.

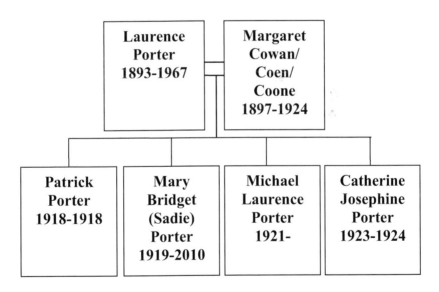

Illustration 2: Family Background of Michael Laurence Porter

Michael Laurence Porter had been born on 3rd October in Tynagh, Loughrea, County Galway, the son of Laurence Porter and Margaret Cowan (Coen or Coone).[20]

Michael's father, Laurence, was the second of 10 children, born in Tynagh village, County Galway, to Catholic parents in 1893. He worked as a small farmer and then labourer.[21] Before marriage in 1918 Laurence had lived with his widowed mother and siblings in Tynagh village, his work helping to keep the family together after the death of his father.

Laurence's wife, Margaret Cowan had been born into a consumption riddled family in the estate Gate Lodge at Pallas, Tynagh. She was the second of seven children. Two of Margaret's younger sisters had died of consumption as well as her father and maternal grandmother when living in the Gate Lodge. The Cowans, however, were able to move into a new and healthier home as a result of the Land Acts.

1.1.8. Land Legislation and New House

In the late nineteenth century, and especially in the early twentieth century the British government belatedly conceded the demands from the peasant tenants in Ireland to purchase their holdings. A series of Land Acts transferred much of the land to the people who had worked it. The British Government provided capital to buy out most of the larger landowners paying them compensation for the loss of their holdings. The former tenants were then offered the freehold on the land they had worked.[22] The graph shows: the miniscule number of land holdings transferred before the formation of the Irish National Land League in County Mayo in 1879 and the subsequent Land War.

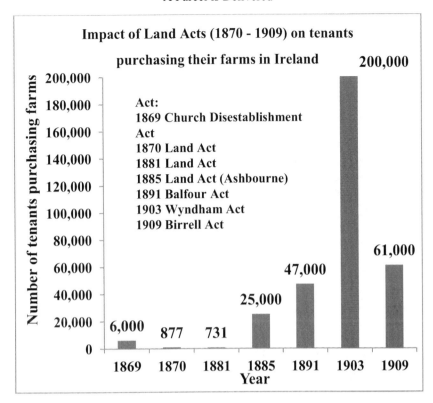

Illustration 3: Impact of Irish Land Acts (1870-1909) on Tenants Purchasing Their Farms

It illustrates the importance of the 1903 (Wyndham) Act that accounted for nearly as many holdings being transferred as the other 6 Acts combined. These Land Acts directly affected at least three of the Quartet's family situations.[23]

Michael Porter benefitted from these changes: he was born in the new 2 storey blue-Bangor slated house erected by his maternal grandmother, Mary Cowan on land gained by Land legislation transfer.

Illustration 4: 'Land Act' New House, c. 1919-Birthplace of Michael Porter

1.1.9. Family Formation and Collapse: tuberculosis

Michael Porter's parents began their married life 'living-in' in the new house (shown above) together with the head of the household, his mother's unmarried brother, John and John's three younger brothers.

Tuberculosis had been endemic in the Cowan family of Michael's mother, Margaret.

'A young person contemplating marriage in Ireland could never forget tuberculosis. Marriage to an infected person could mean a short marriage'.[24]

Laurence Porter, Michael's father, ignored this widespread fear when he married Margaret Cowan. As Margaret was some six months pregnant by the time the couple married in January 1918 this suggests some hesitation on the part of Laurence, and possibly his extended family, to marrying into a consumptive family. The prevailing religious and social pressures to regularise an out-of-wedlock pregnancy obviously prevailed, however, (and quite possibly the genuine love of the young couple for each other).

Laurence and Margaret's first child, Patrick, had died at three months old of whooping cough with no doctor in attendance, suggesting a lack of money for a doctor.[25] Sadie (Mary Bridget) was the second born child in 1919, in the newly built house.[26] Michael Laurence followed in 1921, and a sister, Catherine Josephine completed the family in 1924. By the time of Catherine Josephine's birth in 1924 another of the household, Michael's uncle, Michael Cowan, had died of consumption, at the age of 18 years.

Two vulnerabilities in Michael's family background have been mentioned: infant mortality and endemic tuberculosis in his mother's family. Infant mortality at 12% in rural Connacht, the Irish Province in which Galway was situated, was significantly lower than the 20% rate in urban Ireland in the early 20th Century. Yet Michael's family experienced a 50% child death rate before the age of 5 years when the youngest child, Catherine Josephine, died in her second year of life in 1925. Furthermore the winnowing of his mother's family's continued with 4 of the 7 children of Patrick and Mary Cowan dying before the age of 30 years.[27]

Michael himself was a small child who had contracted polio at some stage in his early life. This left him partially 'disabled' in his left leg. It is not known if this condition occurred at home or after entry to Nazareth House.[28] His sister, Mary Bridget (Sadie), was very short, only 2½ feet tall when committed to care in April 1926 aged 6½ years.[29] She suffered from chest problems and a hacking, whooping–type cough all her life but was described as in good overall health in 1926.

Consumption (tuberculosis) was the major cause of death in Ireland in the first part of the 20th Century: Ireland's 2.8 per thousand death rate compared with 2.2 in Scotland or 1.9 in England and Wales. All countries improved their consumption death rates but the Irish much more slowly. One person in every 200 died of tuberculosis in Ireland in the age group 25-34 in the first part of the century. Not only was consumption the major cause of death in Ireland but ignorance, misunderstanding, and superstitions about its causation and spread greatly heightened the fear of it, and the shame and stigma that carriers and family members felt.

Margaret Cowan's family life well illustrates the perplexing nature of consumption: it took some family members, but not others exposed to the same bacillus that carried the infection. Many people are exposed to the bacillus, as was Margaret, when the droplets laden with bacilli are sprayed out by coughing or spitting by the infected person. Exposure to the infection causes a person's immune system to mobilize against the threat and many build up immunity to infection. A particular risk in Ireland as elsewhere was the near ubiquitous working class habit of spitting. [30] Sawdust in pubs for the gobs of phlegm spat out, dripping spittoons and the very common expectoration of gobbets into the turf fire maintained the risk. Michael's Uncle Frank remembers visiting him and seeing the adult males spitting across the crawling child into the turf fire.

Illustration 5: Michael Porter's Mother: Margaret Porter nee Cowan, c. 1918

Margaret Porter's life contained a number of cumulative risk factors which made her especially susceptible to contracting tuberculosis: she was Irish; she was female; she was a labourer's wife; she 'lived in' with relatives; she was young and probably work-worn, certainly weakened by child bearing and loss of her first child and recent birth of her last;[31] above all had been her repeated life-long exposure to tuberculosis, and her recent pregnancy. A few months after giving birth to her fourth child, Catherine Josephine, Michael's mother died of tuberculosis on 3rd September 1924.

1.1.10. Summary of Michael Porter's Family Disintegration and Eventual Collapse[32]

● **January 1918:** Laurence and Margaret marry. They 'live-in' with Margaret's mother and 4 brothers in Pallas Gate Lodge. Laurence described as farmer. Margaret's mother dies.

● **13 April 1918:** First child, Patrick born in the Gate Lodge.

● **21 July 1918:** Patrick died aged 3 months from whooping cough in the Gate Lodge.

● **C. 1919:** Michael's parents, together with Margaret's brothers and 4 remaining sons, move to the newly completed 2 storey house.

● **17 November 1919:** Second child, Mary Bridget (Sadie) born (at new house). Laurence was a labourer.

● **c. 1921/1922:** Michael's mother's younger brother, Michael, died of consumption.

● **3 October 1921:** Third child, Michael Laurence, born.

● **11 November 1923:** Fourth child, Catherine Josephine, born.

● **3 September 1924:** Mother, Margaret Porter, died of consumption.

● **3 June 1925:** Catherine Josephine Porter died.

● **19 April 1926:** Sadie committed to care in Ballinasloe.

● **23 August 1926:** Michael admitted to care in Sligo.

● **1926/1927:** Father, Laurence Porter, moved in with his mother and brother's family in Tynagh village.

• **C.1927:** John Cowan brought new bride into the 'new' house and started a family.

When examining the families of children who are taken into care, or who are abused, the concepts of 'compromised', 'critical' or 'collapsed' families can be helpful. Many families are compromised by poverty, multi-family occupancy of dwellings, low income, chronic ill-health or other disadvantageous circumstances and yet children do not end up in care. What often saved them, especially at this period, was care from the wider extended family, or, following the death of a spouse, remarriage.

Michael's family had experienced a critical phase when his mother had died. His father somehow managed to keep all three children out of care for nine months. How?

The rearing of young children in 1920's Ireland was exclusively a female responsibility, with the whole domestic sphere, including certain farm activities such as managing the fowl, being the preserve of women. The only female Porter family household member was Sadie, who was two months short of 5 years when her mother died. Who cared for 10 month old Catherine Josephine for the remaining nine months of her life? Or rather which female(s) cared for her? It seems probable that young Sadie would have played some part in the care of her sister, but it does not seem that the paternal grandmother was involved.

1.1.11. Fruitful Errors

Within ten months Michael was the only remaining child alive or not in care when Sadie, then aged 5½ years, was committed to State care until she was 16 years of age in an Industrial School. A clue to what I think may have happened to enable the family to keep Michael out of care for so long, and for four months after Sadie was committed to care, is, paradoxically, revealed in errors in his Nazareth House admission to care records.[33]

Annie Conway of Killeen, Ballyshall (sic) was recorded as Michael's 'grandmother' (sic). Annie Conway of Killeen, Ballyglass was in fact Michael's 'godmother'. She must have been a close friend or relative of the family to have been chosen as a godmother. Aged in her early fifties she was a spinster living on a small farm in Tynagh parish together with her bachelor brother, Michael.[34] The person who gave Annie's name to the Nazareth Sisters, almost certainly Father Bowes, did so most probably because to the forefront of his mind was the person who had been caring for Michael. She is likely to have cared for him since Sadie's admission to care, and possibly since Catherine Josephine's death fourteen months earlier. It may have been that Annie accompanied Michael with Father Bowes to comfort him when he was taken into care.

One further piece of information supports this explanation. Annie Conway's bachelor brother had promised Michael's father that he intended to leave the farm to Michael Porter after he died, indicating some close affinity with the boy (who may have lived with him for fourteen months).[35] This bequest did not occur as Michael Conway died and his sister Annie bequeathed the farm to her relatives after having no contact with Michael during his years in care.

1.1.12. Sadie's Committal to Care

Michael's sister, Mary Bridget (known as Sadie) was placed with the Sisters of Mercy in Ballinasloe, County Galway, some 15 miles distant from home, some 4 months before Michael was taken into care. Extracts from her admission log are given in the following illustration.[36]

No.: 413
Age: Born 3rd March 1920 (wrong)
Date of Admission: 19.4.26
When, where and by whom ordered to be detained: Ballinasloe D.C.
With what charged: Found Wandering

Under what section of Act: 11th
Sentence expires: 2nd March 1936
Previous Character: Good
State if illegitimate: No

15

Mother died of: (Left blank)
Mary not at all strong

Parentage
Names of parent: John Porter (wrong)
Mother dead
Step-parents: None
Address: Tynagh, County Galway
Occupation: Labourer
Character: Good
Circumstances and other particulars: Very poor
Religious Persuasion: RC

Description
Height: Two and a half feet
Figure: Stout
Complexion: Fair
Hair: Dark
Eyes: Grey
Nose: Short
Marks on person and other peculiarities: No

General Health: Good
Educational State
Reads: In Infant School
Writes: (Left blank)
Calculates: (Left blank)
Previous Instructions and for how long: (Left blank)
Mental Capacity: (Left blank)

1.1.13. Deficiencies in Records: Stigma and Children's Reactions

The preceding details of Sadie's admission to care again reveal the problem of bare, contradictory and inaccurate information. These deficiencies in care records, evident in both Michael and Sadie's cases, are commonly found in records of many children admitted into care, not only then, but also well up to the end of the 20th Century, and in Britain as well as in Ireland, and in State as well as Church records. These inadequacies often bewilder and then anger adults who were in care and who later gain access to their files. That was the angry reaction to the limited information about Sadie's career in care, despite my repeated warnings to Michael about the limited nature of many care records in general. His response to these: *My vet kept better records about my dog than they* (the authorities) *kept of my sister.*[37]

The lack or even complete absence of records is often perceived by the former child in care as insulting and further evidence of how little worth they appeared to have when even their 'rescuers' and replacement carers recorded so little about them. The absence of on-going photographs of their career in care was a further source of distress and accentuated their sense of being different, less 'good' or worthy, less valued or respected, than children who had not been in care. Of Residential Care Workers and Social Workers they opined: *We thought they were writing loads about us. They were always having meetings about us*[38].

Above all was the cry directed to the outside world, including schools: *Tell them that we're not toe-rags. People think that you're a criminal when they hear you're in care. It's not our fault that we're in care.*[39]

From the mouths of young people taken into care through no fault of their own was the feeling that they were regarded by schoolfellows and society as tainted. To admit their care status was to invite suspicion, prejudgement and stigma and so they avoided this at all costs. Michael and Sadie avoided talking of their care experiences to each other for almost all their lives, so deep was the shame it engendered in them. Even when they did so they touched on events guardedly, selectively, and fleetingly. Their fear, sadly based on experience, was that the members of society outside their care homes, treated them as depraved when they were actually deprived.

Sadie's care admission details are given in part to illustrate these deficiencies but also to reflect how the language and terms used in the document reflect societal values and concerns in the inter-war period (and beyond). The fear of tuberculosis in Ireland is most tellingly revealed in the admission log by its absence as an entry in

17

the record. The entry *Mother died of* is incomplete. It reads as if the senior nun recording the child's entry did not want the fact widely known and so left it blank. The child was still admitted by the Sisters.

The Mercy Sisters' admission record of Sadie Porter contains the standard question of the period: *State if illegitimate.* Illegitimacy, or more accurately the vulnerable position of the lone mother, and religious and social attitudes towards bastardy, was another significant reason why children might be placed in care, as the case of Patrick Baker, Michael's contemporary at Nazareth House, reveals, and also in the case of William Walsh.

Chapter 1.2: Why the Other Boys Came to Sligo

1.2.1. Paddy Baker's Background[40]

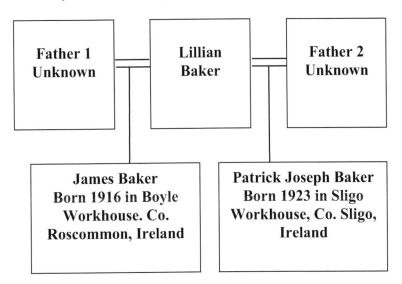

Illustration 6: Family Background of Patrick Joseph Baker

Patrick Baker who is shown second from the left in the front cover photograph was born on 6th January 1923 in County Sligo. He was by far the youngest of the Quartet and he entered care at the age of just 2 years.

Patrick's mother, Lillian Baker, was unmarried when Patrick was born. She had been born in Kansas City, Missouri, in the United States of America in November, 1898.[41] Supposedly orphaned when her parents were both killed in an accident when she was 2 years old, she was taken in by Tom Downes and his childless wife Bea. Downes, a farmer, had gone to work in the United States to generate capital to enlarge his small farm near Culfadda in County Sligo. The Downes couple returned to their enlarged farm holding in County Sligo with Lillian.[42] It seems, however, that they may not have carried out their intention to adopt Lillian. Instead she was reported to have been treated very much as a subordinate and farm servant by Bea, rather than a member of the family.[43]

Lillian became pregnant and in 1916 giving birth to her first son, James, in Boyle town workhouse in County Roscommon. After James was admitted to Nazareth House, Sligo, in 1919, Lillian found a position as a farm servant in Keash, County Roscommon, with a family named Hannon. She again fell pregnant, giving birth to Patrick Baker in Sligo Workhouse, on the Feast of the Epiphany, 1923. In 1925 aged 2 years Patrick Baker was admitted to Nazareth House, to the Nursery Section, in the old Yeats House, to be joined by Michael Porter in August 1926. As in Michael's case the admission to the religious Boys' Home was mediated by the Parish Priest, in Patrick's case, Father Finn.[44]

1.2.2. Consequences of Illegitimacy

Michael Porter's eldest sibling, Patrick, had been born only a few months after his parents' marriage. Marriage was a common ending to a pre-conjugal pregnancy of a young woman in rural Ireland. In cases of a bachelor's reluctance to marry his pregnant companion family and clerical pressure, and fear of social ostracism and stigma, ensured that most premarital pregnancies ended in marriage. Ireland's 2.6% illegitimacy rate in the early 20th century was the second lowest in Europe after Holland (2.37%), and much lower than England and Wales (4.0%) and Scotland (6.74%), and even these latter figures were at the lower end of illegitimacy rates in Europe.[45]

In Lillian Baker's case it appears that the two different fathers of her boys were not in a position to marry her because they were already married. Her pregnancy with James saw a dependent young woman, subdued, 'orphaned' young, exploited by an older, married man. She lost her 'position' in the Downes household, Tom Downes and his wife merely moving to a different parish church to avoid rumour and scandal. Without family, abandoned by her 'adoptive family', without work or income, a source of scandal, and stigmatised, the options for her successfully keeping and rearing her first son in Catholic, rural Ireland in 1916 were extremely slim. What is perhaps surprising is that it took till 1919 until she was separated permanently from him.

The whole saga was repeated when she went to the Keash farm and became pregnant with her second son, Patrick, but on this occasion she lost or 'gave up' her son at the age of 2 years. She disappears from view but re-emerges in the 1930's working in a hotel in the coastal holiday resort of Strandhill, some 5 miles from her two sons in Nazareth House, Sligo Town.[46] Hotel work, work in large Institutions, or other places where bed and board were provided along with a small wage, including farm placements obtained at the hiring fairs, were the common lot of vulnerable young folk of both genders, and on both sides of the Irish Sea at this period.

Attitudes towards illegitimacy in the 1920's help explain why people acted as they did at that time. The following extract, drawn from an influential Catholic publication, outlines the then prevailing attitudes towards illegitimacy, and the reasons for these:

'Nevertheless every illegitimate child that is born represents at least one grievous sin against the sixth commandment, and forebodes many harmful consequences for itself, its parents, and the community. The child is frequently deserted by its parents, or by the father, and is deprived of many of the social, economic, educational, and religious advantages which he would have obtained if he had been born in wedlock. Infant mortality among illegitimate children is at least twenty-five percent higher than among those that are legitimate, while the proportion of criminals among them is also considerably larger. The parents, particularly the mother, suffer a greater or less degree of social ostracism, which, in the case of the woman, often includes inability to find a spouse'.[47]

Interestingly, the extract details the effects of illegitimacy on both child and mother, not just the 'sin'. This extract would have found agreement amongst almost all religious denominations in both Britain and Ireland at that period, and amongst most members of society. Many of these consequences outlined above proved prophetic in the lives of Lillian and her two sons. The extract omits what often proves to be the most damaging effects of illegitimacy, however: the resulting separation of the mother and child, with consequent severe impact upon the child's sense of identity, and in many cases of attachment.

1.2.3. William Walsh

William Walsh, (shown on the right of the Quartet photograph), was the third member of the Quartet. Much less is known about his early life than that of the other Quartet members. Born in 1920 he was the oldest of the Quartet and he hailed from the Tuam area of County Galway. Like Paddy Baker he was illegitimate.[48] That he did not enter care until 1927 suggests that an unintended consequence of the opening of Nazareth House may have been to cause struggling single mothers to 'let go' their stigmatised child. The mother might then forge a new, often anonymous life for herself, especially in England. The loss of his mother at such an age, and the termination of all contact with her thereafter, together with the reasons for his admission to care, would almost certainly have burdened Willie with trauma, shame and stigma.

1.2.4. William Patrick McGowan

The fourth member of the Quartet, suffered the loss of his mother at the same age as Willie Walsh and like Willie Walsh he was then powerfully fused to his mother. William Patrick McGowan, shown on the extreme left of the front cover photograph, had been born on 31st March, 1921 in Gerrib Little Townland, Dromore West Parish, County Sligo. His father, Michael, was a farmer whose farm was typical of the small landholdings in the west of Ireland. He had about 10 acres of land plus turbary rights (turf cutting) to support his family in a two roomed thatched cottage. William, the eldest son, was the second of 7 children born to Michael and Cecilia (nee Feeney) McGowan.

William's mother Celia had given birth to her 7th child, Thomas, in 1928. There had been less than eight years between the birth of her first and her last child. She died shortly after the birth, from septicaemia on St Patrick's Day, 1928. William was present at his mother's bedside when she died. He was not quite 7 years old. This memory with its all-pervading accompanying sense of loss and devastation remained with him lifelong as did the fear and fruitless search for aid for his mother as she lay dying. When child and family saw white froth running from his mother's mouth Willie was sent post-haste to summon help from his uncle Matt, his father's elder brother. Matt refused to come and by the time Willie returned home his mother was a corpse. Willie later confided to his own children that they could never understand the impact of losing a mother at such a young age[49]. This loss and Willie's *cri de coeur* has strong echoes of a notable Irish author's lament about similar loss of mother.

1.2.5. Impact of Loss of Mother

John McGahern, from nearby Leitrim and from the same size family as William, lost his mother at the age of 9 years, and his writings give a proxy account of what it must have been like for Willie McGowan. This theme of the irreparable loss of mother features significantly in a number of his novels. His autobiographical 'Memoir'[50] reads as a paean to her memory and one can sense in his works the continuing effect on him of her death. He sought to recover her presence in both memory, and wish fulfilment, through remembering and recording their shared sight, sounds and smells as he conjured up memories and images of him and his mother walking together through the same, familiar lanes and countryside they had walked when she was alive. The theme of the irrecoverable loss of mother is central to many of his works. McGahern achieved his ambition to be reunited with her by being buried in her grave. William McGowan carried the same mother-loss agony throughout his life, making sporadic references of this to his children.

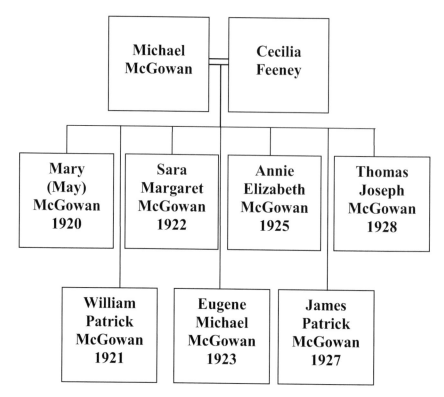

Illustration 7: Family Background of William Patrick McGowan

Michael Porter had lost his mother at a much younger age than William, did not fully remember her and came to believe his memory to have been a fantasy. Patrick Baker was given over to the Sisters when only 2 years old and had no memory of his mother. For all his childhood he believed her dead. When later in life he heard that she was still alive he began a restless, desperate, needy, unsatisfactory search for her. William McGowan's loss was real, raw, and remembered. William was old enough to appreciate the significance of the loss of his mother. Michael Porter struggled with his funeral memory, seeking both to remember and to forget the loss of his mother. She never featured significantly in his life whereas Willie McGowan's mother loss regularly grieved him throughout life.

1.2.6. Collapse and Dispersal of Willie McGowan's Family

The following table[51] details the family disintegration that ensued following the death of Celia McGowan. (Child's known name is underlined).

Child's Name	Date of Birth	Destination
Mary (May)	6th June 1920	Maternal relatives
William Patrick	31st March 1921	Nazareth House, Sligo
Sara Margaret	27th April 1922	Out of family placements
Eugene Michael	10th June 1923	Reared by Mrs Gerraghty, Easky, Sligo
Annie Elizabeth (Lily)	5th Nov. 1925	Out of family placements
James Patrick	7th March 1927	Died in infancy of rickets
Thomas Joseph	8th March 1928	Placed with the Smith family, neighbours, for 6 months then St Michael's Home, Dublin, and then fostered

Illustration 8: Family Disintegration Following the Death of Celia McGowan

After Celia's McGowan's death the neighbours rallied to help Michael McGowan care for his large brood of young children. They offered to share the care of the children during the day allowing their father to care for them at night. These arrangements were opposed by the Parish Priest, one reason being that some of the neighbours were Protestants. The priest may also have felt that the chance of a widowed poor farmer successfully rearing his six surviving very young children in 1920's rural Ireland was very slim, and that the children might fare better being cared for by nuns.[52]

The children's father consented to the priest's advice. May, the eldest child, was brought up by her maternal relatives. Eugene Michael was reared by the Gerraghty family in nearby Easky. Baby Thomas had been cared for by a neighbour, Tom Smith and his wife, for 6 months after Celia's death and they had wanted to adopt him. This was opposed by Michael McGowan and baby Thomas was moved to St Michael's Home in Drumcondra in Dublin, from where he was then fostered throughout his childhood. Margaret and Lily were found out-of-family placements. William Patrick was moved into care on 12th April, 1928,[53] barely four weeks after his mother's death, when he entered the newly purpose-built Boys' Home, Nazareth House, Sligo where he joined Michael Porter and Patrick Baker.[54]

1.2.7. Reasons for Children Being 'Let Go'

To-day, when the importance of the emotional needs and attachment of children to their parents is understood, it is harder to comprehend why all the McGowan children were not kept with their immediate extended family and locality. Then, when the physical care and safety, and even survival, of many children from poor families was often on a knife edge, ensuring that the child emerged into adulthood alive and well was an understandable priority. It is very doubtful that the damaging emotional impact of separation of the boys and Sadie from their families was understood by any of the parties involved, whether family or clergy or Sisters at Nazareth House.

It may well have been that the parents thought that the care decision was the best option for the child. Certainly Michael Porter's aunt, Madge Porter, had believed it to be so.[55] Lillian Baker may well have believed that her sons would fare better away from her. She may also have felt that she had a better chance of a new life for herself unencumbered by the stigma of illegitimacy. However such moves have historically had unintended consequences. Once a child enters care what may begin as a respite placement often becomes permanent. Unless active steps are taken to nurture and sustain relationships between child and family, and vigorous and timely measures are taken to return the child home, the child 'drifts'. Family contact almost inevitably ceases and the child becomes 'lost in care'.

In all three cases mentioned the Parish Priest was involved in the family decision that residential care was the best option for the children. The clergy were the gatekeepers to residential care, certainly where this was voluntary (i.e. not by way of court order). A place could only be obtained via clerical or church mediation. For almost all his life Michael blamed his Parish Priest for what he saw as him prevailing on his father and family to have him placed in care. Clergy were powerful, revered, often feared then and a significant minority of them appear to have been high handed and peremptory in their dealing with their parishioners, especially where these were poor and ill-educated. The anti-clerical strand of some Irish Catholics today seems rooted in their direct experiences of some of these spiritual leaders who misused the power and prestige of their position.

That Michael McGowan and his neighbours fell into line with the alternative plan for the children determined by the Parish Priest is a reflection of the accepting, unquestioning or even deferential cast of mind towards the clergy by Irish then, especially the rural poor. It is axiomatic that a central concern of the clergy in their 'advice' to the parents was to ensure that each child was brought up as a 'good Catholic'. In the case of Willie McGowan and some of his siblings the fear of 'corruption' by Protestants would appear to have been an additional consideration. Yet it may also have been the case that one or all of the respective clergy also sincerely believed that the children's health and welfare would be better served away from their critical or collapsing families. Father Bowes had cited Michael and Sadie's lives having been saved by their removal from the danger of consumption at home. Later William McGowan's choices will be examined to see whether his experiences justified the clerical and perhaps paternal view that his welfare was best served away from home.

1.2.8. Coming Together

Family disintegration following the 'loss' of a mother brought four entirely unrelated boys from widely dispersed area to live together in Sligo. The age of each Quartet member on arrival at Nazareth House was: 2 years (Paddy in 1925); 4 years (Michael in 1926); 7 years (Willie Walsh in 1927); and 8 years (Willie McGowan in 1928).[56] All four boys spent their whole childhood in care but only one of them had any form of contact with their family during this period.

Chapter 1.3: Forming the Formers: the Poor Sisters of Nazareth

1.3.1. Formation of the Formers

The training of a nun was called 'formation' to reflect the process of shaping the trainee to fit into communal life with others. This chapter examines the Nazareth Congregation's philosophy and their moulding of their Sisters to understand how this shaped their approach to child care at Nazareth House: in other words, the formation of the formers.

1.3.2. Bishop Clancy's Workhouse Replacement Plan

John Joseph Clancy (1856-1912) had long been alarmed about the treatment of inmates in the Sligo workhouse following his appointment as bishop of Elphin diocese in 1895.[57] The nineteenth century had seen a number of scandals involving allegations that workhouse staff had sexually exploited inmates and misappropriated their food, goods and money.[58] Bishop Clancy sought to stop the incarceration of children with adults, especially unrelated males. In the first decade of the twentieth century there were no suitable institutions available to care for destitute and orphaned boys in the west of Ireland other than placement in industrial schools, reformatories and workhouses. The Bishop, therefore, invited the Sisters of Nazareth, a religious Congregation whose headquarters was in Hammersmith, London, to staff and run a new boys' home in Sligo to provide more appropriate care.[59]

1.3.3. Poor Sisters of Nazareth Come to Sligo

In 1910 five Sisters of Nazareth arrived in Church Hill, Sligo to occupy *Merville*, a moderately large Georgian House and small estate. To open a home quickly to accommodate both boys and male and female elderly the Sisters took the building at Church Hill, Sligo, on a 5 year lease from the local Tighe family (one of whose members was a nun). These arrangements were always regarded as an interim measure until the Sisters could build more suitable, purpose-built premises.

The first 17 boys in residence arrived on 15th August 1910, taken directly from the Sligo Workhouse. The workhouse authorities provided £10 to be relieved of their upkeep.[60] The scale of need and the rapid expansion of provision to meet this, even in premises that were not ideally suited to accommodate so many disparate groups and ages in one building, is reflected in the numbers accommodated less than a year later. By 1911 there were 53 people living at the Nazareth House Home. Out of this total 7 were Sisters, 5 were elderly men, 4 elderly women, and 4 others (3 female) aged from 16-38 years. There were 33 boys, whose ages ranged from 3 to 12 years, including 4 pairs of brothers. All except the Sisters were classified as paupers under the census statistical return. All Sisters were Irish born, as were most inmates, the vast majority of them having been born in county Sligo, although several boys had been born in Scotland.[61]

The Sligo Home initially accommodated all three groups in the one building: boys, elderly men and elderly women. The Georgian former Pollexfen-Yeats building was subdivided into separate livingcum-dining-cum-sleeping units for each of these 3 groups until a new Home could be funded and built.[62]

This care provision was based on a model aimed at relief of the destitute and needy, 'rescuing' or 'saving' those children in physical and moral danger. These measures represented a radical, pioneering attempt to provide more appropriate care for the destitute young and old. That this provision was in such a large Home, albeit one very much smaller than the workhouse, went against the grain of developing child care practice elsewhere in the rest of Great Britain.

In mainland Britain moves were beginning to be made to reduce the size of child care homes into smaller units, especially those in voluntary care, but also for workhouse children. This was reflected in the rapid development of cottage homes. These were institutions, often in the countryside, where large numbers of children were cared for in a series of smaller cottage-style living units. These were designed to make care more home-like and personal, and to abate the institutional bleakness of the largest institutions. In 1903 there had been 25 such homes in Britain; by 1914 there were 115. Although the new Nazareth House Home in Sligo may have been operating from the outset on a model that was becoming less common in child care provision, it was still several steps up from the care it replaced and was a charitable response to the acute and chronic needs of destitute children and old people.

The arrangements in Sligo conformed with the structure and operation at the first Nazareth House Home in Hammersmith, West London. Nazareth House, Sligo and all other Nazareth Houses were based on the Hammersmith model, which still is, the Headquarters of the Nazareth Sisters worldwide. Some detail of the training of the Sisters at Hammersmith headquarters is given to provide an understanding of their values and priorities. These were the values that would influence their care practices.

1.3.4. Foundation of The Poor Sisters of Nazareth in Hammersmith, London

The Poor Sisters of Nazareth was only established as a separate religious order in the 1860's.[63] The vast scale of poverty and need in nineteenth century London was worsened after the arrival of many post-Famine Irish migrants after the late 1840's. The St. Vincent de Paul Society which sought to help bring relief to these families became unable to cope with the resulting number of abandoned and orphaned children. One of its members, Mr Pagliano, brought to Cardinal Wiseman's attention the need to succour these children,[64] to prevent them being exploited sexually and physically and to preserve their Catholic faith. Cardinal Wiseman approached the Little Sisters of the Poor for help.[65] As their mission was exclusively with the elderly they released a small group of their nuns to begin the work of 'child rescue'.[66]

One of these nuns was Victoire Larmenier (1827-1878), a newly professed French nun from Brittany. In 1851, at the age of 24 years, she found herself in London as the Superior of the handful of nuns seeking to provide care for the children. A decade later she saw the new Congregation of the Poor Sisters of Nazareth established in Hammersmith to care for the destitute.[67] Its mission included the care of children, including foundlings and abandoned children and the elderly homeless, ill and destitute.

The growth of Homes, Sisters and Novices was rapid. Although based in England the labour reservoir the Sisters were drawn from came increasingly from Ireland. In 1901 forty three Sisters were based at Hammersmith, of whom 29, including the Mother General were Irish. Only 2 Sisters, including one whose title was given as 'Victoire le Breton', were now French. Of the 45 nuns in training, styled in the census as 'probationers', 35 were Irish. Three quarters of the Sisters and Novices in Hammersmith in 1901 were, therefore, Irish.[68]

The functioning of the Sligo Home(s) can be best understood by an examination of the functioning of Hammersmith headquarters. [69] The more gentrified environs of Hammersmith today contrast sharply with conditions there in the second half of the nineteenth Century when the Sisters of Nazareth moved there:

'Hammersmith ..... is a vast, busy, shabby and for the most part very poor place, where the slums are said (by Evangelists and those who worked in them) to be as bad as the worst of Whitechapel'.[70]

Both the Socialists and the Salvation Army proselytised in this district seeking to succour the body, but the latter seeking, like the Sisters, to save the soul also. Indeed Sisters, Salvationists and also the established Church of England all poured their efforts into ameliorating the lot of the needy and destitute in the biggest city in the world. The Salvation Army's leader, General Booth, vividly drew attention to the physical and moral degradation he encountered in London in his book *In Darkest England*,[71] deliberately drawing a comparison with Stanley's just published *In Darkest Africa*.[72]

Although the Sisters of Nazareth were involved in care work, 'corporal acts of mercy', they were first and foremost nuns. As such they were subject to the normal discipline and daily ritual of prayers and spiritual devotions common to all who had committed their lives to a Religious Order or Congregation. In their case, however, it was combined with 'deed prayer'. This did not reduce their spiritual duties save for one concession: Nazareth Sisters were not required to break sleep by rising for services during the night.

1.3.5. Formation: Becoming a Nun

There were three phases where a woman discerned whether she was suited to the work of a nun. During these phases the aspiring nun was assessed by the Community of Sisters to determine whether she had the requisite qualities, commitment and stamina to join the Congregation, and especially to make the lifelong commitment needed.

The first phase, Postulant ('seeking') lasted for up to a year. This was followed by the Novitiate of from 1 to 2 years. This latter phase was marked symbolically by the Novice 'taking the white veil'. The woman would then take temporary vows of poverty, chastity and obedience. After a further period, varying from 3 and 5 years, final vows would be taken. The woman would now be a Professed Nun. If she lived entirely within a Convent of an 'enclosed' Congregation or Order she would be known as a nun. If she worked outside, as did the Sisters of Nazareth, she would be referred to as a Sister. (In common parlance the terms nun and Sister are interchangeable).

The process of becoming a Nun involved a series of rituals and sacrifices as the Novice abandoned the world, her past life and, very often, her family as she sought to become a member of her new family, the Religious Congregation. The vows of poverty involved not only money but also a lack of owning clothing, food and other necessaries of life, these being provided by the Congregation. The vow of chastity was made as she sought to become a 'Bride of Christ', even wearing a ring on the left hand, with the consequent permanent denial of the possibility of motherhood. The marriage symbolism was further emphasised by the requirement that each prospective nun (Postulant/Novice) was required to pay to the Congregation a 'dowry' when committing to life in the Congregation, although this could be waived in particular circumstances. The prospective 'bride', dressed in white, was often brought to the altar to make her profession by her father.

33

The vow of obedience involved absolute obedience at all times and subordination of the individual wishes, whims and desires to the needs of the collective, the Religious Congregation. The work of the Spanish Jesuit, Alonso Rodriguez (1526-1616) was commonly used in the training of religious. His most famous teaching example that stressed the absolute need to obey was that of planting cabbages upside down. The perfect Novice was expected to obey this instruction without questioning its illogicality.

Obedience also involved public confession of sins by the penitent nun before her fellow nuns. It would be regarded as sinful, leading to a public confession before the community, if a nun did not report the transgressions of a fellow nun to the Congregation. Lying fully prostrate and kissing the floor in the presence of one's superior as punishment for rule transgression reinforced this culture in an act of extreme self-abasement. The qualities of humility and conformist obedience desired in the postulant were also reflected in the habit of gaze aversion, [73]addressing their superior with bowed head while not making eye contact, this being judged to be challenging.[74]

Before changes brought in by the Second Vatican Council in the 1960's there were a number of other control measures that could be deployed in religious Orders and Congregations. These included: restriction and censorship of letters; refusal to release a Sister to visit sick relatives, even when a parent was in danger of death: having to kiss the floor and accuse oneself when arriving late; and the ultimate test was 'the obedience': being moved anywhere at any time whether one wished it or not.[75]

The nun's new family, the Congregation of fellow nuns, was headed by a 'Mother', and her siblings were the other 'Sisters'. Living lifelong in close communion with a same gender group of strangers the nun needed to possess or acquire qualities of sensitivity, adaptability and forbearance. Prudent management of such a group of confined women was required by their religious superior. The Jesuit, Max Schmid's guide book for superiors, *The Sister in Charge,*[76] gave detailed guidance to the Reverend Mother on the delicate path to be walked in respectfully directing the nuns in her care.

Father Schmid devoted a section of the book to the types of persons generally judged unsuitable for the demands of confined convent life:

'Those who were a threat to the solidarity and emotional health of the whole community; those afflicted with hysteria; those of serious scrupulosity; those with serious defects of character (choleric) who might well prove unbiddable; and, finally, visionaries: St Ignatius says that ninety nine percent of all visions is self-deception'.[77]

Yet none of the unsuitable were to be rejected without serious attempts by the Superior to reform the errant postulant, Schmid, wryly observing that: 'By far the greater number of Sisters in higher positions are of choleric temperament'.[78]

Close personal relationships between Sisters was actively discouraged, not only for sexual reasons, but because it was deemed to fragment the communal solidarity. The sometimes intense, fragile or labile emotional vulnerability of the young women and in particular in the matter of procreation, led some religious orders to extreme measures.

'Young Sisters who visited the sick and poor as part of their work would find themselves stopped from visiting pregnant or post-partum mothers lest this trigger the Sister's own natural instincts towards motherhood'.[79]

The nun would even expunge her Christian name as part of her new identity. A saint's name would be chosen for her, either male or female, both as an example to follow and as a name by which she would be known in future.[80]

Although the involvement of the Nazareth Sisters in begging and care work meant they were engaged with 'the world', the Nazareth Sisters were essentially functioning like their enclosed, convent Sisters. The process of formation of a nun involved her consciously separating herself from past life and from her family, relationships and material possessions. This is most powerfully reflected in the phrase, 'dead to the world'. This death represented both the process of renunciation of past life and attachments and the determination to seek 'the reward' in the next world by sacrifices and denial of self in this. The transition from former life, family and allegiance to the new was described as 'mortification of self'. This conscious 'death' of self and past was marked by the ritual shaving of hair of the would-be nun and by the taking-on of the uniform, the 'habit', of the Congregation.

The Novice arrived to make her vows dressed in white; she left the ceremony clad in dark garb after being re-robed. This new 'habit' was worn to symbolise her confraternity and equality with her new 'Sisters'. It also symbolised her 'death to the world', and this was represented by the colour of the new, dark 'habit', often black, grey or dark blue. Within this habit the individual personality was to be lost. The desired qualities for the professed nun was a person of self-abnegation, even self-abasement, who subordinated her personal wishes to the needs of the collective, and who obeyed without demur any lawful request made to her. A number of these Congregation rules are common in many secular institutions and these will be discussed later.

1.3.6. Care at Hammersmith Nazareth House

The convent day at Hammersmith began at 5am. The Nuns, who slept on straw mattresses, first gathered in Chapel for morning prayers then meditated for half an hour before attending Mass. The Office of the day (formal prayer of the Congregation) and other prayers followed before a breakfast of bread and butter was taken: 'At all their meals they fare like their poor, their food being principally the broken food of alms'.[81] Any nun who had been on duty on the wards during the night was spared none of the spiritual or practical work of the next day.

Alice Meynell, with a woman's eye for clothing and practicality commented on the unsuitability of the Sisters' habits for the practical work they had to carry out. The habit had to be grave, modest and adapted for work. It seems that the requirement for suitable garb was subordinated to the other two, primarily religious, conditions. Consequently the Sisters had to carry out their duties in a habit weighing 20lbs (9 kilograms). These duties involved enduring the heat and damp of the kitchen and laundry, muffled in starched, close caps and with hanging veils. Cardinal Wiseman had designed the Nazareth Sisters' habit; his surname evidently a misnomer, at least in this instance.

The Nazareth Sisters, were Mendicants: as such they relied entirely on begging and soliciting charitable donations to survive and carry out their work, as, in the early days at least, they had no endowments or fixed income to rely on. One contribution to Congregation funds, was the 'dowry' provided by the family of each woman who sought to join the Congregation.

'In this Order there are no lay Sisters. The whole service of the house is fulfilled by these educated ladies–the cooking, the washing and ironing, the making and mending the personal care of the throng of children, some of them infants in arms, their education, the nursing of the sick, the tending of the frequent death beds, and that special work which the Nuns share with very few other Communities– the Quest'.[82]

The Quest involved Nuns going out in pairs with baskets and containers to collect the scraps and leftover food from households, hotels and other premises in London. The Sisters were accompanied by a horse-drawn van to bring the leftover food back to Hammersmith. There it was carefully picked-over and sorted: 'Everything here is made of scraps and yet nothing is made of refuse. The most delicate care is used in the cookery'.[83]

Illustration 9: Sisters of Nazareth on the Quest: London 1910

As well as the care of residents in the Homes in Hammersmith, Nazareth House also provided outdoor relief by means of its daily soup kitchen in the winter months. The Sisters started the cauldrons at 4.30 in the morning. Men, the overwhelming majority of recipients, tramped great distances across London, often in bitter frosts, for their daily dole of hot broth. Several hundred each day came although on one occasion as many as nineteen hundred were fed. The feeding hour had to be changed from noon to late morning to prioritise the food for the unemployed, as poor workmen used to crowd out the even more needy supplicants. The elderly residents of Nazareth House had sometimes elected to give up their food to those attending the soup dole when provisions were short, thereby missing out on one of the few highlights of their long days.

At a time when women were not credited with organisational and managerial abilities, or capabilities for large-scale co-operation,

Meynell, wearing her suffragist hat, argues that the Sisters of Nazareth give the lie to that belief:

'But meanwhile without show or clatter ... of any kind, Religious women have been submitting in large bodies, to rules far more general and inexorable than any dreamed of in the world's affairs; have been resigning all their individuality; have been obeying a woman in union with women; have been organising with a mathematical attention to proportion; have been ..... doing large monotonous work with the precision of machinery..... And all this is done with the difficult cause of charity–, so full of disappointments and disillusions within'.[84]

Any simpering saints among the Postulants and Novices working the large dark institutional building that was Nazareth House would soon have to face reality. Their vocation involved the same physical hard work and domestic drudgery that was the lot of the huge army of poor girls working in domestic service throughout Britain. Mother General's practical approach to the qualities needed by those aspiring to become Sisters was clear: 'There is no poetry in our after-life here, it is hard practical work, and we pray that Heaven may send us none but Novices with sound common sense'.[85]

Meynell compared the lot of the Sisters with other groups averring that the peasant had the boon of nature and the changing seasons while the factory hand enjoyed holidays as some compensation for their hard lives. The Sisters, however, with no income, no holiday, no family home to visit and no restriction in the hours worked, had no such physical or material compensations. Instead they enjoyed a life of daily, unremitting monotony, albeit one that they had 'chosen'. Their days and nights were marked by a regularity only matched by prisons.

After the Sisters of Nazareth added the care of children to their existing remit of elderly care it was decided to completely separate the living, dining and sleeping arrangements of each age group in separate sections of the premises. The reason given for this policy was that the dying love silence. It had been felt that the energy, noise and boisterousness of children would disturb the elderly, especially the many old, frail, sick and terminally ill who lived in Nazareth House. Whether this policy was beneficial to old and/or young residents at Nazareth House, Sligo, where it was firmly applied from 1926 onwards, will be discussed later in the book.

The Hammersmith 'Homes' were very large buildings, almost factory-like in scale, to accommodate the 400 plus inmates. There was also a school and an infirmary on site. One can see glimpses of the efforts made to humanise this large-scale 'warehousing' of so many people with disparate needs.

The very old men read the newspapers while some of the younger elderly chopped wood for the house. Some of the 'old ladies' kept linnets or canaries in bird cages fed from scraps from the table. Many old ladies sewed patchwork pieces to keep occupied. In the Incurable Children's Ward were children who were dumb or blind, the blind being more numerous. A girl born without arms had been taught by the Sisters to write with her mouth: 'An incurable child, once received, need never leave. If her incurable life is long, she grows up and passes into old age and dies there'.[86]

The girls' school on site specialised in preparing the orphaned and pauper girls for work in domestic service to enable them to earn their living in an era well before a welfare state.[87] After they had finished their education they were trained in tasks in the Nazareth Homes until they were ready to enter the world of work as servants at the age of 16 or 17 years. The Mother General reported that the Sisters kept in touch with the girls after they had left. Girls could return to Nazareth House to be nursed back to health if ill. 'We never lose sight of one of them ...we keep up a correspondence with them, and when they have holidays they come and see us'.[88]

The accuracy of that bold statement by Mother General, and whether it held up at Nazareth House, Sligo, will be examined in succeeding chapters.

Chapter 1.4: Care Life in the Old Home Buildings: 1925-1926

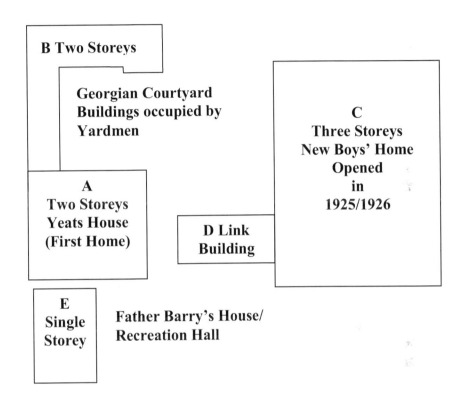

Illustration 10: Diagram of Buildings at Nazareth House Homes, Sligo (not to scale)

A and B. Georgian Former Yeats Home and Courtyard buildings occupied from 1910 by Sisters, Homeboys, Elderly and Yardmen. From 1925/1926 the Yeats House became the Elderly Home only, with Yardmen occupying the courtyard building.

C and D. All the Homeboys, including the babies, were transferred to the new Boys' Home between 1925 and 1926.

E. A stone-built recreational hall for former Homeboys working in the area after leaving care. It was opened in 1931 and always known as 'Father Barry's House' because he funded the building and provided recreational equipment for it.

1.4.1. Overcrowding in the Old Yeats Home

Paddy Baker, although the youngest member of the Quartet, was the first member to arrive at Nazareth House.[89] Already in residence in 1925 was Josie Cummings, a former Nazareth Homeboy, who was employed as a 'Yardman' and, later, the bandmaster who trained the Quartet.[90] Paddy's memories of the early days in the new home are by far the sharpest of all the Quartet and were aided by his conversations with Josie Cummings in later life. Paddy's arrival in 1925 at the age of 2 years occurred when building work on the large new purpose-built boys' building was at its peak.

Illustration 11: Nazareth House, Sligo. Late 1920's

The vast, new, three storey building was located only some score of paces from the old house. From 1910 until the new home building was fully operational in 1926 all residents had been squeezed in together in the old Yeats house and courtyard block: elderly men and women, Sisters, Yardmen, and boys. [91]

The overcrowding necessitated some adjustments to normal segregation of the elderly and children. Some of the 'babies', about 4 in number, slept with the elderly ladies in their quarters at first, despite this being against the Congregation's policy. This had the benefit of increased hands available to feed, change and comfort the babies during the night. The elderly residents were separated by gender within the building, the restricted space resulting in each sex having to eat, sleep and live in the same quarters.[92] The Sisters also had their own separate quarters.

The younger boys including the babies were accommodated and cared for in the Nursery section, separated from the older boys. The younger children attended school in the building until the age of 7 years with their teacher, Miss McGraine. The next oldest group of boys also had a section of the Home for their combined eating, living and dining quarters, while the oldest boys were housed in a temporary wooden classroom. Finally the Yardmen and some of the building workers were accommodated elsewhere in the house, and in the outhouses. The Yeats house and yard buildings had therefore to accommodate at least six distinct groups: the old ladies; the old men; the babies and younger boys; the older boys; the Yardmen ; and finally the Sisters.[93]

The area surrounding the old Home was a building site. The ground between the homes was dug up, rutted and uneven, and would have been very muddy in the frequent Sligo rain. There was scaffolding on the new building, workers on the ground mixed sand and cement by hand and others scurried up and down ladders to the roof like ants. An accident to Paddy illustrates both the dangers the building process caused and how these added to the difficulties that the skeleton staff of Sisters faced in trying to care safely for so many vulnerable old and young people.

Paddy was cared for by Sister Attracta in the Nursery section when he first arrived whom he described as a second mother to him. The immediate area around the home had not yet been cemented. Broken glass bottles had been fixed on top of the walls of an orchard of a neighbouring estate to stop the older Homeboys from scrumping apples. Attracta, rushing about while carrying young Paddy, dropped her charge on to shards of broken glass from the wall. He was cut below the knee and he bled and screamed profusely. Quickly fetching a metal tub from the laundry which she filled with lukewarm water Attracta undressed Paddy and immersed him in a small bath. The blood soon turned the water red. Attracta had to leave him while she summoned the doctor using the only telephone on site in Reverend Mother's room. Paddy, meanwhile, full of self-pity, was studied curiously by the other babies. They also had been left unsupervised because there were no other Sisters available to watch them until Attracta's return. Dr Rouse soon arrived and administered white powder and bandage to Paddy watched by a rather frightened Sister Attracta.[94]

It was the custom at this time for both male and female babies and young children to wear petticoats or dresses, and also to go barefoot. The habit of dressing young boys in dresses continued in many cases until school age. At Nazareth House where the young boys were entirely housed, fed, and schooled on the same premises Paddy remembered that that the boys wore petticoats until the age of 7 years. He was aware of the reason for this and also for the related practice of the lack of underwear for the babies and young boys: to make toilet going easier; to reduce the cost of clothing and the need to clean soiled undergarments; and to make more manageable the work of the few carers looking after them.[95] The petticoat and lack of underwear was common among young working class children of both genders at this period. School age usually marked the rite of passage transition to gender-differentiated clothing for the boys.

1.4.2. Separation of Boys and Elderly

The old men and elderly lady residents sometimes took the toddlers and younger boys for short walks in and just outside the home. One of these, Owen Cummings, showed a fascinated young Paddy from a first floor window the progress that workers were making building the new boys' home. He then took Paddy outside, walking him around the stable yard, with its horse and chickens. The young boy cried when he had to come back inside, handed back to the charge of one of the old ladies.[96]

When the new building was ready for the staged transfer of the boys two elderly ladies escorted Paddy, hand-in-hand, to his new abode. Paddy, then aged about 3 years old, was struck by the size of the building, by the smell of new, polished wood and of paint and by the cool feel of the new floor tiles on his bare feet in the seemingly endless passage. His first impression was that: *I was entering a palace.*

The two ladies guided Paddy up the never-ending obstacle of the great flights of stairs until they reached the summit. When they reached the play room, furnished with a small cloth-covered table and a few forms (hard benches) Paddy was then given over to the charge of Miss McGraine.[97] The old ladies returned to their child-depleted quarters.

The practical support that the elderly residents could give to the care of the babies and younger boys is evident from the recollections of Paddy Baker. Once the new home was fully operational the running of the children's and elderly homes was kept completely separate, even though the two homes were only divided by a small connecting building. The new arrangements meant that the temporary expedient of utilising the elderly to assist in providing supplementary carers ceased. From the opening of the new Nazareth Boys' Home from 1925-1926 the two buildings operated in accordance with the policy of separation of elderly and young that had been determined by the Nazareth Congregation's Hammersmith Headquarters: and indeed as was generally recognised as best child care practice at the time. This also fulfilled Bishop Clancy's desire to separate young children from living with adults, especially men.

This separation of living quarters resulted in exclusion of the boys from contact with the elderly, apart from special occasions. Michael Porter distinctly remembers being forbidden, on pain of punishment, from using the cut-through between the two homes. Where interaction between young and old did occur this tended to be with the older boys and for distinct reasons. These included the elderly attending performances put on by the boys, boys 'watching' by the bedside of the dying, and arrangements where the older boys were used as supplementary helpers to those Sisters responsible for care of the elderly. The mutually beneficial contact between the babies and young boys and their elderly helpers seems to have ceased completely.

This 'apartheid' policy had emotional as well as practical disadvantages, particularly for the younger children.[98] The presence of the elderly had afforded additional caring adults to help nurture and socialise the emotionally needy boys. Having some part to play in helping young boys, and watching them grow and develop, must have been emotionally satisfying for the elderly residents. At Hammersmith the old ladies exercised their post-childrearing maternal and caring instincts by tending canaries and linnets; better, surely, a baby or a boy to help care for, especially when baby and boy were so in need of love, extra care and attention.

Organisations and staff working in them have a tendency to inflexibility: policies, procedures, customs and established practices are followed without reflecting on the wisdom or continuing usefulness of these. Change usually only happens, and then often very belatedly, as a result of crises or scandals, or both. The separation policy meant that the possibility of an informal, organic development of what I would term 'substitute extended family' for boys and elderly was not available to either group at Nazareth House, to the possible detriment of both. It also meant that the Sisters charged with the care of both groups were denied this much needed practical and caring supplementary help.

1.4.3. All Things in Common

The young boys who were able to walk were taken out by a Sister or a pair of Sisters for regular walks when the weather was clement. The boys always walked in pairs holding the hand of a companion in familiar snaking line.[99] The boys walked around the large grounds, chattering, skipping and jumping. A common feature of the boys was their attention-seeking behaviour towards their mother substitutes, the Sisters, as another Nazareth Homeboy observed:

'The younger boys took to these nice nuns and would hold their hands and walk with them. The boys would also be jumping up and down in front of the nun to get their attention. The poor little lads were just looking for a little love. I'm sure most of them never knew what love was'.[100]

The values of sharing and equality were early inculcated in the boys by the Sisters. Although the boys had few or no personal material possessions or presents they were expected to pool whatever they had with their companions. When Paddy and his brother had a brief visit from a man he believed to be his father he had been showered with treats: sweets, chocolate and bananas. These presents hitherto unknown to him were no sooner his than were gone: shared with his companions when out on the Sister-supervised walking line of young paired boys.[101] *They had all things in common.* Whether this be aught or naught, was a clear, socialistic-type approach at Nazareth House. Similar clothing including outfits worn for religious festivals and that for the brass band members emphasised this common 'no-one is superior' approach to the boys.

This approach was underpinned by the Sisters' training and philosophy and indeed by the whole monastic tradition. Church culture at this time lauded the qualities of humility, moderation, and poverty and self-sacrifice, while regarding the pursuit of earthly wealth as inimical to a soul's salvation. A very strong reinforcement of this philosophy had emerged from the influential Papal Encyclical, *Rerum Novarum* (1891). This had been the first to coin the phrase 'The Common Good': this was held out as a central tenet and aim of social and economic policy. A section from this encyclical of Pope Leo X111's captures a flavour of this thinking:

'Therefore, those whom fortune favours are warned that riches do not bring freedom from sorrow and are of no avail for eternal happiness, but rather are obstacles; that the rich should tremble at the threatenings of Jesus Christ.....and that a most strict account must be given to the Supreme Judge for all we possess'.[102]

While the intentions were laudable the attitude perhaps tipped over into an excessively egalitarian approach which insufficiently took account of the needs of such young children, so deprived in so many other ways, for something distinct to call their own. The common good the boys knew and understood; their need was for a degree of personal, individual attention. The low chances of this, primarily because of resources and secondly because of the Sisters well-intentioned ideology, were rendered almost negligible by the policy separation of the elderly from the very young in the new Home.

1.4.4. Separation and Distress

When Paddy Baker arrived at Nazareth House he had never previously been parted from his mother, Lillian. Two years old is a particularly problematic age to move any child. Bonding and attachment between mother and child is likely to have been fully formed. Paddy would have been attuned to the sound of his mother's voice, to her unique smell as well as the sight of his central, and indeed only, comfort figure. Babies and children are necessarily selfish: their lungs demand the world pay attention to their needs. His mother was his world and then abruptly she was gone. Practice at that time was to make a clean break rather than prolong the agony of separation by a phased handover of the child. Yet Paddy had not developed sufficient language, memory or understanding to allow him to store and carry her memory and image with him after they were separated. The trauma of this loss would have been all-consuming for him, triggering bouts of despair and screaming, seeking to call back she who had abandoned him.

The impact of even a short such separation of a previously 'glued' mother child pair is illustrated by the case of a similar-aged boy separated from his mother for about a week when she went into hospital for an operation. Even though he was cared for by an aunt during the day and at night and the weekend by his father and 4 older siblings he remained stunned and vacant, engrossed in trying to work out where his mother had gone. When his mother returned from hospital the boy shunned her to her great distress. He would only go to his father, or to his siblings, recoiling from his mother's attempts to reach out to him. Young as he was, the boy appeared to be punishing her for her betrayal and abandonment of him. For a considerable period thereafter it was clear that the boy was preoccupied with this event that had so disturbed the previous security and certainty of his world. It took some time for him to overcome this wariness towards his mother.[103]

Another Nazareth House boy who arrived at the same age as Michael confirms this withdrawal reaction:

'My mind is blank for a lot of the next two years as from the age of four to six I remember very little. I think I was in a state of shock, a kind of limbo, at being taken from my loving family and now having no-one to turn to'.[104]

This reference to episodic blank memory mirrors Michael's complete lack of recollection of anything of his first few years after arrival at Nazareth House.

The distress of Paddy and the other babies and toddlers at the sudden and permanent separation from their mothers, can well be imagined. These children included his brother, James, who had arrived there at the age of 3 years in 1919.[105] Managing this distress must have posed many difficulties and challenges for the Sisters put in charge of their care. What is sometimes not realised is how variable the reactions of the children to separation can be. Factors such as gender, age at separation, previous history, quality of previous relationships and individual child temperament all play a part. While both genders may manifest anger when hurt it is more common for this response to be shown by boys.[106] Also influential is, of course, how the children were handled and the nature of the institutional regime to which they were sent.

Michael Porter who was nearly 5 years old when he arrived at Nazareth House may well have had his crying, screaming, angry phase somewhat earlier, after his mother had died nearly two years previously. It is possible that Michael's reaction on arrival at Nazareth was quite different to that of Paddy. Withdrawn, watchful, preoccupied with his own thoughts and feelings, bewildered: these are not uncommon reactions amongst some separated, and indeed some abused, children. This different manifestation of distress can often be overlooked either because it is not understood or because overworked staff feel relief at not having a demanding child to attend to. Absence of overt distress can too easily be interpreted as a child having settled or even having become contented. In fact this emotional withdrawal can be much more harmful to the child: a quiescent child may be more damaged and hurt than one who protests.

The emotionally undemanding child is the very one who most needs emotional attention but who is often overlooked and therefore becomes emotionally neglected, becoming in turn less demanding of adult contact and attention. The phrase, 'Shy bairns get nowt', is usually used when referring to material goods; it might equally be used to represent the plight of the emotionally withdrawn institutional child. Discussions with Michael lead me to believe that his reactions at Nazareth House were more of the withdrawal rather than the protesting, demanding type. As such they are more worrying. It is unlikely that the Sisters in charge of these boys had much understanding of the significance of these forms of distress and harm. They would have been doing well to provide safe physical care and limited emotional nurturing to their charges given the lack of Sisters involved in child care.

1.4.5. Child Care Staffing Arrangements

Two Sisters would have been charged with the care of the babies and the boys up to the age of 7 years. One would have to manage the night time feeding, toileting and soothing the babies, and still remain on duty the next day. Some relief for the two Sisters in charge of the younger children and babies would have been provided by the older boys attending the in-house school up to the age of 7 years. As the babies shared sleeping quarters with the elderly ladies up until 1925-1926,[107] assistance from these ladies at night time in particular must have seemed like a Godsend to the Sisters. It is likely that the Sisters chosen for this task were younger and stronger physically than their counterparts. Many of these young women would have had ample experience of child rearing even though their calling prevented them from bearing children of their own. All of them were Irish and many of them would have originated from rural families where small cabins were often filled with large numbers of young children. Child care, including baby care, would have been part of their domestic 'training' by their mothers long before they had ever contemplated taking the veil.

The older boys were also cared for by two Sisters. For much of the period when the Quartet were in residence at Nazareth House, Sister Attracta was in charge of this section, having seemingly moved up from tending the younger children after the opening of the new building. Michael Porter described her as a very large woman; she certainly was to feature largely in the lives of each member of the Quartet during their period at Nazareth House.

Chapter 1.5: Early Years in the New Home: 1926-1928

1.5.1. Opening of New Boys' Home: Unintended Consequences?

By the end of 1926 the new Nazareth House building for boys had accommodated all the boys transferred from the first Yeats building, including Paddy Baker, and the spacious new premises then enabled a flurry of new arrivals such as Michael Porter to be accepted.[108] There remained room for new entrants in 1927, including Willie McGowan and Willie Walsh. The foundation stone was laid in 1921 but the new boys' home was not used to accommodate the Sisters and the boys until after its completion in 1925. Even then it appears that the transfer of boys was phased over a period of time. The first dormitories in the new building were occupied in January 1925 and the Sisters moved into their new dormitories in the following month. It was not until later in 1926 that the new building accommodated all the boys and their child care Sisters. Several hundred boys had been accommodated at Nazareth House by the time the new home was fully operational at the end of 1926.[109]

The former, adjacent Home was then used exclusively as a care home for the elderly of both genders. The Nazareth Sisters continued to staff this Home and both sets of Sisters were under the overall control of a single Reverend Mother. It appears that the child care component was by far the largest part of the overall work of the Sisters.[110]

Parkinson's Law states that: 'work expands so as to fill the time available for its completion'. This adage could be reworked and applied to care placements to read: 'children are taken into care to fill the increased places available to accommodate them'. When there are no facilities available for out-of-home care families usually stagger on in difficult circumstances and retain the child either at home or with the extended family within the local community. Earlier the question was raised as to why Michael had not been admitted to care four months earlier when his sister, Sadie, had been committed to care. After the death of their mother the Porter family managed for two years to keep three, then two, then one child 'at home'. It seems very likely that the reason that Michael was not taken into care simultaneously with Sadie was that there was not yet a place available.[111]

The increased capacity of Nazareth House made possible his removal from home, albeit some considerable distance away. Paddy Baker's mother had kept her two sons with her during the most difficult period of child rearing, giving them up at the ages of 3 and 2 years. Willie Walsh was well into his seventh year before he arrived. The McGowan neighbours had devised a strategy to keep the 6 surviving children with their father yet they were dispersed to other placements available to take them, even though this involved separation of the 6 children into four or five separate homes, one as far away as Dublin.[112] Yet it was not as if anyone was seeking to harm these children. All concerned probably believed that they were doing the best they could for the children, as is evident in Father Bowes' letter. The most serious consequences for children often arise as much from such benevolent and charitably inclined policies and provision than they do from carers deliberately seeking to inflict hurt upon them. Well intentioned social policies may have unintended detrimental consequences. Did the new child-care places at Nazareth House meet a pent-up demand for care or did they create a vacuum that sucked boys in to fill these additional places available; or perhaps both? Certainly the significant expansion of care places at Nazareth House had fateful consequences for both Michael Porter and Willie McGowan; whether there were other compensatory benefits arising from their period in care, will be illustrated in the outline and discussion of how their later lives developed.

1.5.2. Resource Needs Mismatch

There was a significant shortage of carers at Nazareth House, Sligo. In 1910 there had been 5 Sisters and 17 boys at Nazareth House.[113] By the following year the numbers of Sisters had increased to 7 to look after the total of 46 boys and elderly residents.[114] Michael Porter, Paddy Baker (and William McCormack in the late 1940's and early 1950's), all commented on how few Sisters there were to do the work in the Home and how overworked many of them were. According to the Quartet's recollections it seems that the overall number of Sisters to run both homes varied from 9 to a dozen or so during the 1920's and 1930's. Michael remembers counting them all in his mind when they sat at the back of the in-house chapel. Sister John reported that the total number of Sisters at Nazareth House, Sligo, may have reached the low teens at this period.[115]

The number of boys in the home varied. Willie McGowan reported the number of boys there in his time as 72; Michael's impression was that the numbers were never less than 70, never more than 100.[116] Sister Attracta listed 95 boys during her time there, but this seems to have been the maximum number accommodated there at any one time.[117] Then there were the residents of the adjacent Home for the elderly men and women, taking the total number of residents to be cared for to well over the hundred mark. This would give a staffing ratio of Sisters to residents (both young and elderly) of about 1 to 10. That does not, however, reveal the true chasm between residents and the staff available to care for them.

To understand the challenges faced by the Sisters in caring for these vulnerable residents it may be useful to compare their circumstances with present day practices and standards. Present day staffing ratios of child care staff to children would commonly be 1 staff member to 6 children, or 1 to three with babies. Because staff to-day work 40 hours or less, and take holidays and sick leave, and there is sleeping-in cover at night, a total care staff complement of almost 100 might be required to safely care for that number of dependent old and young residents. In addition, as care staff today would not be expected to carry out the domestic chores that the Sisters did, with help from the boys there would need to be employed perhaps an additional 20-30 plus domestic and ancillary staff to cover the year round operation of the two Homes. Furthermore the Sisters and the few Yardmen who did the heavy outdoor manual work did not enjoy the advantages of lighter and better clothing for themselves and the residents, labour saving cooking and cleaning equipment and the smaller, more suitable buildings to service that are available in present day child care facilities.

The staffing situation was even worse when two additional factors are considered. Two of the Sisters were constantly out of the Home begging, and much of the Reverend Mother's time was taken up with raising funds to keep the home operational in addition to her overall management of the Sisters and the two Homes. The Sisters still had their religious duties to perform and that inevitably meant periods of the day when they were withdrawn from their care duties,[118] even though some of these religious functions occurred both before and after the children went to bed. Summarising the above factors, and trying to make comparisons with today, it seems that the staff available to care for residents was between one tenth and one fifth of what would be regarded as necessary today to provide acceptable safe staffing numbers.

This enormous resource gap was met by the Sisters working continually, not being relieved by another shift of workers coming on duty, nor taking holidays or days off. Working relentlessly and rarely being off sick (unless they broke down) they still had their religious duties as nuns and members of a religious Congregation to attend to.

It was also met by involving the boys in some aspects of the work (kitchen, laundry, cleaning and care of elderly) even though this was in clear breach of Congregation policy.[119] The significant human resource shortage at Nazareth House, Sligo, makes more understandable why the older boys were used to provide additional hands to cope with the scale of work. It was also a contributory factor to the Sisters use of regimentation and shepherding of the boys in their care practices.

1.5.3. Daily Routine in the New Home

An outline of the daily routine in the new Boys' home during the period when the Quartet lived there illustrates these aspects of Home life. The boys rose early, but after the Sisters had commenced their religious duties. The babies and younger children were cared for and educated in their own nursery section of the building. From the age of 7 years these were transferred and allocated to one of three dormitories: Sacred Heart; St Joseph's; or St Patrick's. The two larger dormitories, both age based, were very large, the other considerably smaller and not age based.[120] This was reserved for those boys who were bed-wetters, a not inconsiderable number. Boys are statistically more likely than girls to develop bladder control later and to persist in bed wetting until a much older age, even into teenage years. Trauma such as the loss of family suffered by the boys in the Home made much more likely that this distress would exacerbate problems of bladder control. Although the iron bed frames and mattresses had protective sheeting for the bed-wetters in order to minimise staining and smell that this problem caused, washing of stained sheets and sometimes the heavy woollen blankets was a daily necessity.[121]

Paddy Baker described the process of transfer, a rite of passage from petticoat-garbed and protected infanthood, to becoming a 'big boy' at 7 years of age and wearing shorts. His new Sister carer questioned him and a small companion who was also to be transferred from the babies' dormitory with: *Do we wet the bed?* Patrick Columb Monaghan, nicknamed 'Domsey', and like Paddy born in 1923 and also one of two brothers at Nazareth House, said that he was dry at night. He was given his night-time cocoa. Paddy, so schooled by the Sisters to tell the truth, admitted that he sometimes wet the bed. He was not given the night time tin mug of cocoa provided to his young companion and all the older dry boys. Instead Paddy was given a small handful of currants on the bare table as a substitute. Paddy bemoaned the awful habit of truth telling ingrained in him by the Sisters, young as he was that had denied him the cocoa:

The nun clapped her hands which summoned us to stand up, saying grace after meals, line outside on the passage and walk silently two by two to our respective dormitories. I very nearly made the mistake of walking in to the babies' dormitory for I had known no other. I landed in St Joseph's.[122]

Despite his confession of bedwetting Paddy had not been sent to the bed-wetters dormitory, the Sister instead using the currant-for-cocoa substitute as a preventive measure. While in St Joseph's Paddy had to listen to the older boys' ghost stories. They claimed that attic ghosts came down: *to cause havoc amongst us boys* and that is why the attic was always kept locked. Paddy's fear of the ghosts prevented him using the toilet and the inevitable bladder failure ensued resulting in his transfer to St Patrick's (patron Saint of the incontinent). Despite Paddy's prayers to his namesake: *he didn't bestow a sweet smile on me,* and Paddy remained in St Patrick's until the natural ageing process resolved his problem.[123]

Michael Porter was not an habitual bed wetter but once, in his teens, he wet the bed. He was mortified to be allocated to the small dormitory for bed-wetters for this one slip. Michael cannot ever remember moving out of the dormitory and he felt a great sense of injustice that he was there and permanently stigmatised after just one incident. In that dormitory they had plastic sheets under the mattresses. He tried to help the other boys in there by getting them up in the night to see if they could relieve their bladders and not wet the bed. Toileting was with a potty. He felt a great deal of stigma attached to this and being there was an invitation to mockery from the other boys.[124]

The older boys were not supervised when they got up and were expected to take wet sheets to the laundry area if necessary, and be bathed or sluiced in cold water and disinfectant to remove the smell of urine. All had to wash and dress themselves after prayers. They attended daily Mass in the chapel which was then in a large, bow-windowed room on the ground floor corner of the Home. The Sisters sat in a bench at the back where they could keep an eye on the 70 to 100 boys in the benches in front of them. Each boy was trained to serve Mass and to recite the basic Latin needed for this. Willie McGowan, when older and a student at Summerhill College, had to serve as many as three Masses a day before breakfast. He was consequently in a state of collapse from hunger by breakfast time.[125]

Breakfast was eaten in the dining room at the end of a long corridor. Tin plates and mugs were used and also tin spoons. Hammersmith visiting inspections laid great stress on improving manners and eating habits. The visitors were not always impressed by what they took to be lower standards in these areas in Sligo.[126] This was no doubt regarded as another example of supposed English superiority and snobbishness by the Irish, Sligo-based Sisters, even though Ireland was now no longer part of Britain.

1.5.4. Diet and Nutrition

For breakfast the boys always had salt-seasoned porridge and a slice of bread. Half a mug of cocoa was drunk. The dried cocoa powder, like the porridge, flour and many other cooking supplies, was bought in large quantities in hessian, hundredweight or heavier, sacks.[127] Storage of these inevitably attracted mice and the supplies were also susceptible to damp. During a school week the boys were given a slice of bread, usually with dripping, for lunch. They had to return from Quay Street Marist School, queue up in front of a Sister at the front entrance, and she dispensed a slice of bread to each boy. The boys hurried to get their dinner because late arrivals had sometimes found that there was no bread left for them.[128]

At weekends, and on school day evenings, a cooked dinner was provided. This included some form of meat or mince in gravy, a couple of potatoes in their skins (the near-universal Irish manner of serving them) and a seasonal vegetable, usually cabbage or turnip. For weekend tea the boys might have two slices of bread and dripping followed by a dessert.[129] This was usually one of the common milk-based staples such as rice pudding, semolina, tapioca, or carrageen moss. The carrageen was made from sugar, milk, egg, vanilla and sea weed.

An occasional treat was bread and butter pudding. This depended on the amount of leftover bread gathered from the elderly residents whose teeth, or lack of them, were unable to cope with the crusts.[130]

Not eating the food resulted in the food being re-presented until it was eaten. Michael remembers having difficulty eating food when younger and thought he might have suffered from a digestive problem. The more common problem for the growing boys was lacking enough food to digest, especially during the school day, when from breakfast to tea time they were fortified by just one piece of bread and dripping.

The most difficult food to provide to the boys, because of its cost and limited availability was, unsurprisingly, that which they enjoyed little of: fruit. Jam on bread briefly appeared at lunchtime. Like the vegetables, fruit and berries for the jam were only available seasonally. In the summer the Sisters took the boys to the seaside and also in the autumn to Lough Gill. The boys gorged, blue-lipped, on the berries they gathered around the Lough side and the remaining gathered fruit was made into jam on return to Nazareth. This treat was all the more memorable because of its rarity, a*nd when it was gone it was back to the old dripping again* for the lunchtime bread as Paddy regretted.[131] Before retiring to bed the tin mug of cocoa was again given, with the St Patrick's dormitory boys eating their compensatory currants. The great religious, seasonal festivals were similarly marked by a variation of the diet. At Easter the boys, appropriately, were given hard-boiled egg; at Christmas, sausages.

Boys who were ill, as in the case of many in Michael's dormitory who contracted measles in the early 1930's, were dosed with home-made barley water. Senna and castor oil doses, standard treatment for children in many domestic as well as institutional settings, were also administered regularly to the boys.

The boys' diet was the same for all children in Nazareth House Homes, the Sligo Sisters following instructions and example from Nazareth House in Hammersmith. The diet is remarkably similar to that recommended by Seebohm Rowntree, and is almost certainly based on the 'scientific' recommendations in his policy-changing study report into poverty in York at the end of the nineteenth century.[132]

1.5.5. 'Scientific' Nutritional Standards: Background

Seebohm Rowntree, a director of Rowntree's Cocoa and Sweet Factory in York, England, had carried out an extensive study of poverty in his home city. Studies of poverty in London in the late 1800's by Charles Booth[133] and the Salvation Army's William

Booth[134] had outlined the massive scale of poverty and destitution in the then world's largest city. When Rowntree's York study revealed that poverty was endemic in an attractive historic city in Britain at the height of its imperial power this was unexpected and so had more impact in changing government policies.

Rowntree had found that 28% of the overall city population and 43% of the 'wage-earning class' were in poverty. More than half of the worst, primary poverty was not the result of unemployment but caused by those in regular work earning insufficient wages. For many workers, therefore, they and their families lived insecure, poverty-blighted lives despite working full-time, in often arduous manual work. Infant mortality in the poorest sections of York was 25%.[135]

To improve the health of the population and to maintain health and to enable children to grow properly Rowntree recommended dietary changes. His 1901 report had the benefit of timeliness. His recommendations echoed with leaders such as Winston Churchill who had been shocked at the unfit state of the military. Large number of British recruits to the Boer War (1899-1902) had been rejected because of stunted growth and/or nutritionally related health problems.[136] Many recruits failed the already low height and chest measurement standards. In the First World War special Bantam regiments had to be created in some industrial areas of Britain. These had even lower physical requirements to enable regiments to be raised and the height requirement was reduced to as low as 4 feet 8 inches. The correlation between social class and height and weight was shown by Rowntree's York study and also revealed during war: British officers were on average some 4 to 5 inches taller and proportionately heavier than their working class men.[137] In Ireland the health and height of the rural population was generally better than that of the population of industrial mainland Britain.[138]

The title of the 1903 government committee set up to address the problem neatly encapsulates its nature: The Committee on Physical Deterioration.[139] The earlier poverty reports had not produced concerted government action; problems and failings resulting from the feared deterioration of the race were acted upon only after they damaged the country's ability to conduct a war. As with many changes, including those in child and elderly care and protection, actions usually occur long after the initial problems, and almost always triggered by crises, disasters or scandals. The Nazareth House residents, both children and elderly, and many others in institutional care in both Britain and Ireland, were the unwitting, indirect beneficiaries of these changes.

Nazareth House menus bear the imprint of Rowntree. His nutritional analysis of foodstuffs, and examples of diets for different household members was used by public and charitable bodies to provide cost-effective, balanced nutrition for inmates of institutions, including workhouses. He made precise calculations, based on professor Atwater's work, of the energy requirement for different groups,[140] at different ages, and how best to achieve the carbohydrate, protein and fat components necessary for this. He paid attention to the need to provide the necessary vitamins and minerals as well as how to do this most economically given the restricted circumstances of many household budgets. Sample menus were given. These included cocoa, so extensively used not only at Nazareth House but also in many working class homes.[141]

1.5.6. Rowntree's Nutritionally Balanced Menu

The following table, compiled from Rowntree's first study, enable the foodstuffs and a sample diet to be compared with the boys' fare at Nazareth House. The menu is for a child aged between 8 and 16 years old.

	Breakfast	Dinner	Supper
Sun	Bread, 6oz Margarine, ½oz Tea, ¾pt	Boiled bacon, 3oz Bread, 3oz Potatoes, 8oz	Bread, 6oz Margarine, ½oz Cocoa, ¾pt
Mon	Bread 3oz New milk, ½pt Porridge, ¾pt Sugar, ½oz	Potatoes with milk, 16oz Bread, 2oz Cheese, 1½oz	Bread, 6oz Vegetable broth, ¾pt Cheese, 1½
Tues	Bread 3oz New milk, ½pt Porridge, ¾pt Sugar, ½oz	Vegetable broth, ½pt Bread, 3oz Cheese, 1½oz Dumpling, 6oz	Plain cake, 6oz Milk, ¾pt
Wed	Bread 3oz New milk, ½pt Porridge, ¾pt Sugar, ½oz	Boiled bacon, 3oz Bread, 3oz Potatoes, 8oz	Plain cake, 6oz Milk, ¾pt
Thur	Bread 3oz New milk, ½pt Porridge, ¾pt Sugar, ½oz	Cocoa, ¾pt Bread, 6oz Cheese, 2oz	Bread, 6oz Broth, ¾pt Cheese, 1½oz
Fri	Bread 3oz New milk, ½pt Porridge, ¾pt Sugar, ½oz	Boiled bacon, 3oz Bread, 3oz Potatoes, 8oz	Plain cake, 6oz Cocoa, ¾pt
Sat	Bread 3oz New milk, ½pt Porridge, ¾pt Sugar, ½oz	Suet pudding, 12oz	Bread, 6oz Milk, ¾pt
(In addition to the above; lunch in the form of bread, 2oz; butter, ½oz; cake, 2oz; or biscuits, 2oz, is allowed on weekdays only).			

Illustration 12: Sample Rowntree Menu for 8 to 16 Year Old Child[142]

63

1.5.7. Nazareth House Diet Compared with Rowntree's Recommendations

When comparing the former Homeboys' memories of Nazareth House diet to the Rowntree example certain differences are evident. The boys do not record eating dried beans and pulses, which formed the base for vegetable soups and broth, or suet or cheese. Local circumstances in Sligo and different food preferences in Ireland compared with England may account for some variation of diet from the 'model'. Although the boys' recollections do not include the above foods it is extremely unlikely that their memories are comprehensive on this matter.[143] It seems probable that these foodstuffs did form a significant part of the diet. It is most unlikely that meat was given every day to the boys because of its relatively high cost. Cheese and dried pulses are likely to have been substituted for the meat course, as they were a cheaper way of supplying protein to the children. Willie McGowan's lifelong liking for dried pulse based soups and broths is almost certainly a further testimony to his Nazareth House diet as such fare was not a feature of his food at home,[144] and at least three of the Quartet members maintained a lifelong habit of making porridge for breakfast.[145]

A further factor that is likely to have influenced the boys' diet is the somewhat unpredictable nature of foodstuffs gifted by businessmen to the Nazareth Homes. The begging for the Nazareth Homes was carried out not only by the pair of travelling mendicant Sisters, but also by way of advertising, at both Headquarters and in regional Homes. The example given here is taken from *The Times* newspaper:

'The Sisters of Nazareth beg to return sincere THANKS to Messrs Nurdin and Peacock of Wells Street, Oxford St. for their ANNUAL gift of eggs, butter and lard and hope that this generosity may be followed by other firms, as having upwards of 400 inmates entirely dependent on them for food, even the smallest contribution will be gratefully accepted'.[146]

1.5.8. Fund Raising

Whatever the gifted foodstuffs happened to be would be incorporated into the diet of the residents. The above example of regular donations from Nurdin and Peacock, a firm of egg and butter importers, illustrates the imaginative use of publicity and, propaganda by the Hammersmith Mother General, and also the precarious nature of Congregation finances for feeding the residents. The Congregation sought to develop a network of supplies to keep the Homes running. Of especial benefit were the regular donations such as this one, as these enabled the Sisters to plan their provision of food and care more predictably. Both donor and recipient benefitted from the arrangement; the donors more so for not appearing to blow their own trumpet.[147]

Fund raising for the Sligo Nazareth House Homes encountered both setbacks and progress. The disturbed conditions in Ireland in the early 1920's, because of the revolt against British Rule and the subsequent Irish Civil War, created problems for the running of the Homes including that: the Sisters at the Collecting had many set-backs...the roads were dug up. The sheltered, oasis-like life in Nazareth House is reflected in this extract from its history. *It was a sad time in the country as civil war raged but life went on for the Residents.*[148]

After the end of the civil war compensatory funding was raised through the efforts of the Sligo Fund Raising Committee of Nazareth House. Local Sligonians, *who were by now getting very interested in the new building,* [149] were able to see the newly opened building at a Carnival in the grounds of the Home in May 1924, organised by the Committee. This three day event raised £1, 651. With this bounty the Sisters were able to purchase, at auction, a nearby field belonging to the *Merville* property, hitherto held by a Mr. B. Frazer, for the sum of £320. They were also able to install an electric plant for the Homes in December that year, with the chapel lighted for the first time by electric lighting at Midnight Mass.[150] This very early availability of electric lighting in Ireland was not something the boys commented upon, as it formed part of their taken-for-granted life in the Home, yet it was a considerable improvement on facilities enjoyed in their family homes. The Shannon Hydro Electric Scheme begun by the new Irish Free State took many years to reach the rural Homes occupied by the families of the Nazareth Quartet.[151]

These improvements in premises and facilities were largely funded by charitable donations, primarily from Catholic sources but also from Protestants, a Mr Lindsay gifting £15. There were even contributions from those of no religion, including an English, self-declared 'freethinker', Herbert Quinton, a Dental Surgeon, who provided free dental services to Nazareth House. True charity knowing no denominational boundaries. The daily operation of the Homes, including feeding the boys, was still, however, dependent on the success of the Collecting Sisters' widespread begging journeys.

1.5.9. Dietary Summary

Reviewing the nutrition of the boys, it does seem that the dietary regime at Nazareth House was based on established best dietary and scientific guidance at that time. In many respects it was superior to the diet of many working class children in Britain, and in Ireland, especially in urban areas. The potato rich diet of the peasantry in Ireland, especially if supplemented with milk, would have been of greater volume and almost as healthy, but monotonous and much less varied then the Nazareth House diet. The Sisters managed to achieve a balanced nutritional diet despite constant anxiety about their uncertain and fluctuating income. I rather doubt that their charges were aware of this, or that they regarded their still somewhat Spartan diet with appreciation.

Chapter 1.6: Schooling: Quay Street and Summerhill College

1.6.1. St John's, Marist Brothers' School at Quay Street, Sligo

Nazareth House boys began to attend schooling outside the home from the age of seven. They then followed the daily routine of the older boys, leaving the grounds when Sister Attracta had dismissed them after morning assembly. The boys made whatever arrangements suited them to get to the Marist Brother's School on Quay Street. This was attended by almost all the boys except for the handful of older boys who were receiving a secondary education at nearby Summerhill College.

After school the same freedom to come home was granted the boys and they would dribble home, and were even able to go into town and into the shops, if only to 'eye shop' and envy. The only imperative was to be back in time for the evening meal. When not at school, or engaged on organised or approved activities outside the Home, the boys were expected to remain within the extensive Home grounds.

The 'Homeboys', as they were referred to by their schoolfellows, would have been identified as such immediately they entered Church Hill because of their uniform Home clothing. In the 1920's and 1930's this was blue coloured shirts and denim shorts, patched where necessary, with boots worn only in autumn and winter.[152] In the 1940's and 1950's the colour was khaki.[153] The uniform, rather like military garb, served as a rallying point to a boy under attack. Pairing or joining larger groups of other Homeboys would occur if a Nazareth boy was in one of the disputes or even fights that periodically flared up between Homeboys and 'Townies' (the Homeboys' term for their schoolmates).

Sometimes Homeboys made common cause with Townies as on the occasion when a Town boy cheeked a rag and bone man. Michael and the other boys were in Church Hill en route to their school in Quay Street, a poor, dockside part of town. The rag and bone man in a light, horse-driven cart rounded on all the boys, Townies and

Homeboys alike, lashing out at them with his long whip. He pursued the fleet-footed boys all the way to school.[154] The boys knew where school was situated by following their noses for the adjacent tannery's stench pervaded the area, and their lessons and playtime.

St John's National School, situated down by the docks in Quay Street, was run by the Marist Brothers. They had first established the School there from 1868-1880, re-starting it there on their return to Sligo in 1898. It was a single sex school and all teachers were male. In a number of Nazareth House Homes elsewhere, and in other Irish children's homes, care and education occurred on the same campus. For the Nazareth House boys this taste of the world beyond the Home grounds, albeit limited, was still invaluable in widening their range of experiences and contact with the outside world, that world in which they would eventually have to make their way.

Although a National School, St John's, Quay Street, was still church controlled, the Headmaster and a number of teachers being Brothers, with assistance from lay staff. A significant element of staffing of Irish schools and colleges was provided by religious of both genders, and by priests. Even where the 'National' schools were not staffed by religious or clergy, their management, control and staffing decisions were vary largely determined by local clerics.

1.6.2. Marist Brothers and Education

The Little Brothers of Mary, more commonly called Marist School Brothers, were a religious institute founded in France in 1817. Their recruitment specifically excluded anyone with aspirations for the priesthood as: 'their aim is to secure recruits who are likely to develop special aptitudes for the mission of teaching'.[155] The Marists also ran boarding schools, industrial schools, orphanages, and homes for working boys: any function that involved education or training of boys.

In 1934 the Marist Brothers bought part of a field along Church Hill for £100. Situated immediately below Nazareth House, nearer the town, this was developed for their living accommodation (their 'monastery').[156] Despite this proximity to Nazareth House, and despite meeting a Brother on Church Hill, Michael Porter never realised that Marist Brothers lived there. Although this home was behind a high stone wall, and hidden also by woods from Nazareth House, Michael's lack of awareness of his teachers living immediately next door to him suggests that one aspect of institutional life may have been to foster a heightened degree of self-absorption in some of the boys.[157]

Paddy Baker listed the teachers he recollected at school as:[158]

Class 1: *Brother Charles*

Class 2: *Mr Harte (nicknamed 'Badger Harte')*

Class 3: *Mr Cahill (elsewhere given as 'Kabel')*

Class 4: *Mr Shine (known as 'Daddy' Shine)*

Headmaster: *Brother John*

Many decades later five teachers, three of them Brothers, were convicted of sexual abuse of boys in their care, the abuse occurring in the 1960's to the 1980's, after the Marist Brothers School had moved to Temple Street after the Second World War.[159] The Quartet's experiences do not suggest that this was a problem during their school days. Michael Porter reports not a suggestion of anything improper against any of the teachers. Paddy described two of the Brothers, Brother Charles and Brother Benedict, as the best teachers. Michael recollects a Brother Francis and another, younger Brother who prepared him for his bursary examination, and yet a further Brother who organised plays at Nazareth House, whose names he could not remember. When Paddy first started Quay Street about 1930 the Headmaster, Brother John, used to supervise the boys playing in the stony schoolyard. Paddy, always moved by music, used to: *creep up behind Brother John and listen to him humming a song.*[160]

1.6.3. Gaelic and Nationalist

Although Michael always referred to Sligo as 'an English town' there was a strong Celtic tradition there fostered by the Gaelic

69

League whose leading national luminaries included notable Sligonians, W B Yeats, Countess Markievicz and Lady Gore-Booth. The former Bishop, who had invited the Sisters to Sligo in 1910, John Joseph Clancy, was also a very keen promoter of Hibernian language and culture, and also a member of the Gaelic Association. These figures sought to save and promote Irish language, culture and tradition and to rebut or repress what was regarded as the foreign, overweening, Anglo-Saxon influence as a result of centuries of occupation and dominance by Britain.

The suppression of the Anglo element resulted in anyone playing competitive 'garrison' games being excluded from participation in Gaelic League games. The garrison games were so-called after the games played by the British soldiers, such as Association Football (Soccer) and Rugby Football (Rugby). Sligo Rovers, whose ground was opposite Nazareth House at the upper part of Church Hill, and the roars from which were regularly heard by the boys of Nazareth House, was a very famous and well supported Irish Soccer club. It managed to attract famous English League players such as 'Dixie' Dean to play for them, usually at the tail end of their career. Anyone who did play such garrison games would know they risked being banned from playing Gaelic games. So soccer players often went under assumed names, sometimes, ironically, in Irish form. Sport, music and dancing were the central elements, after language promotion, in the post-independence push for producing Celtic-cultured children and youth for the newly formed Irish nation. All three elements featured heavily in the Quartet's boyhood experiences, more so indeed than the Irish language.

Nationalism and national politics intruded into school in February, 1932. The general election of that month saw Eamonn De Valera's Fianna Fail party challenge the incumbent Cumann na nGaedheal party that had been in power in Ireland since the civil war. The school windows were open, the stench of the nearby tannery pronounced. Suddenly there came a great roar from the townsfolk and Paddy Baker heard them singing, but couldn't make out the words. He memorised the melody, however, and asked a schoolfellow next day for the words which he remembered as:

Up de Valera,
He's the champion of our right.
We'll follow him to battle
With the orange, green and white[161]

This Hibernian element was inculcated in the Quartet as soon as they entered St John's School where roll call required boys to answer to their Irish names: Liam for William; Micheal for Michael; and Padraig for Patrick. At school the Brothers adopted the then near universal boys' schools practice of addressing the pupils by their surname whereas at Nazareth House the Sisters always addressed the boys by their Christian names.

1.6.4. Punishment and Mr Shine

A pupil at St John's School in the 1940's and early 1950's, when it had moved to Temple Street, wittily gives his view of the discipline and ethos then:

'Just before the school summer holidays in May 1952 everything was as normal at St John's National School in Sligo town. The swish of the cane could be heard from every classroom as each Brother and as each lay teacher carried out their God-given duties at assaulting helpless children they were supposed to be teaching. Was there any other way they could teach? No they knew no better. Punishment was their method. They were too ignorant to know any better'.[162]

Caning was standard as a form of punishment when the Quartet were pupils at Quay Street in the late 1920's and much of the 1930's. It was also in widespread use in boys' schools in Britain and Ireland then, and indeed until much later. The recollections of the Quartet, though varied, give a generally different perspective on the ethos in the school in the 1930's. Paddy Baker bemoaned a number of matters: having for school wear the blue Home uniform outfit of denim shorts and short-sleeved shirt; going barefoot in spring and summertime; and the lack of pencils and books to do his schoolwork. Otherwise, with one exception, relating to punishment by one lay teacher, Mr Shine, he exudes a warm feeling about his years there. And even when complaining about Mr Shine:

71

*and the most notorious and feared was a Mr Shine, who didn't
spare the cane and incited the boys to fear,* he recognises that:
*Shine no doubt meant well with me and wanted no doubt to mould
me into a master schoolboy. Had it not been for his cruelty I might
well have achieved this.*[163]

Michael's perspective of Mr Shine adds an interesting dimension to
Paddy's recollections:

*Mr Shine was very tall and lean, well over six feet in height. He
would stand with his back to the coal fire in the room warming his
backside while firing questions at us. He would cane you if you
were slacking. He wanted us all to do well and showed great
perseverance, even with the slower learners. One thing though; he
would always give it to you on the hand, never on the backside.
And he wouldn't jump up when caning you to make it harder. He
would never punish you for nothing. There was always a reason.*[164]

Paddy, two years younger than most of his classmates, was at least
as much afraid of being punished than of the punishment itself.
Fear and the preoccupation it causes can block a pupil's ability to
learn, a variant of the 'frozen watchfulness' manifested by
physically abused young children in domestic environments.

Mr Shine had been a Brother himself before marriage and a family.
He was known to some as 'Daddy Shine', possibly ribbing by some
of the still celibate Brothers of their former colleague who had
taken the family path out of religious life.[165]

There is a standard tune and doggerel familiar to many a schoolboy.
This was chanted by the boys at Quay Street, *sotto voce* one
presumes. That our 'hero', Mr Shine is chosen would indicate that
he was the pre-eminent, most feared and punitive teacher to the
boys.

*Mr Shine is tall and thin
He goes to Mass on Sunday
He prays to God to get a cane
To beat the boys on Monday*[166]

The worst punishments are not always physical, however, more lasting harm often arising from the tongue rather than the fist. Mr Shine seemed to have it in for a Town boy called O'Brien. This boy came from a poor family in a slum district and habitually arrived at school dirty, poorly clothed and smelly. Mr Shine regularly humiliated O'Brien in front of the class, ordering the boy to go and wash himself. The boy's mother intervened, arriving at Mr Shine's classroom door to tell him: *Mr Shine, my son is no rose. Don't smell him. Just teach him.*[167]

1.6.5. Teachers' Ambitions for the Boys and Eclipsis

The same teacher's other qualities were shown when he gave Paddy a whole shilling, an enormous sum then, for reciting the Credo without making a mistake. Although the Homeboys did not have pocket money, and rarely had money of their own, it appears that Quay Street staff sometimes gave out cash prizes for good work or to encourage the boys to greater efforts. The Headmaster, Brother John, instituted an English essay competition where content and presentation were assessed. He gave two pence for the first prize and he judged the boys' efforts. Michael won the competition. Dr Jekyll again metamorphosed into Mr Hyde when Mr Shine, charged with doling out the reward to his pupil, told Michael: *Well Porter I wouldn't have given you first prize.* He gave Michael only one penny.

Paddy Baker, young, handsome, with a good singing voice, conjectured that Mr Shine's promotion of him was because he had designs on adopting Paddy. Mr Shine already had a son, a student at Summerhill College, where he was due to be ordained to the priesthood. The son used to teach Mr Shine's Class 4 on occasions under his father's supervision as part of his external placements from Summerhill:

The cane was never used when he was present. The son had been sick for a long time and his father knew that his days were numbered. He died while I was in the fourth class and Shine wore the black armband on his arm.[168]

There is absolutely no suggestion that Mr Shine's interest in Paddy was improper and Paddy may, or may not be correct in his belief that he was to be the replacement for his only son. The earlier statement about Mr Shine's motivation having been to mould him into a *master schoolboy* has a compelling ring to it. As such it swings the Shine pendulum back towards the Jekyll personality, corroborating Michael's view that behind the cane was a man who had a genuine desire to see each of his pupils fully apply their abilities: *he wanted us all to do well.*

That last statement would seem to typify the approach of the Brothers and teachers at Quay Street generally; and in particular their efforts to help the more academically able pupils progress beyond elementary education. What is interesting is that one person, Mr Shine, features so significantly in the accounts of life at St John's National School, and that the extremes of life, especially caning, dominate to the exclusion of almost everything else. Much of the mundane is either forgotten or, quite probably, eclipsed by the extreme, either good or bad. This too is a feature of the recollections of life at Nazareth House, and of some of the Quartet's memories of childhood generally. The effect of caning or severe physical punishment, and the fear that this engendered, seems to have had a continuing dual legacy, and not only in Sligo: it features disproportionally in later recollections of childhood: and it eclipses many other memories, including the positive ones. It can make it more difficult to cut through the thicket of such memories to discern the more common pattern of daily life.

1.6.6. Education, Nationalism and the Catholic Church

Almost all aspects of the Quartet's childhoods were dominated by the Catholic Church. Their admission to care had been mediated by their parish priest. They were cared for by Sisters in a religious institution and taught by Brothers in a religious controlled 'National' school. Yet these welfare and educational functions had been established during the long period of protestant British rule in Ireland. During the nineteenth century the British Government increasingly ceded state patronage and control of education, welfare and training to the Catholic Church. This had come about because the British Government sought to influence the Catholic Bishops to exercise a moderating influence on the usually latent, sometimes violent, opposition to this rule by their flock. The Catholic Church generally did exercise this buffering and moderating influence against violent revolution and it was delivered in spades in 1888 when Pope Leo X111's encyclical, *Saepe Nos,* condemned the Irish Land League policy of boycotting and withholding of rent.

This moderating role was very evident in Sligo where Bishop Clancy faithfully followed the papal line:

'Dr. Clancy was a strong Nationalist but took no active part in politics except on the occasion of agrarian agitation, which he did his best to discourage. He was largely responsible for the defeat of the 'No Rent' campaign on Lord De Freyne's estate some years ago. On that occasion he strongly and constantly warned his flock against the operations of the paid organisers of the united League'.[169]

The Catholic hierarchy appears in many respects to have been a more effective force in abating violent agitation and revolutionary energies than the combined military, judiciary and police establishments in Ireland during the nineteenth and early twentieth century: their ideological control giving them the *de facto* power and influence that the Imperial Government lacked.[170]

The transfer of funds, patronage, premises and personnel from state to Catholic Church control was attacked by a catholic barrister, Michael J. F. McCarthy in a series of trenchant publications that illustrated the scale of what I would term 'institutional capture' of state functions by the Catholic Church.[171] In Connaught (Mayo, Sligo, Leitrim, Roscommon and Galway) the numbers of clergy, religious and teachers under Catholic Church control amounted to 4,825 in 1901. This contrasted with the size of the Imperial and Local Government establishment (including Civil Service and Police) of 3,083.

The number of clergy and religious in Ireland increased from 5,995 in 1861 to 15,397 in 1901 despite the Catholic population declining by a quarter in this half century, largely because of emigration.

75

This resulted in the 1861 ratio of clergy and religious to laity of 1 to 751 reducing to 1 to 210 by 1911. Much of this growth of church personnel was in schools, industrial schools and other training facilities, hospitals, workhouses and other care facilities for children and the elderly that were funded or part funded by the British Government.

1.6.7. Advancing the Orphans: Secondary Education and Summerhill College

Despite the early years of education at Quay Street School having occurred during British rule in Ireland, the opportunities for secondary education were, like England, very limited for working class children.[172] Had any of the Quartet remained at home with their families it is most unlikely that they would have progressed to secondary education let alone attained a university place, where only a tiny proportion of Catholic children went on to secondary level education (and a high percentage of these did so by pursuing a religious or clerical career). One route to education for the poor but able child was to join a religious order. Candidates for the secular priesthood tended to come from the better off families because of the costs and fees involved. Even more significant was the consequent loss of the labour or income that the boy or girl contributed to the poor and often large family. Individual ambition and educational aspiration came up against the reality of the need to contribute to family finances as soon as legally able to do so: in Ireland, and also in England, economics usually trumped educational aspiration.

Both the Brothers at Quay Street and the Sisters at Nazareth House tried to alter this in-built educational barrier to the poor and doubly disadvantaged Nazareth House boys. A particular way for the poor, able scholar, called in Scotland the 'lad o' pairts', to advance educationally was to secure a bursary or scholarship to a secondary school. In Sligo boys successful in entrance examinations could progress to the College of the Immaculate Conception. Summerhill College was its better known name called after the district of Sligo in which it was located after 1892, having earlier been in Quay Street. Founded in 1857 by the local Catholic Bishop its purpose was to prepare scholars from the Diocese for entry to seminary, as well as providing what would have been regarded as grammar school education in England for other day-pupils, not destined for seminary. It was staffed by clergy. In 1911 the 6 priest professors taught 67 scholars in residence. Most students were aged from 14 to 18 years with the 4 younger boys being 12 or 13 years old. In addition to the above complement of students were the day scholarship students from Sligo and its environs. [173]

1.6.8. Puritan Rigorism and Gloom

The uniform, congregational membership, discipline, and vows marked Marist Brother and the Sister of Nazareth alike as different and 'superior' to the laity; yet they in their turn were 'inferior' and subordinate to the clergy and male hierarchy, their gender and non-ordained status indicating a marked hierarchical gap from the 'commissioned', ordained caste above them.

The laity had only one way to look: upwards. There they found the many NCO (non-ordained religious) and commissioned officer ranks (priest and the many other gradations above them) in their rigidly hierarchical Church. The NCO class, however, looked, Janus- faced, both ways: both subordinate (and often markedly, even deferentially so to priest and prelate); while to those below them, they could reverse roles and be excessively controlling. Push, or appropriately challenge, upwards, and respect those in one's sphere of control, did not seem to be the dominant *modus operandi* in the late nineteenth and early twentieth century Roman Catholic Church; rather the reverse. This was often accompanied by a manner and stance more postural than pastoral, especially among the more clericalist shepherds of the flock.

Salus extra ecclesiam non est, St Cyprian of Carthage's third century statement (outside the church there is no salvation) was believed and followed by Sisters and their charges alike: all determined never to leave the barque of St. Peter, the one sure vessel to heavenly bliss.

All, bishop, priest, Brother, Sister and lay person alike, were subject to the weight of the rather dour, un-joyous, sin-centred, Puritan moral rigorism delivered in Church teaching in Ireland at this period. This left its consequent impress: guilty mind and dirty soul. Penitence and punishment, both here and in the hereafter, were the miscreant's lot. Soul-cleansing punishment now would prevent further sin in the future: even more importantly it would shorten time in Purgatory, and help avoid the even worse fate. Purgation and punishment; it is not hard to see why the overall message led to an additional, heightened response to youthful boisterousness, high spirits and pranks. Catholic, Presbyterian and some other non-conformist sects added an extra layer of control and punishment to the already quite censorious and controlling, climate in Ireland and the United Kingdom. Most harmful, perhaps, was the infliction of this message on children, so intensely and when they were so young.

1.6.9. Current Consequences of Past Attitudes and Policies

The results of successive British Governments allowing, or even encouraging, the secular expansionism of the Irish Catholic Church in the areas of care, education and training in particular is even now being worked out. The many scandals and inquiries into institutional abuse in Ireland are a result of this Church domination of institutional care in Ireland. Care in Ireland became almost synonymous with Catholic care. Children's homes and schools, and indeed any residential settings whether for children or adults, are more likely to harbour, perhaps even foster abuse, than non-residential settings. Because most such institutions were Church run, and many others Church managed or controlled, it was inevitable that these state responsibilities would eventually redound upon the providers of care, in Ireland usually the Catholic Church. This proxy provision of care by the Catholic Church had two very important benefits to the Irish State: the exchequer and taxpayers were saved an enormous amount of money throughout most of the twentieth century; and blame for abuse and exploitation could be laid almost exclusively at the door of the proxy providers of what, on the other side of the Irish Sea, would have been increasingly accepted as state responsibilities.

1.6.10. Scholarship and Summerhill

In Sligo the Church control of education was evident to the Quartet at Quay Street and at Summerhill schools. Michael Porter had always been keen to learn and he loved Mathematics in particular. An education at Summerhill, although heavily denominational in content, would have enabled him to develop this passion. One thing Michael looked for was getting an answer that was exactly right. He experienced great pleasure when either music or a mathematical equation came out perfectly. He loved the concrete but had no time for the more ethereal, and was always more keen to read something factual such as history or biography, having little time for stories or fiction. Mathematics seemed to him to be the nearest thing to perfection. Get it right and no one could argue with you or contradict you, you were right, summarised Michael's feelings about the complete satisfaction that Mathematics gave him.

He seemed to have a particular aptitude for it and he often helped some of the Townies with their Maths homework, usually before school. In exchange he was sometimes given money, more often comics or other goods from the boys he had helped. Doing the Townies' homework appears to have been quite a common practice among the more able Nazareth House pupils who also garnered money or goods this way.

Michael knew that he needed to get a good education if he was to make his way in the world as he intended to do. He enjoyed school and was always one of the boys at the top of his class. The preparation for the scholarship examinations had been conducted by a young, enthusiastic Marist Brother new to the school. He coached Michael and the other scholarship candidates that included his Quartet colleagues Willie McGowan and Willie Walsh, as well as some of the town boys. The first examination, conducted outside school premises, was confidently tackled and Michael knew from his answers which were checked later with the brother that he had done well. On the day of the final examination Michael commenced the paper as usual then stopped very early, having long decided to deliberately fail this exam, his best subject, Mathematics. He looked around, handed in his paper early and on the way out asked another boy whose new bicycle he had seen outside: *Can I have a go on your bike afterwards?*[174]

At school some time later the Brother who had prepared him for the examinations said *Now we know who's been copying his homework.* The Brother then came up behind him and struck him on the back with a cane several times, hard enough to make him jump out of his seat. Michael knew what he had done and the Brother also knew what he had done. He had deliberately thrown away a scholarship to the notable Summerhill College, with all the life and career enhancing opportunities this afforded him. He had also wasted the efforts of the Brother to advance his education. The die cast the Brother did not query Michael's motive for flunking the exam. Sometime later he met the Brother who was coming out of the Marist Monastery on Church Hill as Michael was walking down from Nazareth House on the other side of the road. The Brother crossed to speak to him: *Porter you're a very foolish boy, you missed a great opportunity.* Michael understood the Brother's reactions. The Brother evidently did not broadcast Michael's misdemeanour as there was no mention of this by the Sisters at Nazareth House.[175]

Michael bore no resentment to the Marist Brother to whom Michael's deliberate failure to complete his exam paper must have seemed wilful, perplexing, short-sighted and self-harmful: a waste of a great opportunity. Although Michael claims to have no regrets about his childhood decision, he does lament that he did not advance much further in the study of Mathematics.

Young though Michael was he had long formulated a plan in his somewhat unworldly head to leave Nazareth House and school at the earliest possible opportunity. He did not know what he would do when he left care or where he would go, but he would be 'out' and free, and so set his mind to leave care at the earliest possible opportunity. Although he didn't know exactly how long you had to stay at Summerhill he knew that the secondary pupils stayed at school much longer than those in elementary school. Indeed his ignorance of what Summerhill entailed led him to believe that he might be resident there: *I was in an institution and I was due to go*

to another institution if I went to Summerhill.[176] Summerhill was
indeed a part-residential College and Junior Seminary but Sligo
boys and Nazareth House boys attended there as day pupils.[177]

A further reason for Michael's actions was the rumours he had
heard from Quay Street pupils about the teachers at Summerhill,
though this was very much a secondary consideration. He had
heard tales from other boys about the ill treatment meted out to
boys by the priests at Summerhill, severe physical punishments and
beatings plus oblique but repeated, sexual innuendo such as: *you
wouldn't want to go near him ...don't let him get near you.*[178]

1.6.11. Irish Language and Accent

At Quay Street School Irish was taught as part of the school
curriculum, but all lessons were still conducted in English.
Competence in Irish became a requirement for all public sector jobs
and so there was an inducement to learn it. The initial decision to
teach every school child Irish after independence in 1922 proved
very difficult, not least because of the lack of competent Irish
speakers to teach it. The percentage of Irish speakers had declined
slightly faster than the overall population in the half century before
Irish independence in 1922. In 1926 just over half a million were
listed as native Irish speakers (22% of the population) compared
with over a million in 1861 (24%). Michael's family had not been
native Irish speakers. Paddy's mother was American. Willie
McGowan's parents had been Irish speakers.[179] The remaining
native Irish speakers were to be found predominantly in the poor,
western counties, especially along the western seaboard. Michael's
school Irish has long since disappeared.[180]

Reference to the Irish language did not feature at all in the extensive
communication between Paddy and Willie McGowan. The only
evidence of Irish I encountered in any correspondence was by a
nun, in Sister Gertrude's correspondence to Willie McGowan where
she used the Irish spelling for personal names. The dominance of
the English language as the *lingua franca* in the world of work and
commerce appears to have been the greatest reason for the decline
of the Irish language, this effect continuing after independence

despite the best efforts of government, school and carers to sustain it.

The language revival efforts of the new Irish government had been designed to foster a great sense of Gaelic heritage and identity. Somewhat surprisingly Michael did not regard his teachers or nun carers as Irish, despite their considerable efforts to inculcate in him this respect for all things Irish, including music, sport and dancing. Although most of the Sisters, and all the Brothers and lay teachers, were Irish themselves Michael saw them as neutral in terms of nationality and also accent. They were just, he said, the sort of people one was involved with when you were being educated or brought up. Nor does he recollect being attuned to their different accents even though some of the Sisters, including Attracta, came from the northern counties of Ireland whose strong accents are very different to the southern and western counties.

This neutrality in accent was mirrored in his attitude to the Sisters' gender. He didn't regard them as women, rather some gender-neutral kind of being. *I didn't have any experience of women when I was growing up either in the Home or at school.* When reminded about his Sister carers he said, *but they weren't women.*[181]

The Sisters' large voluminous habits and wimples obscured much of their face and body, and also their feet, rather like Muslim women today. Michael remembers having being fascinated by how the Sisters seemed to glide along without any evidence of feet. He tried unsuccessfully to see whether he could see a pair of shoes.[182] Paddy made similar observations including the standard analogy of the Sisters' habit and gait reminding him of penguins. Uniform as a barrier and distance between wearer and others is a common experience. Michael found the barrier a little more pronounced with the Sisters compared with the Marist Brothers, gender perhaps partly explaining this.

1.6.12. Mischief and Play

Michael and Paddy were both keen sportsmen, and liked the rough and tumble of boys' playground games, and fights, unlike Willie

McGowan. Paddy describes the differences between Willie and himself. Willie didn't seem sports minded and never:

got involved in a fight. You were always cool and collected. Unfortunately I cannot say the same thing about myself and my broken right hand thumb always reminds me of my aggressiveness and lack of self-control.[183]

Neither would Michael say no to a scrap or a fight or an argument and he was subject to bouts of occasional, but near uncontrolled, temper in childhood and in later life.

Yet Paddy Baker's image of Willie as a plaster saint was not entirely accurate. Willie McGowan managed just the once to be a scamp during his period at Quay Street School when he found a full packet of cigarettes on his way to school. He detoured away from school, playing truant while he searched for a match. Eventually he found one, but only the one, and went into a field where he lit up. Knowing that he could only light subsequent cigarettes from each preceding one, he smoked the whole packet, and passed out unconscious. He awoke to find himself in the Infirmary at Nazareth House. He had smoked both his first and last cigarette that day.[184]

Paddy complained of being verbally abused by a fellow pupil when asking to share his book, the boy rebutting him and his efforts and abusing his mother as a whore, and Paddy as a bastard.[185] Michael reports himself having had *a happy schooling* at Quay Street with the overall quality of education as good as was available in Ireland at the time. He valued the freedom he got going to, from, but also at school, away for a period from the sometimes stultifying atmosphere in the Home. He also greatly enjoyed mixing with the other boys at school. He describes them mixing freely together with very little friction or bigotry, the periodic disputes between Townies and Homeboys occurring on the way to or from school and usually confined to cat calling. He found the problems related less to boy-to-boy interaction and more to the attitude of their town boys' mothers, some of whom discouraged their children from playing with the Homeboys.[186]

One such example happened when Michael and his classmates were returning home after school. They had been playing tag after school on the road leading up to the turn to Church Hill. The game involved trying to tag or touch a companion, sometimes lunging at them as they sought to run away. Michael was called to see Sister Attracta, rehearsing in his mind the usual litany of misdemeanours he had committed to see which of them had been found out. He was confronted by a Mrs McGoldrick with whose son he had just been playing tag. She accused Michael and another boy of roughing up her son and tearing his clothes. Sister Attracta asked Michael to give his account of events and he was then dismissed without rebuke or any other action taken against him, to the evident disappointment of Mrs McGoldrick. Thereafter Michael never played with or spoke to McGoldrick again and crossed to the other side of the street from the boy's home when going to and from school.[187]

'Audiatur et altera pars'-'Get both sides of the question' was a much honoured principle even in pagan Rome[188]. So too was it at Nazareth House, Sligo, in the 1930's. Several issues arise from this episode: the Sisters had inculcated truth telling in the boys to the point that it had become second nature to them; Michael's repeated experience that the Sisters were just, always asking for your account before taking any action; finally that the Sisters could also tell whether a boy was telling a lie or the truth. It also shows, most unusually for that time, that a child's word, what is more a Homeboy's word, would prevail against the complaint of an adult. This echoes Sister John's comment that: *Attracta fought for her boys.*[189]

The walled playground at Quay Street School was full of sharp stones and as the Nazareth boys went barefoot in spring and summer, games were often a painful experience. Quite a number of their Townie fellow pupils were similarly shod, or rather not shod, and a number of them much worse dressed, less well fed and some of them verminous as Willie McCormack observed of the School even as late as the 1940's and early 1950's:

'You could always tell the very poor boys. They came to school with no shoes on their feet, winter or summer and were easily recognisable from the other boys of the town. Some had patches on the seats of their trousers and some had no such thing as underpants. If they had an overcoat it was probably too big or too small for them'.[190]

Several matters are suggested from this extract: the 'orphanage' boys being better dressed than some of their Townie fellows; the patches on some of the Nazareth House boys described by Paddy Baker in the 1930's had disappeared: and the material conditions of the Homeboys were superior to those the poorest class boys in Sligo town.

The stony playground did not deter the boys from play and sport. Michael loved any ball sport and had acquired, probably through doing a Townie's homework, a new handball. This was stamped with an elephant brand image and he often played handball practice by himself in the school ball alley. Handball is a distinctly Irish game played with a hard, small ball against a high flat wall with two end side walls. It is a variant of squash. These handball alleys can still be seen all over Ireland, often standing alone in rural areas.[191] When practising his skills alone Michael was alarmed when summoned to the classroom of a Marist Brother, one who hadn't taught him. The Brother told Michael that he had observed him playing handball, was keen on the game himself and would try to give him a game sometime. Michael cannot remember whether this happened, but he well remembers the elephant ball, and the sense of joy that owning something so special gave him.[192]

1.6.13. Getting on: Mixed Blessing?

Willie McGowan and Willie Walsh, used the opportunity that Michael had rejected, and worked assiduously to fulfil the hopes and aspirations that the Brothers and Sisters had for them. Both passed their entrance examination to Summerhill College leaving Paddy and Michael to continue at Quay Street School. The two Willies were not the first Nazareth House boys to make the move from Quay Street to Summerhill. In 1930 the Sisters recorded that:

This year there are three boys at College as day boarders free of charge. The College staff continued to take a great interest in these boys whilst the Marist Brothers gave us the school books free of charge

Another Homeboy, J. J. Burke had followed the church path to education, winning a bursary to the Jesuit Mungret College, Limerick in 1929, later being ordained in Rome, in 1932, at the Propaganda College.[193] The two McGuinness brothers, John and Michael, younger than Willie, both went to College, then to seminary, with John even graduating from the University of Cambridge.[194] So there appear to have been a number of 'From Log Cabin to White House' achievements of Nazareth House boys, usually via the route of church and church schooling.

Willie McGowan and Willie Walsh's achievement of secondary education was a rarity for poor boys in inter-war Ireland: in 1924 the percentage of pupils enrolled in secondary schools was only 5% of those in primary schools.

When the two William's went on to Summerhill College, Michael had cause to examine the wisdom of his decision to fail his entry examination. All indoor activities at Nazareth House occurred in the age-appropriate playroom. For the older boys this was a very large room on one of the upper floors, furnished with table and chairs. Many different activities, including children's games and play, reading and homework occurred in this single room. When Michael, freed from onerous homework in the last years at Quay Street School, saw Willie McGowan come back from Summerhill he knew that he had made the correct decision by scuppering his own chances of a place there. He remembers Willie looking weary, somewhat down in the mouth, having to unpack his homework and try to concentrate against the noise of the others in the room. Willie Walsh was similarly deeply engaged in his homework. Paddy remembered the two McGuinness brothers who seemed to him somewhat privileged. As College boys, one of whom was destined for the priesthood and the other for the religious life, Paddy remembers that the Sisters found them a private place to study.[195]

Willie McGowan had confessed to Paddy in later life that he had *hated College.*[196] This had amazed Paddy to whom Willie represented what he aspired in his dreams to be; dignified, cool and collected, respectful, diligent, academically able and successful. Paddy recorded how he had always: *had a deep admiration towards* Willie, wanting to emulate him. Having been advanced two years in his schooling may, in retrospect, have been disadvantageous to Paddy both educationally and socially, in having to compete with his older Quartet colleagues.

The unhappiness at Summerhill is not entirely surprising. Michael regarded the 'College boys' as: *way above us* in the social and educational spheres. The Homeboys normally had little contact with them and Michael felt that: *as Homeboys, at the bottom of the pile, we had a natural dislike of those in the higher grade.*[197]

One day after Michael had left school he had been walking along the pavement in Sligo when he found his path deliberately blocked by a trio of College boys in 'civvies'. He was surprised to be slapped in the face by one of the trio, a thickset boy, who told him: *Don't call me names.* There was some reference to 'Archibald', a name Michael had never heard of, and which indeed he thought was an Italian name. As the boys were all much bigger than him, and there were three of them, Michael, most unusually for him, did not retaliate deciding that discretion was the better course of valour on this occasion. The slap did not hurt much, and that in itself was even more hurtful than a punch would have been. The *de haut en bas* action signified condescension to Michael, the contempt of a superior to a lackey. He had no recollection of having verbally abused the boy, but did confirm that name calling did occur, and that he engaged in it. That he hadn't even been given the opportunity to explain himself was a further indication to him that the College boys viewed the Homeboys as lower beings, unworthy to even be talked to.[198]

While hardly representative of Summerhill College pupils as a whole the above incident does give an intimation of the inherent difficulties faced by the two Willies at College. The sensitive Willie McGowan would have been highly attuned to his socially vulnerable position at Summerhill where it would be surprising if his Homeboy status was not used against him by some of the boys.

It appears that Willie McGowan may have continued the able Homeboy tradition of doing other boys' homework. Paddy had teased him that when in the playroom: *You were perhaps under the table counting the L.S.D.[199] you collected from the more fortunate friends in College.[200]*

The implication of cash in exchange for doing homework is there; that it was done at all does suggest a difference in social status between the doer and those for whom the work was done.

The two College boys, the two Willies, continued their education until the age of 16 years, the two Quay Street boys leaving school some eighteen months to two years earlier than their band fellows. At Nazareth House and especially in the band, but also in dancing, music, drama and sport, and in general play and activities in the Home they continued to have a great deal to do with each other. Despite this contact in the home the College and Quay Street separation prefigured the somewhat different life chances for the respective pairs.

Chapter 1.7: Recreational Life at Nazareth House

1.7.1. Freedom to Play

Within the large walled grounds of Nazareth House the boys were both constrained but also free. Unless they were attending school, or otherwise had some particular need to leave the premises with permission, they were required to remain within the Home grounds. Otherwise they were free to play outdoors, or in bad weather, in the huge upstairs playroom/all purpose room. Although the boys were not supposed to leave their playground field they often ignored this requirement.

At the back of the home was a very large field that doubled as a playground and sports field. This was large enough for a soccer match to be played, either up and down or across (so probably between two and three acres in size). The field had some remaining tree stumps in it, was rather hard baked and dusty in summer, and fell away sharply from left to right. It had one soccer goal only at the end nearest the Home, near the rear hallway. The left to right declivity meant it was less suited to Gaelic football for which there were no goalposts, and the steep slope in any case made it more suitable for soccer, which was the game usually played. Gaelic football was played there, however, and the Home had a Gaelic football team.[201] Michael loved all sports and valued such a large playground and field to play in, especially after the more confined playground at Quay Street.

The number of boys in the Home meant that there were always playmates of varying ages and sizes available to make up teams, and to test one's skills against. The shouts and cheers of the crowd across Church Hill at the neighbouring Sligo Rovers soccer ground on Sunday afternoons enabled Michael and his playmates to imagine their skills were receiving the approbation that they deserved. The sounds of the town also penetrated the secluded Home grounds, indeed daily, from the nearby Catholic and Church of Ireland cathedral bells. At 12 o'clock and 6 o'clock every day the ringing of the Angelus bell always resulted in the boys stopping whatever they were doing, even if engaged in a soccer match, to recite the Angelus. Throughout Ireland, especially in rural areas, workers would similarly stop and bow their heads at the sound of the Angelus bell.

1.7.2. Medical Matters

In the photograph of the Quartet Michael's left boot can be seen curved up at the front. As far back as he can remember Michael was aware of a problem he had with his left leg, but he had no idea what had caused this. Not until he was nearly seventy years old did any doctor diagnose the cause of his problem. He was then told that he had nerve damage that afflicted the whole of his left leg and hip as a result of childhood poliomyelitis.[202] He was then fitted with a calliper and now wears a more suitable light plastic ankle and leg brace that fits inside his shoe. His polio afflicted left leg had never been bad enough to prevent him from participation in any sport but it meant that he had to make adjustments. He could not kick a soccer ball with any degree of control with his left leg if the ball was on the ground. When the ball was airborne in either soccer or Gaelic football he could kick it well enough, and kick it out of hand in the Gaelic game.[203]

At the age of 10 or 11 Michael had been given a cursory examination by the Nazareth House doctor. When the Home sports day arrived, Attracta's assistant child care Sister had requested that the doctor assess Michael after she observed his gait. He told her that he couldn't run sprint races, despite fully participating in all ball games at the Home and school. The doctor asked him to walk up and down a few times. Michael believed that the doctor was assessing his fitness to enter the sprint races and whether it was safe for him to run. He was excused participation in these.[204] No treatment was prescribed at the time for his problem, nor was a calliper prescribed for him, nor can he ever remember having been referred to hospital. He has never allowed his problem to stop him tackling any sport or indeed any physical activity. Nor has he ever regarded himself as having had a 'handicap' let alone being classified as handicapped. In childhood he could run well enough to play football, hurling and Gaelic football and tennis. Later in life he enjoyed golf and ping pong (table tennis) and he has always been fiercely competitive. If anything he felt that his problem leg made him even more determined to prove that he was as good as anyone else. Indeed that phrase would afford a neat summary of Michael's overall approach to life.

1.7.3. Fund Raisers and Supporters

Over a period of time the Home records show that the Sisters had been able to improve the facilities at Nazareth House in three main areas: play facilities for the boys; general facilities in the Home; and religious improvements. These depended upon special fund raising events or legacies or donations as the money raised by the efforts of the Collecting Sisters went towards the day to day living costs. A further form of 'donation' was the free services provided by Sligo professionals to the Home, including medical provision. A number of these professionals were eminent men in their respective fields.

When the Home had first opened professionals had rallied round to help the Sisters care for the boys and elderly. Medical services had been provided *gratis* by a Mayo born, Catholic doctor and member of the Royal College of Surgeons, Patrick Joseph Flanagan of High Street, and later Union Street, Sligo.[205] The Dental Practitioner, Herbert Quinton a member of the Royal College of Surgeons of England, who also provided his services free of charge, was an unusual character. The Surrey born Englishman, of 15, Wine Street, Sligo, declared his 'Religious Profession' as 'Freethinker' in the 1911 census. His London born wife, Elizabeth Sarah, nee Levington, a former nurse, declared herself as 'Independent', the same title given to the religious persuasion of the couple's 1 and 3 year old sons, and a Wicklow born female servant.[206 207] Such public declarations of agnosticism or even atheism were unusual enough in Ireland in 1911. What is even more surprising than the offer of services to a religious charity by Mr Quinton was the acceptance of these by the Sisters. The needs of the residents would seem to have prevailed over the scruples of the Sisters in this instance, who, in a small town like Sligo, must have been aware of the beliefs of this benefactor.

91

A further boon to the Sisters was the provision of free services for the Home's brass band. The Sisters of Nazareth developed bands in most of their children's homes, either brass or ceilidh. In Sligo a brass band had formed with the very costly instruments, beyond the resources of the Sligo Sisters, provided by Nazareth House Headquarters in Hammersmith. The Home records in the early 1920's show that: *the Band continued to develop under the guidance of Mr Depew, who is a devoted Band Master,* [208] *and who also provided his services free.*

In 1928 great advances were made when the Bishop, following an official 'inspection' visit to the Home, told the Sisters to order a set of gymnasium equipment that he would pay for.[209] Paddy Baker remembers with childhood excitement the opening day for this equipment, and the stir it caused for the boys. What Paddy described as the *gymnastic accoutrements* had been erected in the senior boys' park. Paddy, 5 years old at the time, was still in the Nazareth House School under the care of Miss McGraine. The older boys, for whom the equipment had been provided, were out at Quay Street School so the 'babies' had the first chance to play on the equipment, and Miss McGraine took photographs of them:

We had great fun climbing the ladders and being bounced on the seesaws where many of us not being able to maintain our balance fell to the ground. Most of all we enjoyed the swings and there was many a struggle between us as to who would be next. [210]

Paddy had mistakenly believed that the equipment had been provided by another Nazareth House benefactor, Father Barry. His mistake was understandable, however, as Father Robert Barry did provide much for the boys and the Sisters. Father Barry had retired to live at Nazareth House in 1927 following service as parish priest in Oldcastle, Meath, after his health had broken down. Paddy remembered him as: *a nice grey headed old man whose thoughts were centred on us children,* this judgement borne out by his actions. He presented a Christmas crib to the Home that had cost £100. It was used for the first time in 1927 when: *after Midnight Mass the boys stood around it and sang the Adeste Fideles.* [211]

1.7.4. Father Barry's House: Youth Club

Father Barry made a notable contribution to the welfare of former Nazareth House residents when he assisted the Sisters' effort to provide a facility for the increasing number of boys who had finished school or who were working in positions in Sligo. He funded a single-storey, stone building erected next to the old Yeats building. It acted as a youth club and recreational hall for the former Homeboys in town, who often found themselves alone and at a loose end, and especially at Christmas. Opened in 1931 the building had ping pong and other recreational games and from 1931 billiards facilities were provided when a Passionist Priest, Father Costelloe, gave a billiard table: *It was seen as a great boon to them to have a place to meet and play games on Sunday evenings and free times.*[212]

Such a provision, not very common then, showed considerable forethought by the Sisters. It also confirmed that they saw their responsibilities to the boys continuing well after they had left the Home, just as a family would. The boys always referred to this as: *Father Barry's House.*

Illustration 13: 'Father Barry's House. Situation Boys' Recreational Hall

At Christmas 1931 the Sisters recorded that: *The recreational Hall was well used over the Christmas Season.*[213]

Father Barry's influence in broadcasting the needs of the boys and his ability to secure funding for these was further demonstrated in 1931 when his nephew donated the then very considerable sum of £700 to have a ball alley erected.[214] This was placed at the back left corner of the playground field. Michael spent many hours in the

Nazareth handball alley, honing the skills that the Quay Street Marist Brother had observed he possessed. Father Barry died on 8[th]June, 1935, his last eight years of life having been fruitfully deployed in improving facilities at Nazareth House, including improving the grounds, planting shrubs, helping acquire a new organ for the Chapel, contributing to the painting of the Stations of the Cross, and having a Summer House constructed for the Sisters.[215]

1.7.5. Discrepant Memories

In evaluating a range of sources of memory it is quite common to meet contradictory accounts and one is then left having to 'adjudicate', as best one can, as to which, if any, memory to prefer. Not uncommonly the accounts, sincerely given and not intended to deceive, conflict with official records. This has been a feature of Michael's tested and challenged recollections over four years plus research, leading to significant modifications of his understanding of events and motivations. The issue of what type of ball was used at Nazareth House illustrates this dilemma. Paddy Baker, in one of his first 'stream of consciousness', 40 foolscap pages, missives to Willie McGowan bemoaned never having had a proper ball to play with at Nazareth House, stating that they only possessed a ball made of rolled up rags.[216] Michael Porter is *absolutely clear* that they had proper balls to play with.[217] These were the customary leather balls with a leather knotted lace covering the gap where the separate internal bladder was inflated. The knotted lace could hurt and cut the head when heading the ball and the ball was covered with dubbing to protect and preserve the leather. The Gaelic football was larger than the soccer ball. Rolled up rags or stockings were used as a ball, Michael recollects, when the boys were confined in the large upstairs playroom in inclement weather. The boys could not use a proper football there but were allowed to play a mini kick about game with a rag ball substitute. [218]

Michael's detailed account is preferred for a number of reasons. Although his recollections can also be mistaken he is not generally given to invention, to fudging or to giving information of which he cannot be certain. He will not fill a knowledge gap with a 'it would have been.' Paddy's initial letters to Willie McGowan had not a little of the 'poor little orphan Annie' tone to them, with an understandable degree of attention-seeking, hyperbole and self absorption, as he had not had a 'confidant' previously to whom he could decant his memories and experiences. It is notable that, as the correspondence between the two former Homeboys, Paddy and Willie McGowan, developed, Paddy's perception of his experiences changed, and it subsequently appears more balanced and more reflective. This process of perspective shift was also a feature of Michael's recollections, after he was given the opportunity to test his memories against other records over a period of years.

Reflecting on the above suggests the benefit to adults who were formerly in long-term institutional care of having other relevant people with whom to discuss their experiences. If this occurs over an extended period of time, the process of sifting and testing recollections can produce not only a clarification of what actually happened and what is mistaken, but also lead to a more concrete, consolidated and chronologically secure memory, with the emotional benefits this carries with it. Significantly, it can also achieve a degree of perspective about the person's experiences that is not usually available to the raw, and sometimes incontinently expressed, personal 'memoir'.

1.7.6. Gaelic Football

The practice in the Nazareth House playing field, with proper leather ball, bore fruit when the Nazareth House Gaelic Football Team won the Sligo Juvenile Football Challenge Cup in 1936 under the auspices of the Gaelic Athletic Association.[219] Michael was a member of the winning team whose success, understandably, produced: *great excitement* in the Home. Michael's highlight memory of the day was scoring a goal, a fluke, with his weak left leg when his high shot just beat the goalkeeper's outstretched hand under the bar. No congratulations from his team mates ensued: *We didn't go in for all that backslapping stuff in those days.*

The Lord Mayor of Sligo, Alderman M. Nevin, presented the winning trophy at a tea party at the Cafe Cairo in Sligo.[220] Yet Michael, then aged nearly 15 years of age, remembers not one thing about this halcyon event despite being old enough to have stored this significant event in his long-term memory. Nor does he remember his confirmation about the same time in Sligo Cathedral, illustrating yet again the somewhat perplexing, selective and sometimes idiosyncratic nature of memory.

From 1930 onwards, the flood of new inmates that had followed the opening of the new boys' Home building in 1925/26 markedly reduced. This period of stabilisation coincided with Nazareth House teams enjoying success in varied fields: sporting team games; athletics; brass band playing; music and singing including plainchant; dancing; and recitations. Individuals also gained educational bursaries and scholarships.

The 1936 Sligo Town Gaelic Football victory led to Nazareth House representing their area against the winners from another county. They travelled away to Ballaghaderreen in County Roscommon. Though Ballaghaderreen is now in County Roscommon, having been transferred there from County Mayo in the Local Government Act of 1898, it was then classified as being in County Mayo by the Gaelic Athletic Association. The GAA had maintained the pre 1898 location of Ballaghaderreen in County Mayo. As the competition was played under its auspices Nazareth House represented County Sligo, and their opponents, County Mayo.

Memory fails Michael about any aspect of the journey to Ballaghaderreen. Indeed he can recollect nothing of any of the many journeys he made with the Nazareth House band or summer trips to Rosses Point and Strandhill with the Sisters, or what form of transport, whether bus, train or charabanc, was taken. He does, however, remember the match. The opponents were a secondary school team, probably St Nathy's College, which was a large diocesan seminary and secondary school, the equivalent of Summerhill College in Sligo. The weather was cold and very wet and the pitch muddy. Michael and his teammates were eager, excited and flushed with their previous success. They were impressed when they entered the changing rooms by a strong unknown smell. This emanated from the large bottle of

Wintergreen liniment that their opponents were liberally applying to their limbs from a large bottle. The Nazareth House boys eagerly accepted the proffered liniment, feeling even more ready for the fray. When they looked more closely at some of the opposition players their confidence began to wane because these seemed to be much older than the Nazareth House team, a head taller and much heavier.[221]

The Nazareth House team's ability to compete effectively at this level would have been compromised by a lack of older and bigger boys to choose from as Gaelic Football used 15 players compared with soccer's 11. The overall height and weight of the average institutional Homeboy would have also been less than the average for an opponent of the same age from the more advantaged College. The opposition's organisation and football togs were also better. Michael remembers the only tactical refinement for his team as: *you go there.* He cannot recollect what outfit they wore but does remember the boots: these were the normal boots worn for school in autumn and winter and not soccer boots at all; a big handicap in the wet, greasy conditions. A Gaelic pitch is much larger than either a soccer or rugby football pitch measuring from 142 to 159 yards long (compared with soccer's 100 to 130 yards) and from 87 to 98 yards wide (compared with soccer's 50 to 100 yards). The ball is also larger than a soccer ball.

Did the Homeboys show pluck, perseverance and skill to overcome the disadvantages of conditions, pitch size, inappropriate boots, tactical vacuum, height and weight inferiority and age disadvantage too? Hardly. Michael recalled that: *we got an absolute drubbing,* his team losing by a cricket score. *They were firing the balls into our net like it was a tennis match.* Willie McGowan was the lad vainly trying to stem the tide of goals, until replaced by Michael: *They even put me in goal, small as I was, but it made no difference; the goals kept raining in.*[222]

Michael remembered not only the superior height, weight and skills of the Ballaghaderreen boys but also their efforts to crush the Nazareth team by the size of the score, to let their opponents know that they were *superior beings.* No residual English legacy of,

97

'that's enough chaps, don't humiliate them' came from the future seminarians: rather a sustained effort to: *let us know they were better than us and put us in our place.* This message included giving the Homeboys a good physical pasting to boot. Michael bore no resentment at his opponents' humiliation of his team, confessing that: *I would have done the same to them if I could.* After they had administered a reality check to the pre-match euphoria of the Homeboys, the College boys' thinking might well have echoed the Scottish anthem against the English 'We sent them homewards tae think again'. Michael certainly thought again, deciding that he was too small and otherwise unsuited for Gaelic football. Ballaghaderreen was the last Gaelic football match that he ever played. Thereafter, although he continued to play soccer, he concentrated on games of individual skill such as golf, tennis and table tennis, where he could rely on himself, not his team mates.

1.7.7. Boys Will Be Boys

The boys often wandered from their playground field behind the Home to explore the out of bounds areas: the nearby estate house yard and orchard, and the Sister's field well away to the back left of the Home. The next large house to the Home had the irresistible lure to all boys of an orchard. That it was protected by a high stone wall topped by broken glass only added to the allure and increased the boys' determination to scrump the forbidden fruit. They would creep up in concert, lifting one of them up and over, with that boy lobbing over the small, bitter, crab apples to his colleagues. The excitement and challenge, the desire for the forbidden, but especially the frisson of fear and danger the raid produced was their Pied Piper lure, not the apples themselves. Often they found a large lady who wore boots in wait for them. She would chase them all the way back to the Home grounds, shouting after them and trying to grab a boy, the other boys helping fend her off. Michael was distinctly impressed with this lady's fleetness of foot, especially as she was encumbered by wearing big boots, from which he took her to be a domestic servant. On one occasion she caught one of the boys by the leg as he tried to clamber back over the wall. His colleagues pulled their fellow in return shouting at the woman to: *Get off him. Leave him alone. Leave him alone*, eventually prising the bruised boy free. Michael does not remember ever having been taken to task by the Sisters for these raids, the only punishment being the stomach cramps and worse that the raid's bounty inevitably produced in the boys.[223]

The Sister's field where a cow was kept was well out of sight of the Home. Nazareth House was not an Industrial School and the Sisters had specifically decided that they didn't want the children to work on farmland. The Sisters had not wanted the acres of land that they were gifted, until later, during the Second World War, they began to realise the benefit of it for growing food during wartime shortages.[224] They had some tillage on the land worked by the yardmen to produce vegetables for the residents, and kept chickens, horses and one or more cows. The large field for beasts was where the boys often played. It had the great advantage of also being a safe place out of sight of the Sisters. Should a fight break out between any of the boys, as happened with Michael and the three Farrell brothers, it could proceed to the end without adult interference, from either the yardmen or the Sisters.

Michael had started to fight with Kevin Joseph, the eldest of three Farrell brothers at Nazareth House, in the field. The usual pushing and shoving turning more serious, with the other Homeboys urging on the protagonists. Kevin Farrell was a year younger than Michael but bigger than him. When the other two Farrell boys saw that their brother was losing the scrap they joined in to help him. Donald Patrick, a year younger than Kevin, and the tiny Desmond Peter, four years younger than him, began to pummel an increasingly maddened, Michael.[225] The tiny Farrell's contribution was to kick the back of Michael's legs incessantly. Turning on the boy Michael picked him up: *and I dumped him in the horse trough and that cooled the little blighter.*[226] That appeared to cool the fight too and the youngsters covered up their bloodied faces and clothes as best they could, and fabricated a cover story for drowned Desmond's waterlogged state should it be necessary, former combatants now conspiring together against the adults. Michael soon had cause to observe the results of his blows when, sitting immediately behind the Farrells in chapel, he saw the swollen, scratched and reddened ears in front of him, his own features similarly bearing evidence of the encounter. Two thoughts were prominent in his head: relief that the Sisters immediately behind him hadn't questioned why all the combatants were in such a state; and deep satisfaction at the visible results of his handiwork.

The difficulty that the skeleton staff of Sisters faced in trying to control and monitor the boys is revealed by a serious incident that had occurred when Michael was throwing stones in the playground. Maurice Walsh was one of the boys Michael was friendliest with at Nazareth House, and at Quay Street School, where they were in the same class. Maurice, like Michael, Willie McGowan and Willie Walsh (no relation) was one of the top scholars in their class. Born in 1921 he and his younger brother, Patrick, originated from Swinford in County Mayo.[227] One day when Michael was wandering around the playground, throwing stones as hard as he could, one of these, a large one, accidently struck Maurice in the head. He immediately fell unconscious to the ground, a large bloody cut above his ear bleeding profusely. Michael immediately thought that he had killed him. Aid was quickly sought from the Sisters and doctor and Michael was relieved when Maurice recovered and that no action was taken against him.[228]

Maurice Walsh left Nazareth House in the same year as Michael, both he and his brother returning to their family home in Mayo. His father had remarried and there was now a home available for him. Maurice died in December, 1940, at home in Swinford with his family.[229] When Michael heard of his death he felt guilty: for many years he believed that the death might have been a result of the delayed effect of the head injury he had inflicted on him.[230]

The boys took every opportunity to get up to mischief; the adults sometimes too. One of the yardmen had brought out the large, unbridled horse from the yard, asking Michael if he would like to sit on it. Thrilled he was sat up on it when the yardman smacked its rump causing it to bolt, galloping several hundred yards with the terrified boy clinging to its neck. On another occasion a yardman told Michael to: *Catch hold of this, and give us a hand here.* He pointed to an old, two handled metal bath half filled with water and potatoes. Michael touched the handle while the yardman held back, unaware that the bath had been wired to an electric source. He heard the yardman's laughter as he took the electric shock: strong enough to make him dance but not severe enough to uncurl his thick shock of wavy hair.[231]

Michael also took his chance to play pranks on the adults. In front of the Home was an enormous tree with a vast canopy of leaves. Sometimes the boys would climb up there and hide. On one occasion one boy had taken a trumpet up with him, knowing that the Sisters were accustomed to walk to and fro below it while reading their breviaries. The young scamp waited, hidden up in the foliage, until a Sister appeared below, ready to add sound effects to the biblical readings. Taking the 'and the trumpet shall sound' as a commandment, he blasted the nun with his trumpet, delighted at her startled response (feigned for his benefit perhaps?)[232]

Michael took it into his head to play a really serious prank and have that same tree felled. He fabricated a tale to the home yardman-gardener that Reverend Mother had given an instruction that the tree had to be cut down and she had instructed him to tell the gardener to do this immediately. The gardener, who had no inkling that the tree was causing any problem, consulted the Sisters. They confirmed that no such instruction had been issued. Again Michael wasn't punished for his prank but was referred to by the gardener thereafter as, *Father John*: this nickname having attached itself to him following a recent theatrical debut in that role.

The large stone staircases at Nazareth House surround a huge open stairwell that goes all the way to the top of the building. The Sisters repeatedly forbade the boys to slide down the wooden banister rails because death was likely to ensue if a boy fell; indeed one boy had been killed in this way at another Nazareth House. Michael recalls the boys, himself included, taking the quickest route downstairs whenever a Sister was not in attendance: *Sure we were fearless in those days.*[233]

The Maurice injury, the tree felling and the other incidents of mischief that Michael and Paddy especially were involved in, illustrate the adage: 'The devil makes work for idle hands'. At Nazareth House it was not just a saying, it was acted on as a core principle by the Sisters, both in their own work and prayer lives and also in their approach to the boys in their care: *They realised that we needed to be occupied all the time to be kept out of mischief.*[234]

1.7.8. Prevention of Harm

Having escaped either detection or punishment on a number of occasions for misbehaviour or pranks Michael was surprised to be called before one of the Sisters when he felt he had not done anything wrong. Although the boys did not have pocket money or access to comics or films in the Home they were able to obtain these from Quay Street schoolmates in exchange for services, then swapping these for other items. They therefore knew about Cowboys and Indians and read the standard comics of the period such as *Gem, Magnet, Comic Cuts, Film Fun* and *Boy's Own.* Two of the most popular games were 'tag' and 'Cowboys and Indians', but Michael cannot ever remember going to the cinema to see these. 'Horse and Jockey', one boy up on another's back, and then charging a similar couple to knock the 'jockey' off was another popular game they played. When geeing up his horse; one day in the playground Michael was surprised to be called up to see one of the Sisters who had been observing the playground from a first floor window. Again examining his conscience haversack to see which transgression must have come to light, he was puzzled by the ensuing conversation: *What game were you playing? Cowboys and Indians and piggyback, Sister. Then he was dismissed by the Nun, nothing more having been said.*[235]

Michael could never understand what it was that had caused him to be summoned before the Sister when he had been so innocuously playing. I suggested to him that she may have been concerned at the playing, the close proximity of the boys together, having sexual overtones. If so it suggests that the Sisters, even in what were days of great ignorance about sexual exploitation and abuse by adults, had at least some glimmering awareness that boy with boy sexual experimentation, or boy on boy sexual exploitation, could occur there. By the actions in this case, unnecessary as it turned out, it does further suggest that, with the limits of their knowledge and understanding at that time, the Sisters sought to protect the boys from sexual harm from other boys. It would also indicate a preventive as well as protective culture in the Home in the area of sexual exploitation.

None of the informants about Nazareth House, Sligo, for this book have suggested that sexual exploitation while they were there had been something they were subjected to, or were aware of during the 1920's or 1930's. Peer on peer sexual abuse did occur at a much later date in Nazareth House. Despite no records of such behaviour occurring during the 1920's and 1930's it would be very surprising if such peer abuse incidents did not occur then, as they did in all such male residential establishments whether Church or State run, whether public school or orphanage as: 'Children abuse each other too. Possibly half the total of abuse reported in institutions is peer abuse'.[236]

The running of the Home by women rather than men greatly reduced, but did not entirely exclude, the risk of adult sexual exploitation of the boys. The incident above, puzzling as it was to Michael at the time, seems reflective of an adult regime that sought to prevent, rather than facilitate, sexual exploitation of the boys; at least within the limited range of knowledge possessed by carers then. I think it most probable that the extreme stress then by religious, clerics and teachers about modesty and avoiding sexual talk and contact, including close physical proximity, and of avoiding 'occasions of sin', was the prime reason for this intervention by the Sister.

Chapter 1. 8: Family and Identity

1.8.1. Contact and Information About Siblings and Family

The Preface of this book outlined the three central concerns that Michael Porter had as a result of his time in care. My concerns are three fold:

- *Lack of family life, family information and contact when in care*

- *Lack of love*

- *Lack of information and communication*

Why did Michael have these concerns but Willie McGowan did not? Paddy Baker, Willie McCormack and Michael Porter all complained about lack of information about their families, and lack of contact with them during their stay at Nazareth House. Willie McCormack and Paddy, who each had a brother in the Home, described almost negligible contact with them during their stay there. Michael and Paddy report having had no contact at all with their family of origin during their stay at Nazareth House; they also alleged that their families were never mentioned to them. These deficiencies they attributed to either lack of emotional intelligence on the part of the Sisters or deliberate Home policy. [237]

Three of the Quartet's members, Willie McGowan, Michael Porter and Willie Walsh were in the minority 35% of Nazareth House boys who had no siblings living there. Paddy Baker was one of the 45% of boys who had one brother there. The Farrells, Michael's combatants, were one of the 20% of boys with 2 brothers living there.[238] The Farrells clearly had contact with each other and obviously a strongly developed and maintained sense of fraternal identity, as Michael's bruised features could testify, despite the inevitable age segregation that would have meant day to day separation from each other. Referring to his brother, James, Paddy recorded that:

My only regret is that we never got to know each other whilst in Nazareth. Contact with each other was forbidden which led me to conclude that I didn't have a brother. We were isolated from each other as though we had some serious disease. The age difference of seven years seems to have been a drawback. The house had its strict rules and everyone must adhere to them. To be isolated from one's own brother all those years, not even allowing us to walk together in the park is to say the least absurd. I would have thought that an arrangement could have been made between Attracta and the Sister in charge of me for both of us to come together occasionally where we as brother and brother could have a little chat.[239]

Despite the presence of siblings in the Home the structure and operation of the Home did very little to preserve or foster sibling contact. Paddy later detailed two other reasons for the lack of contact between him and his half-brother. Firstly that: *Attracta didn't have the foresight.* Secondly he refers to pressure of work on the Sisters. He described the occasion when Attracta and another Sister were managing an access visit by the man that Paddy believed to have been his or his half-brother James's father.[240] That had also been the first contact with his brother that Paddy could remember. After managing this brief visit, Attracta and the other Sister made arrangements for Paddy to join his age group on a walk, while one Sister attended to the father and Attracta dealt with the other immediate demands:

There was a bench in the middle of the passage next to the other entrance which was mainly occupied by the old and very poor people of Sligo town who sometimes had to wait a very long time for a Sister to pass by and listen to their problems. She would then go to the kitchen and bring them some bread.[241]

1.8.2. Not Quite an Orphanage

Paddy's account captures the Sisters' seeming lack of appreciation of the importance of siblings to the emotional welfare and comfort of the boys, allied to the precedence they gave to institutional structures and routines. Contacts between the boys, whether living, schooling or sleeping arrangements, were age based and so almost inevitably led to the segregation of siblings. Both Willie McCormack's and Paddy's objections to how the rigidity of this structure militated against contact between them and their respective brothers are, I think, well founded: their further assertion that this resulted from a deliberate policy to deny such contact is not.

The lack of carers, so tellingly brought out in Paddy's account, does give an understanding of the pressures the Sisters were under to juggle manifold, often competing demands. The impact of the Sisters' training, discipline, giving up of their own family and general self-abnegation may have resulted in some deadening of their awareness of the emotional needs of the boys. These considerations do not fully explain, however, this seeming failure to understand the need of the boys for time together with their nearest kin, unless one seeks to operate a policy of complete environmental determinism. Although Nazareth House was not an orphanage it seems that as far as sibling contact within the Home was concerned it was little different from one. Indeed it was recorded as such: 'Convent of Nazareth. Superioress. Mother M. Kevin. This is a home for orphan boys and for aged men and women'. [242]

The emotional imagination of the Sisters would appear not to have been nearly so well developed as was their physical care of the boys in their charge. They appeared insufficiently attuned to needs of the boys for sibling and family contact. Though they did not promote this contact, there is abundant evidence that they did not seek to deny it as Willie McGowan's case illustrates, and indeed the evidence of one of the complainants, Willie McCormack.

Willie McCormack details a number of instances when he was able both to visit his sister in care of the Mercy Sisters Home in Sligo and be visited in return, with the pair going off alone around Sligo. He also describes visits to his grandmother in Sligo and some trips out around Sligo itself.[243]

Willie McGowan went home reasonably regularly on weekends to stay with his widowed father at the family farm in Skreen, Dromore West, County Sligo, and to work there in the summer at harvest time. A protestant, Bertie Shaw, who owned a holiday cottage near Willie's father, had a shop in Sligo where he, his wife and two daughters resided during the week. On Saturday, after the shop had closed, he usually drove with his family to spend the remainder of the weekend at the holiday cottage. On many occasions Bertie Shaw called at Nazareth House to collect Willie on Saturday, taking him home to his father in Skreen.[244]

Knowing that a male Irish farmer's catering skills were rudimentary, and no doubt assuming that Willie would be hardly over-fed at Nazareth House, this Samaritan's wife always insisted that Willie first came to their cottage. There Willie was always given a hearty cooked dinner before Mr Shaw dropped the boy off at his father's house. Willie was driven back to Nazareth House on Sunday night when the Shaws returned to Sligo. The Shaws seemed to have acted as a type of surrogate, back-up family for Willie, affording him some of the emotional sustenance that was not available to the other Quartet boys. They, and he, maintained life-long contact with each other, and this included the Shaws' daughters, Vera and Elizabeth.[245]

Where family were nearby or where they wished to maintain contact, the above examples show that there were no barriers put in the way of this by the Sisters. This also applied to parents who wanted to reconstitute their families where circumstances had changed, as in the case of the three Farrell brothers, Kevin, Donald and Desmond. They had all been placed in care at Nazareth House in 1929 at the ages, respectively, of 7, 6 and 3 years. Michael Porter remembers his astonishment when the parents of the Farrell boys arrived at Nazareth House in 1936. They had come to retrieve their sons and to take them with them to the United States of America.[246]

1.8.3. Communication Deficiencies

In his early years at Nazareth House Michael thought that his mother was dead and that his nightmare related to her funeral and his home. The longer he stayed in the Home, however, the weaker and more doubtful this memory became, so that he eventually concluded that this memory must have been, like the drowning memory, a nightmare and a figment of his imagination. He retained no other memories of family, however, nor was he ever told that he had a family or relatives living. During his entire stay there he believed himself to be an orphan. No family member ever visited, nor did he ever visit them, and he never received any correspondence from anyone. Nor was he ever encouraged to write a letter to anyone. Despite the Nazareth Sisters knowing of his father and grandmother and where they lived in County Galway no mention of them or any other relative was made to Michael, save one oblique and one direct reference, which he could not or did not process or understand.[247]

Two nuns, Sisters from a different religious order as Michael noted from their habit, called one day to the entrance door of Nazareth House. Michael when he had been sent for, as usual scanned his conscience for recent misdemeanours, becoming increasingly anxious at the unknown, impending outcome of his summons. The two foreign Sisters were waiting for him in the tiled entrance lobby. A brief 'conversation' ensued. He gave monosyllabic answers, or nods, to their questions; they, speaking softly and quietly, told him that they would be visiting his home and family; they may even have mentioned Tynagh. After a short period they told him that *they would tell his family that he was well;* then they left. Michael remembers them walking off immediately afterwards, not communicating with the Nazareth Sisters. His whole energy had been preoccupied with whether he was in trouble; his only feeling afterwards was relief.

Afterwards he brushed off his peers' queries about this unusual event with: '*nothing*'. He did not mull over the visit, immediately casting it out of his mind. It was entirely inexplicable to him. Although he remembered *family* and *home* and *telling them* about him, he did not digest this information, nor did it impact in any way on his belief that he was an orphan and without any family. The Sisters who visited, and the Sisters of Nazareth also, would presumably have thought differently. That he had been told about his family but evinced no interest in them or asked questions about them would, it seems, have been their natural reaction. The whole episode is yet further evidence about the communication and understanding gulf between adult and child, and between Sisters and boys in the 1930's. When I queried what he made of the mention of *Tynagh* Michael said: *It meant nothing at all to me. It was just a word. It might just as well have been 'Mars' they were talking about for all the impact it had upon me.*[248]

The earlier chapter has detailed the priest's letter about Michael's sister, Sadie, having been being placed with the nuns in Ballinasloe. I wonder whether these Sisters who briefly visited Michael, when he was about 12 or 13 years of age, were Mercy nuns from Sadie's Industrial Home in Ballinasloe, on a visit to another of their Convents and Homes, close to Nazareth House in Sligo. Michael is absolutely clear that the word *father* was never mentioned; neither had *sister* been mentioned. I, and he, doubt whether his entrenched orphan belief, allied to his hyper-anxiety at this totally foreign, unexpected and very brief encounter, would have allowed him to process this information.[249] The Sisters at Nazareth House had never mentioned his sister to him and Michael can never remember being aware that he had a sister. It is likely that the Nazareth Sisters never realised that Michael had forgotten that he had a sister; certainly no one ever took the trouble to find out what he thought.

1.8.4. The Boy Who Believed He Had Never Had Parents

The above incident reveals how different understanding by adult and child can occur. Michael was absolutely clear that he believed himself an orphan for his entire duration at Nazareth House. The Sisters would have been equally clear that this was impossible because; they would not have realised that he would have forgotten his sister and father; they had thought he would have understood the communication from the other Order Sisters[250]; and in a later incident where one of their Sisters told Michael about his father. A not uncommon problem where conflicted understanding occurs. Michael was factually wrong in stating that he had never been told about having a family; substantially correct, however, because the assumptions, and perfunctory and poor quality of communication, did not trouble to ascertain anything about his understanding of this.

The following describes Michael Porter's changing memory and perception about parents and family during his stay at Nazareth House.

● *I had a mother but she died. My nightmare about her in the box is about her leaving me when I was little. (I never ever thought about a father or a sister or any other family member. I never believed that I had any of these).* (Age from 5-9 years old).

● *My memory about a mother was false; it was only a nightmare.* (Age from about 9 years old till well after leaving Nazareth House).

● *I had never ever had a mother or father. Nor had I any relative at all. I was totally alone in the world. I was an orphan (but I did not know what this word meant) and so I believed were all my fellows at Nazareth House.* (Age from about 9 years old to well after leaving Nazareth House).

Despite many years working with numerous children in care I had never previously encountered this scarcely credible phenomenon about a child believing that he had never had parents; and holding this belief until he had left care.[251] Michael describes it thus:

Strange as it may seem, I felt that I had never had any parents, and so it changed from I had lost them to I had never had them. We never ever discussed our families with other boys, the nuns or anyone else at the Home and I didn't believe that any of the Homeboys had families outside. It came as more than a surprise when we were told that the three Farrell brothers had been collected by their father and taken to America. I and the other boys just couldn't comprehend that anybody in the home had parents. You might say 'surely as a child you would think that you would know that you had parents', but when you have never heard of them, or any talk of them, you came to the conclusion that you had never had any. And in the catechism it gave the answer to the question 'Who made you?' as 'God made me'. So I came to believe that not only didn't I have any parents, but that I had never ever had any.[252]

1.8.5. Boys Locked in Their Own World

Michael was most surprised to hear of the Farrells' destination; absolutely dumfounded to hear that they had parents or indeed anyone belonging to them in the world outside Nazareth House boundaries. Throughout his entire stay at Nazareth House, though

Michael was not aware that any boy there had parents until the Farrell visit, he was aware that some of the boys had brothers in the Home. He thought only a minority had brothers at Nazareth, he reckoned only about a fifth, whereas nearly two thirds of the boys had at least one sibling at Nazareth House; so singletons were very much the exception.[253] Above all he had never heard any boy at Nazareth House mention parent, or any relation outside the home. He knew that the Farrell boys were brothers but thought that they were orphans like him, and like every other boy at Nazareth House.

The only people that Michael knew who had parents were his school fellows at Quay Street School. He came to associate the Home boundaries as delineating those who had someone to belong to, and care for them, and those who did not. At the age of 15 years Michael had been introduced for the first time to the almost incomprehensible fact that a boy at Nazareth House, a Homeboy, had parents. Furthermore, these parents had come to take their sons away with them. His fellow Homeboys were similarly mystified by the apparition of the Farrell parents, the boys regarding this as some kind of miracle.

Michael can never recollect any boy having been visited by a family member. Paddy Baker later wrote to Willie McGowan to express surprise at the news Willie had given him: *I didn't know that you were a family of seven and I cannot recall you ever having a visitor.*[254] Willie's regular absences at weekends and holidays had not been noticed by two of his Quartet colleagues, Michael or Paddy. Nor had the appearance of Bertie Shaw's car been noticed by the boys despite this being a rare enough sight in those days, especially at Nazareth House.

This does confirm Michael's judgement that he and his fellow Homeboys enjoyed a substantial degree of self-containment and self-absorption: this left them, like the Sisters too perhaps, somewhat blinkered emotionally and insufficiently attuned to the emotional life of their colleagues. Nor did the boys think laterally. Michael did not project this new knowledge of boys and parents onto the other boys and question whether they, let alone he, also might have parents. Nor did he think more widely about this. He

took it to be an exceptional, indeed unique, event. It didn't affect
him and so was forgotten. That Michael was unaware of Willie
McGowan's occasional trips home is not entirely surprising. Willie
was at Summerhill, Michael at Quay Street in their latter years at
Nazareth House. Michael describes a degree of only limited
camaraderie amongst the boys as each one was so preoccupied with
his own thoughts and difficulties. *You had pals, playmates but you
were never close to anyone,*[255] was how he summed it up.

1.8.6. Protective Ignorance

There was comfort in everybody being in the same boat as far as
family was concerned. Deprivation can be absolute such as the loss
Willie, Paddy and Michael all endured with the deaths of their
mothers. It can also be relative. Many of the boys appear not to
have been kept informed about their family members. This lack of
information about their families produced a paradox: ignorance
could be emotionally protective. Where all were equally
'deprived', no one felt the additional burden of being different. The
Farrell family's departure for America did not really change this as
it was regarded by Michael as such a unique, incomprehensible
event, that this comet would not strike earth again.

There was the further paradox that those who believed themselves
to be parentless, such as Paddy and Michael, did not have the
anguished feelings of enforced separation from family to contend
with (although they had the feelings of total loneliness and absolute
bereftness to deal with). Those boys like Willie McGowan and
Willie McCormack who had been separated from still living adult
carers and siblings, and whose siblings were scattered had to endure
this emotional pull and confusion: this sorrowing for what they had
lost but was still partly available, at least as an option in their mind.
This clearly bothered Willie McCormack. With no family to pine
for, Paddy, Michael and boys like them were at least spared this:
'useless sorrow'.[256]

A study of long-term inmates in maximum security prisons
produced rather surprising findings, that confirm the above
observations: [257]

'Those who had few contacts with the outside through letters and visits were low in suffering, those who had medium contact suffered a great deal, while those who had high contact were again found to be low in suffering....The middle state in which relationships are only tenuously maintained seems least bearable.....Farber ...found clear evidence of prisoners who cut off all contact in order to reduce suffering'.[258]

These findings replicate empirical experiences of social workers and carers who have had to deal with family contact for children that is intermittent, unpredictable, or promised and then not fulfilled by parents. The disappointed child commonly responds not by blame directed towards the parent but either angry and disruptive discharge of disappointed emotions towards the carers or withdrawal into itself. This behaviour often in turn leads to repeated breakdown of placements especially where the child is in foster care. While one would hardly advocate cutting off parental contact to children in long-term care, it is at least some consolation that those who believed themselves orphans were not tortured in the same way as those who had some limited contact with their families, such as Willie McCormack. Yet their plight is, I believe, much greater than that of those who know they have families, as the following section shows.

1.8.7. Identity and Information

In Ireland at this period, four components would have been central to the formation and maintenance of a boy's identity: clan; community, nationality and creed. In the early teenage years, about the age the boys were when they won the Sligo Feis competition, young people usually begin to explore in more detail their sense of identity. Very commonly they commit this to paper, practising also various styles of handwriting, often on geography exercise books. These for Michael and Paddy's, had they been still at home, might well have been recorded as:

Michael Laurence Porter, Tynagh, Loughrea, County Galway, Eire, Europe, the World, the Universe. Date of birth, October 3rd, 1921. Age 12 years and 6 months.

Patrick Joseph Baker, Sligo, County Sligo, Eire, Europe, The World, The Universe, Outer Space. Date of birth, January 6th, 1923. Age 11 years and 2 months.

Except that at Nazareth House neither boy could have written this, or anything like it. Willie McGowan, however, certainly would have been able to do so, both because he was much older when he entered care and because his continued family contact and home visits meant that the fundamental components of his identity were available to him growing up.

Neither Michael nor Paddy knew their date of birth. Paddy operated for almost half his life in the mistaken belief that he had been born in 1921. He was actually born in 1923. Not knowing his birth date, and with birthdays not being celebrated at Nazareth House, he had no way of knowing his actual birthday. In an extraordinarily illuminating illustration of the creativity and uniqueness of a child's imaginative thinking, he tethered an actual fact to his memory store. This would appear to have been done to meet his need for concrete knowledge, his mind abhorring the vacuum that was there previously. He took the foundation stone date of the new Nazareth House building, November 21st, 1921, to be his birth date.[259] He did not make this up; rather it seems that when regularly passing the stone in his early years at Nazareth House, this concrete date somehow became interwoven into his mind as his actual date of birth.[260]

Michael, much less imaginative than Paddy, responded in a different way; he assumed a batch age, roughly estimating his age (never actually knowing it) from that of his classmates at Quay Street School.[261] Many of the other boys would not have known either birth date or family background if, like Michael and Paddy, they had been very young when they arrived at the home.

Neither Paddy nor Michael knew their place of birth either. Again, intensely concrete thinking Michael did not assume that he must have originated from Sligo town or County Sligo because he lacked information to the contrary. He did not fill in a knowledge gap with a likely explanation to help him make sense of things. He simply never ever wondered about his originating place of birth or indeed about there being a family living there.[262] Neither Paddy nor Michael knew who their parents were, indeed whether they had any still living, and they had no conception of the possibility of having a wider extended family, other than Paddy's awareness of a brother at Nazareth House (who was in fact a half-brother).

When I tried the 'geography exercise book' question with Michael Porter, he had no idea what I was talking about.[263] He had never carried out this exercise. His son Michael, however, fully understood what I was talking about. Indeed he had been punished by his teacher, for an over-florid handwriting attempt at identity forging trial on his school books.[264]

I outline below what Michael and Paddy knew in April, 1934 to enable comparison with the actual information stated before:

Name: Michael (********) Porter. Place of Birth/Origin: *****, County ******, Eire, Europe, the World, The Universe. Date of Birth: ********. ***. Age: ** (The same as my classmates at Quay Street School, whatever that happened to be).

Name: Patrick (******) Baker. Place of Birth/Origin: *****, County Sligo, Eire, The World, The Universe, Outer Space. Date of birth, November 21st, 1921 (Wrong). Age: 12 years and 4 months. (Some 14 months older than his actual age).

One of the most profound forms of deprivation is to be deprived of one's identity, or important aspects of this, particularly in childhood when this should be formed. The lack of information about this, or incorrect facts, is probably less harmful than the complete absence of information. The old adage -*what the eye does not see the heart does not grieve over*- suggesting that ignorance is bliss is wrong in this case; indeed the opposite is true for Paddy and Michael. Michael, and Paddy lacked any relevant information to form a distinct identity; the consequences of this were they did not tackle the issue of who they were in the same way as other children. They were unable to mentally and emotionally attach themselves to significant persons or places. This identity information vacuum, at the critical time for identity formation, is likely to have had a constraining effect upon their ability to shape a solid sense of who they were. That needed to be, but was not, grounded in their family and local community. They had needed this knowledge constantly when growing up in order to absorb it naturally, gradually, even imperceptibly.

Having to acquire this fundamental, essential, personhood-shaping knowledge in post-care life, makes it much less likely that a person would be able to splice this knowledge into their sense of who they are.

Acquisition of identity information later in life may well produce the residual long-term effects of the person feeling that they do not truly belong, or deserve to belong, leaving them with a pervading sense of differentness, of inferiority, of being an imposter; of always looking in on their family as an outsider. This became a marked feature of Michael Porter's personality; and, to a lesser degree, of Paddy Baker too.

1.8.8. Remembering, Forgetting, Confusing and Misleading

Interviewing or reading the accounts of boys in care can be a confusing experience. Both Paddy and Michael repeatedly described themselves as believing they were orphans, despite their own evidence to the contrary in other statements. In Paddy's case he had the visit of his 'father' to Nazareth House when he was very young.[265] He knew he had a brother, James, 7 years older than him, with whom he reports having negligible contact when they were at Nazareth House. Paddy complained that Sister Attracta had lied to him, telling him when he was about ten years old that his mother was dead.[266] This, I presume, was in response to Paddy asking about his mother. Paddy describes two occasions where he was withdrawn from school photographs at Quay Street School that may be connected with his mother (or possibly even his father). That was most definitely the reason for his withdrawal from a group activity at a later date when he was not allowed to go on a band trip to a Strandhill hotel to play at a wedding reception.[267] The best band players, such as the Quartet, used to be invited to perform at functions such as weddings. At the very last minute Paddy was withdrawn by Attracta from going with his band mates. No explanation was given him. Later in life, in 1965, he learned from his bandmaster, Josie Cummings, the reason for this late withdrawal: his mother, Lillian Baker, had been working at that very hotel as a waitress.[268]

Paddy seems never to have explored further the various possible reasons for his withdrawal, or relate this incident to the fact that his mother had never visited either him or his brother at Nazareth House. It is most likely that Lillian would have known that the Nazareth House Band were booked to play. Was she eager to see Paddy? Was she terrified that the new life she had built for herself would be prejudiced, her hard won restoration of reputation imperilled if evidence of her past emerged? Was she in a new relationship? Had she agreed that she did not want to be traced? She seems not to have attempted then, or later, to contact either of her sons. Did she feel that they would be better off not knowing her? Did she not wish to encumber her new life with these 'blemished' reminders and handicaps from the past? The photographs and hotel incident combined read more like Attracta's intention was to prevent the still waters of Paddy's life at Nazareth House from being disturbed by the emotional maelstrom that contact between mother and son might produce; sparing Lillian, too, the pain of such a brief glimpse of Paddy and also from the shame of her secret coming out.

Attracta's actions over the Strandhill appear to have been an attempt to resolve a difficult dilemma. She did not have the luxury of time for reflection, or much professional experience and training on the complexity of such matters. Always over-busy, constantly badgered by the needs and management of so many needy boys, she made her decision. Her handling of the withdrawal from Strandhill seems to have been an action, 'sufficient unto the day', resolving that immediate problem with some aplomb.

That she had on another occasion told Paddy that his mother was dead as he claimed, was, however, if true, a step too far. That applies whether or not Lillian herself had wished this message to be passed on to her son. It was an action that could well have produced fateful, life-long consequences; indeed it did. I doubt very much that this was done to hurt him; indeed it is probable that

Attracta believed her actions to have been in his best interests. This decision was of much greater significance, an entirely qualitatively different type of action, because Paddy Baker left Nazareth House in the erroneous belief that his mother was dead, only later learning that this was not so. [269]

Harmful consequences often occur, not from deliberate attempts to hurt or harm ,[270] but usually because of well-intentioned actions that are compromised by all or some of the following; insufficient relevant training, consultation and support; insufficient information about, or failure to think through, the consequences; lack of time and pressure of other work; lack of similar situation experience; lack of sensitivity; or the opposite: a desire to avoid mentioning the subject of family and loss to spare the child. Above all is the failure to put oneself in the position of the person who will be most affected by your decisions. Indeed, that summarises well, my feelings about some of the deficiencies, at least those that stand up to scrutiny, that Michael and Paddy identified; sincere and well intentioned efforts by carers for the most part, but insufficiently sensitised or thought through on occasions; rarely deliberately designed to hurt or harm; almost all having to be made *en passant* to other work; done in the vernacular, 'on the hop'.

1.8.9. Decision Making Resources and Process

It is worth considering how such decisions would be taken to-day, comparing this with the different circumstances at Nazareth House in the 1930's. At the present time the child would have a field social worker of their own, based in the family's home area. That social worker would be responsible for the child in care and for liaising with the family of origin, and the parents. Parents would be routinely involved in decisions and Conferences about their child. On matters of significance or dispute, a Case Conference would be called. The child would be interviewed by the social worker and asked for their views on matters. The courts might have appointed a Guardian ad Litem, specifically to represent the views and interests of the child. The Conference might well include; the parent(s); the field Social Worker and their Senior Social worker; the residential care worker and their manager; the Local Authority legal adviser and possibly a solicitor for the child; any specialists or therapists involved; medical and nursing services; and sometimes police. The meeting would be chaired by an independent chairperson, reports and recommendations would be available to the meeting and the membership present would deliberate over the range of options available, and of the unintended consequences of some of these, before reaching recommendations.

Considered, planned, collective; time and resource plentiful; not quite comparable to Nazareth House in the 1930's. None of this battalion of inter-agency professionals were available to help shape child care decisions, or resolve problems or dilemmas, or to support the child in care, or the Sisters caring for him. As far as much general child care practice in Irish Religious Voluntary care Homes was concerned in the 1930's, including the boys at Nazareth House, many of the children were 'warehoused', parked in care until either their parent(s) or family reclaimed them, or, far more commonly the case, they had to make their own way in the world after they had left school and care. I have constantly tried to think what it must have been like for the boys in care at Nazareth House; but also what it must have been like for those caring for them, and especially under such resource pressures. Overall I find it unsurprising that 'errors' of judgement were made; the greater surprise is that more were not.

1.8.10. Religion, Identity and Allegiance

All the Quartet boys shared with their peers elsewhere in Ireland Irish nationality as central to their identity and also their religion, their Catholic faith. Yet even here, the effect was likely to have been markedly different, certainly for Michael and Paddy, but also for Willie McGowan. For Irish Catholic schoolchildren the emphasis in their home, at National School and in the Parish Church was of acquiring a life-long allegiance to the 'faith of their fathers'. This, in common with the non credal aspects of identity has two elements: 'like to' and 'different from'. The 'like to' emphasises the positive attachment, affiliation, and bonding component of identity, of one's likeness and particular attachment to family, community, and country, and the importance of this throughout one's life. The 'different from' emphasises how one's identity is secondarily shaped by what one is not, or by what one is opposed to or threatened by.[271]

All the boys had this positive national message repeatedly reinforced at Nazareth House and at Quay Street School; negatively too in the emphasis of their non-Englishness or even a degree of anti-Englishness, including their learning of history, and in their acquisition of song words. These two identity-determining forces, the positive one binding, and the oppositional one dividing, were interwoven into all aspects of learning and life. The socialisation of the boys included a much more overtly and unapologetically indoctrinating element, both in terms of nationality and nationhood, and also, but to a much more intense degree, in terms of religious creed; and of course the tendency of many Irish to conflate Catholic and Irish as part of their identity had each aspect reinforcing the claims of the other 'creed'.

Had the boys remained in their home area for schooling they would have attended National schools, which, as argued in chapter 1.6, were clerically and Church dominated. Yet those schools such as Quay Street that were staffed and run by religious such as the Marist Brothers, had an additional intensity of emphasis upon the Catholic and credal aspects of identity.

Of greatest significance for all the Quartet was the reality of living in a Home staffed by religious, and the degree to which faith and Catholicism were incorporated into, embedded might be a better word, every aspect of life, ritual, and thinking. At night the boy composed himself after kneeling by the bed in prayer, lying in bed arms crossed in imitation of Christ on his cross, praying yet further prayers against improvident death and the lures and wiles of Satan.[272] In the morning, bedside kneeling prayers were later followed by morning prayer in Chapel and daily Mass. All meals were begun and finished by prayers. At twelve and six o'clock daily all movement and activity stopped for the recitation of the Angelus. At Quay Street, morning and afternoon sessions would have been prefaced by prayers, and followed by the boy learning the core components of Catholic faith; these were enshrined in condensed form in an educational and doctrinal masterpiece: *The Catechism of Christian Doctrine*,[273] or Penny Catechism, as it was known. And on Holy Days of Obligation, and actual holidays, as on the trip to Strandhill, a Rosary or two was never far away from being started by the Sisters, although the latter also would have featured daily in their family homes.

The catechism, a common tool of many Christian denominations at this period, was designed to communicate the core elements of Christianity and of Catholicism, in question and answer format. The class chanted the answers to the simple questions, imbibing sometimes complex aspects of faith or theology in clear, short gobbets of information. In essence it provided a skeletal framework of 'approved', 'correct' belief that could be used to defend a Catholic if challenged by another person from a different Christian denomination. Michael summarised the thinking at that time of his childhood in Ireland:

The biggest thing to the Sisters was that we stayed true to the faith, that we didn't go over to the other side. That was their greatest fear, that we might stray; that was what drove them the most. All their work was to that end. Not only that but that we should continue attending Mass and say our prayers after we left Sligo. The worst thing of all would have been to have become a Protestant. That would have been much worse than not attending Mass. It would have been the ultimate betrayal by us, and they would have seen it as them having failed. 'Does he go to Church' would be the first question they would want to know about one of us.[274]

'One of us'; to retain the boys as one of us, Catholic and Irish preferably, or at the very least, Catholic, was the mark of success for the Sisters, and they mustered all their efforts to achieve this, as, had they failed in this quest, this mission, they would have believed that the boy's soul would have been imperilled for eternity. At this period Church teaching emphasised the doctrine that outside the Church there is no salvation. Remaining in the Barque of St Peter was seen as the surest, indeed only, way to navigate safely through the stormy seas of life: *until we reach the shore.*

At the Requiem Mass the perils of eternal damnation for the soul who died in mortal sin outside the Church, were made fearfully clear in the Sequence: *Dies Irae* (day of wrath or anger). The following extracts from the *Dies Irae* are given to illustrate the pervasive atmosphere in which sin, death, heaven and hell were spoken of, and of the climate of fear, even terror, that it was designed to invoke in the mind of the faithful, eager to avoid the fate of those outside the Church.[275]

One need not look far to find parallel texts and tone in a number of protestant Churches and sects of the time, especially those in Northern Ireland, Scotland and Wales echoing Akenson's assertion that there are *small differences* between southern Catholic and northern Protestant. Although the *Dies Irae* was a Catholic prayer of mediaeval origin its content would have been agreed by many protestants of the period:

'Lo the Day of Wrath, that day
Oh, how great shall be the fear,
When at last, as judge severe,
Christ the Lord shall reappear!

Death and Nature then shall quake
As the Dead from dust awake
To their Judge reply to make

So before the Judge enthroned,
Shall each hidden sin be owned,
Naught of guilt left unatoned

Guilty, lo, I groan with fear,
Whilst with shame Thy throne I near
When the cursed at Thy behest,
Go to flames that never rest,
Call me thou to join the blest

Sad indeed shall be the day
When the guilty, cast away,
Fall in to eternal gloom.
Save us, Lord, from such a doom.

In Thy mercy, Jesus blest,
Grant Thy servants endless rest' [276]

A journalist criticised Mother Theresa of Calcutta, arguing that her priority in life, the saving of souls, was the wrong priority, and that attending to the physical and material needs of the poor should take precedence. Although Mother Theresa and the Sisters of Nazareth would have rejected the simplistic duality suggested by the critic, they would have agreed that the central purpose in life was the saving of souls. Each members of the Quartet would also have seen that as the central purpose of his life. Although at least two of the Quartet lacked a past life, in terms of knowing aught of family or place of origin, they retained a central purpose, and a destination, throughout their life; this was centred on the religious and faith aspect of identity that had been inculcated in them at Nazareth House and at Quay Street School. I find it difficult to evaluate to what degree the absence of core aspects of identity in childhood was compensated for by an increased intensity of adherence to the faith component.

For Michael Porter, this religious grounding has acted as a compass for him in navigating his life, keeping always before him a hope, a belief that he had a destination, and a final and permanent home to go to. He still retains the Catechism answer below that summarises the philosophy and priority for his carers, teachers and Church; it has remained the guiding principle of his life:

'What doth it profit a man if he gain the whole world, yet suffer the loss of his own soul'.[277]

Chapter 1.9: Institutional Care and the Sisters of Nazareth

1.9.1. Four Questions

This chapter addresses four questions throughout:

• What was the standard of care at Nazareth House in the 1920's and 1930's?

• How did this compare with other institutional child care?

• Why was it as it was?

• Can a large institution ever really become a home for young children?

The first three questions are framed to guide an exploration of the nature and quality of the care of the boys by the Sisters of Nazareth in Sligo, related to the context and to the era when it was provided, the 1920's and 1930's. This last question is stood up but not directly answered; rather it is introduced as a wider question for reflection, both here and throughout the book.

1.9.2. Commonalities of Institutional Care

Institutions dealing with large numbers of inmates, especially with small numbers of staff, do so by ensuring that the inmates do not challenge the authority of staff. Ensuring compliance with the rules is instilled into each new inmate. Absence of individual possessions, wearing the same clothes as one's fellows, communal dormitories and ablutions, lack of privacy or personal space, are all aspects of the institution designed to make management easier and more efficient; they also have the effect of weakening individuality and individual identity. They also make smoother the process of compliance-moulding of the new inmate. The regimentation of the daily routine, and the immediate response to whistle, bell or command, drill home in the inmate's mind the pattern expected to assist the smooth running of the institution. Resisting, rebelling, or protesting by inmates is almost always futile and usually produces painful consequences. Keep your head down and keep out of trouble. This mortification of self by any 'inmate', be it child or adult, was the self-same process undergone by the Sisters of Nazareth during their training at Hammersmith.[278]

In total institutions, where the resident, inmate, patient or prisoner never leaves the confines of the institution, the restrictive and oppressive aspects of 'incarceration' tend to be greater than those such as Nazareth House in Sligo, where care and daily life occurred in different places. This is because the boys in Sligo engaged to some degree with the outside world, at school, or in outside activities, usually organised. In some other residential care homes, including some other Nazareth House Homes elsewhere, the children were educated on site. One would expect that the 'freer', more open model in Sligo, would do less harm to the children and better equip them for life after care than the completely closed institution.

Institutions vary greatly in size, location and structure. Many of the Irish Children's homes were vast in physical scale and housed in rather forbidding, workhouse style buildings, including some of the Nazareth homes in the north of Ireland. Perhaps an even greater child care challenge was posed by the enormous numbers of children housed in some of these institutions. It is axiomatic that staff working in such homes, and more importantly the children living there, would find it hard to relate to others, or to be treated with any degree of individuality. In general the larger the numbers of residents, the smaller the chance of individual personal attention for them, particularly emotionally.

1.9.3. The Religious Dimension: Sisters

The uniform, whether prison, hospital, or religious habit, makes immediately overt who is charged with authority and power, and who exercises control; the Homeboy uniform equally marks those subject to this control. Compared with a non-uniformed institutional staff member, those in uniform can often seem to the inmates: to carry greater, and instant, authority; to stand at a greater distance from them; and to lack any aspect of a human personality, or even face. The inmate sees the uniform, and rarely, sometimes never, sees the human being within it: the person within the profession.

The religious dimension, and the Sisters' habit that resembled a female Muslim-type exclusion of all body and head parts, meant that only one area of the person was visible: a part of the face. Or rather, it was obscured in practice, because of the stricture on the boys that forbad them making direct eye contact with the Sisters; this was adjudged a token of challenge or defiance.[279] This sanction exacerbated the tendency of the boys to see a uniform rather than a person in the figure before them. The dark coloured, heavy, enveloping uniform, designed to represent the Sisters' death to the world, conveyed to the boys a similar dour, even smothering, impression. All factors contributed the tendency of the boys to see a depersonalised image of their carers.

The Sisters were also charged with the moral and spiritual care of the boys, in addition to their corporal care of them, to a much greater degree than other institutional staff. Furthermore this moral care was meant to be evident: right conduct by the boys was a sign of their success; conversely, wrong or bad behaviour was a manifest sign of the failure of the Sisters, or Brothers, and should be checked or eradicated.

1.9.4. Catholic Church Ethos

Both the Nazareth Sisters, and Marist Brothers operated their care of the boys imbued with the Church culture at the time, the tenor of which was touched upon in earlier chapters. This ethos could be, and was not uncommonly perceived to be: clericalist in mood, clerically dominated and tightly controlled; confident, dogmatic and imperious; somewhat implacable; and distinctly unwelcoming of challenge or dissent. Indeed challenge or dissent risked adding additional sins, because church canon law added manifold, additional, intra-ecclesial sins to the already considerable testamentary tally. The Church at that period seemed to convey an impression of greater concern with struggle against aspects of sin and human darkness than the other side of its message: light, hope and redemption; more often a Good Friday sepulchral feel; less often Easter Sunday joy.

The 'Jansenist-derived', negative, guilt-ridden, Christ-crucifying, hell-avoiding, devil-tempted, sin-fixated culture that could be evident in the Church tone at the period would have been conveyed to the boys at Nazareth House, as to Catholic children everywhere in Ireland, but to a less intense degree for the latter. The effects of this sin-fixated culture that was seared into the minds of young and impressionable children is evident in both Michael Porter and Paddy Baker's accounts of their lives at Nazareth House (and also from William McCormack's life there in the 1950's). In consequence Michael carried his cross of guilt around with him, expecting sanctions, even though these rarely occurred.

Michael Porter's constant memory of Nazareth House was his pre-occupation with being caught out by the Sisters for doing something wrong, and avoiding punishment for this. He remembers committing plenty of misdemeanours and infractions of the rules. On a number of occasions he was either called before the Sisters to explain his conduct, or not interviewed at all. He felt he could always rely on being given the opportunity to put his side of the story to the Sisters. Yet when I queried the source of his anxiety about punishment, he could never remember a single instance of actually being hit or even punished by them during his entire career at Nazareth House, although he would be told off, or be *given a look*, for misdemeanours.

He also remembers the same atmosphere of needing to avoid getting into trouble when he attended Quay Street School: for example, taking care not to hit anyone with the handball when playing in the school yard. He was punished by caning at school and yet this did not really bother him, certainly not frighten him. He always felt that this had resulted from a transgression, and that the caning was not sadistically or wilfully applied. *It was how things were done at that time: you knew the rules and therefore couldn't complain if you broke these.*

One would imagine that an atmosphere of continual concern with avoidance and purgation of sin, of securing indulgences to lessen suffering in Purgatory, of constant fear of dying in mortal sin and going to Hell for all eternity would entirely knock the spontaneity, joy and laughter from young boys. It seems not to have done so for the Quartet, save in one area: guilt. For Catholics of this period, the terms *guilt-ridden* and *Catholic* may be taken as synonymous, and the term *guilt-ridden Catholic*, renders redundant the hyphenated adjective. Fear of punishment, even if not factually grounded, becomes *de facto* reality to the child, to Michael, and to many other Catholics of the period who never saw the inside of any residential institution. Although Michael, and Paddy too from his letters, would agree with the above description this did not mean that they doubted the major tenets of their faith. These, then and now, for all of the Quartet, and most especially for Willie McGowan and Willie Walsh, formed a central core of their life, even for Paddy in his later ruminating years. They all seem to have been able to understand that deficiencies of the organisational Church and the conduct of some of its pastors did not invalidate its core message.

Religion seems to have added an additional layer of distance in relationships between Sisters and boys. The uniformed aspect of institutional staff is reminiscent of Russian dolls. Staff position, staff uniform and religious habit, each creates a barrier, hiding the human within. To the three dolls just listed were further hidden doll-type barriers: probably that of gender; and certainly that of religious authority which further separated Sisters from boys. Michael felt these latter two elements created additional distance between him and his carers.

Overall, however the Quartet members regarded Catholicism as a binding element between them and the Sisters, and the Marist Brothers: in terms of identity (as shown it the preceding chapter); in terms of faith; and in terms of a common patrimony that helped them connect with their fellow Catholic *sufferers* both within, and when they had left, the Home.

1.9.5. Institutional Abuse

'There is no such thing as a bad boy'.[280]

'The experience of the Review has seemed at times a crash course in human (predominantly male) wickedness and in the fallibility of social institutions'.[281]

The first quote above came from a Sligo educated priest, working in the United States, in the early part of the twentieth century. The second quote was taken from an Inquiry in to abuse in Children's Homes in England and Wales, at the end of that century. The priest's early century optimism had given way to an end century pessimism, the change worked by the unfolding knowledge about the extensive sexual exploitation, and other forms of abuse, of children in residential care, both historically and currently.

Residential care has tended to be the *Cinderella* element in care and welfare provision, attracting the least qualified people and requiring them to do the hardest of care tasks. The amount, quality and nature of residential care at any given period mirrors the values, priorities and health of the society in which that care is provided.

In post-independence Ireland residential, and indeed hospital care, was provided primarily by religious and charitable organisations, much more so than in the United Kingdom. Yet even in the UK state support and responsibility for the welfare of children was decidedly patchy, and voluntary and religious organisations still substantially buttressed state provision, as the Curtis Report (1946) concluded:

'Due to the inadequate care provided by governmental authorities, neglect, abuse, and the efforts to prevent it or care for those that suffered it, was provided by a plethora of charities and philanthropic societies. The care and measures used by the various societies prior to the 1948 Childrens' Act, varied greatly in quality and practice; many failed to attain the basic criteria stressed by child care professionals of the day, yet they continued to practise due to the simple fact that the only alternatives in existence were the poor-law institutions'.

The child rescue model of care that led to the formation of the Sisters of Nazareth in Victorian England had been a voluntary and philanthropic response to social need at a time when state intervention in family life was regarded as undesirable, indeed even harmful. This was not only because of the general policy of *laissez faire,* but also because of the primacy that was given to parental autonomy over their family. This was especially so in Ireland and reinforced by Catholic social teaching, and where intervention in family life by the state was discouraged, only to be permitted in cases of extreme abuse or neglect of children.

Some historical context to attitudes to children, especially vulnerable ones such as the Nazareth House ones, gives an idea of the prevalent social attitudes to children in the 1930's that would have influenced their carers. The works of two authors, Maslow and Kempe, show how society's understanding of the needs of children has evolved since then, albeit slowly and somewhat unevenly.

1.9.6. Hierarchy of Needs

Abraham Maslow's hierarchy of needs[282] enables care at Nazareth House to be compared with a model to assess any strengths and weaknesses. The five needs are arranged in order, the most fundamental first:

1. Food, warmth and shelter

2. Safety

3. Love and belonging

4. Esteem

5. Self-actualization (i.e. self-fulfilment or achieving one's potential)

The first two fundamental standards appear very well met at Nazareth House, the third barely or not at all and the fourth somewhat mixed: although individual attention was lacking the varied cultural, recreational and, especially, musical activities provided a collective forum for development of self-worth. I would not even attempt to try to ascertain whether level 5, self-actualization, was achieved: to do so would be to expect people to deliver something they did not understand nor had the time to deal with.

When Paddy left Nazareth House he pined for the clean, safe, secure environment he had left behind. The earlier chapters have described the efforts made to provide a balanced, if hardly over-generous, diet and to secure medical and dental services. Michael had been one of only two children in his family to survive childhood, both of the survivors having been taken into care. He now believes that he and his sister would probably not have survived childhood if they had remained at home. Providing this quality of physical care is a not inconsiderable feat; that it was achieved with so few staff, and largely based on uncertain and charitable giving, is remarkable.[283]

The great void in Michael's and Paddy's life was the third stage of Maslow, that of love directed towards them as individuals and of lacking a sense of belonging to parents or to a family group. It does not appear that this was a priority for the Sisters. Had it been so, the staff numbers and overall demands leading to batch care would have made this difficult to have carried out effectively, or consistently.

The prime, indeed the overwhelming reason for the lack of individual attention to the boys was the massive mismatch between the very small number of Sister carers and the large number of boys to be cared for, as detailed in Chapter 5. The practice, if not policy, of the Congregation never to refuse entry to a request to accommodate a needy or destitute child was undoubtedly well intentioned, seemingly rooted in a deep commitment to the needy; so too was the Hammersmith Mother General's stance that the Lord will provide when money and resources were not available to meet the scale of need.[284] The practical consequence of this mismatch between need and resources, especially Sister carers, was that need was met by the Sisters running faster and further to try to close the gap. The material care of the boys appears extraordinarily well met, given the limited number of carers. The number deficiency meant, however, that the emotional side was the one that was much less well dealt with.

1.9.7. Evolving Understanding of Harm to Children

The understanding of children's needs has changed considerably since the period of the 1920's and 1930's: indeed even since the 1960's, and is changing still. In the sociological jargon it is *socially constructed*, with these needs being perceived differently at different times and in different societies. In the early 1960's an American paediatrician, Henry Kempe, attracted controversy and much criticism for claiming that a number of children admitted to hospital with serious injuries that they had received at the hands of their parents; like Father Flanagan, he met a disbelieving world. The same disbelief marked the unfolding evidence of sexual exploitation and abuse of children; within the family; within institutions including care homes; and in church settings. Societies seem reactive and then slow to act until repeated scandals and incontrovertible breaches of trust force change: and this applies to all organisations, all countries, and all religions.[285]

1.9.8. Conformity and Compliance

The training of the Sisters, allied to their pattern of compliance and obedience, meant that there was never any chance of upward pressure from the Sisters to the Reverend Mother in each Home, or to the Hammersmith overall management of the congregation to obtain extra resources to care for their young or old charges, although they did ask for items such as a cooker that were needed[286]. Even had they challenged the significant human resource gap the philosophy outlined in Chapter 1.3: 'There is no poetry in our after-life here, it is hard practical work, and we pray that Heaven may send us none but novices with sound common sense'[287] would have prevailed. You're here to work and to do God's will not to complain; God gave you two hands and two arms, so roll up your sleeves and get on with it; such a response might well have been predicted. They largely seem to have got on with it uncomplainingly.

1.9.9. Emotional Bleakness

Although the mismatch between needs and resources would seem to be the major reason for the lack of individual attention it cannot fully explain it. It is disturbing that Michael Porter can only remember a single act of personal warmth and kindness directed towards him during his entire career at Nazareth House by his Sister carers: the 'shy Sister' episode described later in this chapter. The emotional bleakness Michael Porter felt at Nazareth House, Paddy

Baker experienced too: and this emotionally austere climate is my overall impression of what it must have been like for the boys living there in the 1920's and 1930's. A look, even glancing, a smile, an encouraging or kind word; any, or all, of these could have made so much difference, as would putting themselves into the shoes of the boys, thinking, *there but for the Grace of God go I*. What makes the situation of the emotional care of the boys harder to understand is that I believe that the Sisters did feel genuine care for the boys.[288]

Other factors, less critical than resources, but still influencing the culture of care include: lack of training; insufficient emotional sensitivity on the part of some of the Sisters; the Sisters' training and culture leading them to manifest a pattern of veiling their emotions; and the need to exercise authority and control, usually for the needs of the boys. The greatest deficiency was one common to all organisations to some degree: communication, and in particular the lack of communication and information about the family of origin, and the boys' sense of identity. This barely featured, if at all.

1.9.10. Cultural Life

In contrast to the emotional bleak climate (Level 3 of Maslow's hierarchy) was the vibrant cultural life with considerable, sustained, innovative and varied efforts made to provide some degree of esteem for the boys through collective recreational, cultural, spiritual and sporting provision (Level 4).[289]

1.9.11. Physical Abuse by a Sister at Nazareth House

Physical chastisement, let alone abuse, was explicitly forbidden in the rules of the Sisters of Nazareth, and it seems that this was not, despite the serious one listed below about Sister Attracta, a common feature of life there during the inter-War years. (Indeed when the prison warder Mahon's brutality towards the boys was discovered he was instantly dismissed by Reverend Mother).[290]

Paddy Baker describes two instances of physical abuse and degrading treatment when at Nazareth House; one from Sister Attracta; the other from a former Sligo prison warder, named Mahon. Michael Porter also instances his only physical ill treatment abuse incident, again at the hands of Mahon.[291] The two Willies missed this Mahon ill treatment, according to Paddy, as they were attending Summerhill College.

Paddy described the incident with Sister Attracta having occurred when he had accidentally broken a window when trying to close it with the window pole during a storm. He records being slapped and sent to obtain money for this at night from his brother working in Rose Hill Nursing Home. His brother also gave him sixpence. Paddy kept the sixpence:

To have money at Nazareth and not give it up was equivalent to a mortal sin, so with this on my conscience I had to battle with the Devil and the Almighty as I lay in bed with the 6d still firmly clasped in my hand. The Devil of course won the battle. He secreted the little silver promise of treats-to-come in various locations in the Home, eventually hiding it in an attic in the scullery where he helped Sister Agata (Agatha). Unknown to Paddy he was spotted by Sister Felim and reported to Sister Attracta. She called him to the classroom prior to going to bed, locking the door. He denied once possessing the coin, then twice, then thrice. He recorded that Attracta turned him upside down, pulled down his trousers, and beat his bare backside with a stick that she got from the medicine cupboard. He got dressed and was then taken by the ear to retrieve the sixpence from the scullery attic. On return to St Patrick's dormitory he cried bitterly: *Not because of the pains but because of my lost sixpence.*[292]

Michael Porter could easily identify with this sense of coveting something of one's own; in his case the elephant stamped handball had performed this function. *Even half a swapped comic made you feel special*, he recalled.[293]

The morning after the beating Paddy found that he had wet the bed and there was blood on the sheets. He then reported being given a cold water bath in an aluminium tub, together with the other bed wetters. Of Sister Attracta Paddy variously recorded:

The little love I had for her was extinguished.....Who was invariably prone to kindness, but who now changed her tactics in the treatment of the older boys. Who would have thought that the same nun who once held me in her arms as a child....could be so cruel to me 12 years later.[294]

A slightly earlier escapade with the Sister who had reported Paddy's hiding place to Attracta, may have also contributed to the severity of Paddy's punishment for lying about the sixpence. Sister Felim worked in the laundry and Paddy reported being threatened with a punch on the nose and dared by the older boys to find out whether the Sisters shaved their heads; their wimples and head gear prevented any sight of hair. Paddy also reported that he was at the age of puberty and was becoming curious about sexuality. Carefully planning his move Paddy concealed himself above her when she was changing in the drying room and he saw that her hair was very short. When she looked up to button her hood she saw Paddy. *She must have been as terrified as myself.... She reported me to Attracta for me having dared to intrude on her privacy.*[295]

The tendency for those in institutions, or uniform, including army and police, to fail to act upon examples of abuse or even report crimes, seems in my experience to be greater than that in the wider civilian population. In chapter 1.3 the extreme stress in the training of the Sisters upon obedience and not challenging authority has been outlined. It is extremely unlikely that Attracta's abuse of Paddy, although conducted behind locked door, would not have been known to some of the other Sisters, and indeed Reverend Mother. Indeed Paddy reported Sister Felim smirking after he had been caught, proud to have detected his disobedience. Attracta's actions may therefore have been sanctioned by the silence and inactivity of the rest of the Congregation of Sisters in Sligo.[296]

There is a further element in abuse that I think applies to those religions such as Roman Catholicism that employ sacramental confession. It can lead to what I have elsewhere termed a *confessional wipe-out mentality.*[297] Sin, confess; sin confess; and so the pattern is repeated. I believe that this has been a contributory factor to some clergy's repeated abuse of children, including within, and immediately after sacraments. The offending cleric then expunges the *sin* in confession, before continuing the sin/sin expunging process. Would this have been an element with Attracta?[298]

Attracta's severe loss of control, though, opens up the wider issue of workload and work environment as contributory factors to the ill-treatment of children, or indeed of any inmate. Where the workload is far too great, where there is no time to think or relax, where large numbers have to be corralled together by few shepherds, where there is no holiday or weekend break, can this lead to a mechanical response to those in one's charge and to a dullness of emotion by the carer? Can, then, anything which interrupts the smooth operation of the organisation receive a disproportionate response? Further, is it not it a truism, that the staff and *inmates* in any institution tend to become like each other, with the adults sometimes acting like children? A weary body and mind depresses the soul. Such musings, I think, not only give a context to Attracta's brutalisation of Paddy, but are, I believe, a feature of the less serious acts of spitefulness or pettiness evinced by some nuns and other carers towards children in care. It is human nature to release anger and frustration somehow: it is much more likely that this will be directed to those *below* you in the pecking order than to those more powerful.

1.9.12. Physical Abuse by a Lay Helper at Nazareth House: Unintended Consequences

It certainly appears that even the more experienced Sisters were aware of their difficulties, deficiencies even, in handling the older boys, and also in providing only a female role model for them. It may even have been the incident with Paddy that triggered the decision to introduce a new male figure into the boys' lives, as a Mr Mahon, a Sligo prison warder was introduced to Nazareth House at this time. Mahon, a man about five feet nine inches in height and of medium build, aged in his thirties, took the boys for Physical Exercises and also drill, usually for an hour or so periodically, not on a weekly basis.[299] Both Michael and Paddy recall being brutally beaten by him, for no reason. In Michael's case he was accused of entering a forbidden area of the grounds for the Elderly Home, and summarily punished without the right of questioning or reply by

Mahon. His punishment method was to lay the boys on a wooden table, pull down their trousers, with their feet touching the floor and thrash their bare buttocks and thighs, with a thick cane.

Michael describes Mahon as the first person he ever truly hated: *If hate could kill he would have been dead.*[300] Michael refused to cry out on his beating, knowing that this was what Mahon wanted from him, to break his will, and he refused to give him the satisfaction by uttering a sound. Silence was defiance, a refusal to surrender. But the real harm had already been done. He had been stripped naked and beaten in front of his peers; that this had happened to some of them was no consolation to him. The shame of this was the real punishment. It is notable that none of the boys thought of telling the Sisters, the Brothers at school, the Yardmen or any other adult, not even Josie Cummings, about Mahon's brutality. The majority of children do not tell.

So extreme was the hatred engendered by Mahon's brief regime that the boys planned to stop his brutality. Both Paddy and Michael describe Mahon as a sadist who loved his *work*. Paddy, who met a few of them in the war when serving in the British army, described him as Nazi-like, revelling in the harm he inflicted on others. Michael recalls the boys ganging up together to plan to kill Mahon. When I challenged this as a figure of speech he corrected me:

We actually intended to kill him, not just to hurt him. We planned how we would do it, but before we got the chance he was gone. I think the Sisters must have got wind of what we were up to, for he went just as quickly as he came. I always believed he had left because of us. There was no one leader. We were all leaders, all of us in it. We snatched conversations in huddles together in the playground, at school, wherever we could. We knew when he was next due to visit and made our plans. We had no weapons, as the Sisters would have detected these. We had decided to attack him, either in the playroom, or out in the playground, depending on the weather. We were all to jump on him, pin him down and beat him till he was dead.[301]

That the boys' plan would have succeeded is fantastical; that it was deadly serious is not. The effects of Mahon's brief period at

Nazareth House was not just bruised bodies and crushed spirits. The brutality, and the injustice of punishment without trial, that was a feature of Mahon's approach, resulted in Paddy running away from Nazareth House. Two years younger than the other Quartet boys, intimidated by Mr Shine at Quay Street, Paddy was not as old or resilient as Michael, or the older plotters against Mahon. His response was flight. His disappearance, and the reason for it coming to light, appears to have been the trigger for Reverend Mother to instantly dismiss Mahon when she found out what he had been doing.[302] So a move, presumably well intentioned, to introduce a positive male role model for the boys had so spectacularly failed. The greatest victim was Paddy: as a result of him absconding he may have lost the chance of a career in music, under the sponsorship and tutelage of Count John McCormack, the Irish tenor.

1.9.13. Struggles with Control

Paddy himself seems aware that the Sisters struggled more with their relationship and control of the boys as they got older and bigger and as they reached puberty. Attracta, herself, also seems to have been aware of this, as a 1968 letter from her, in *retirement* at Nazareth House, Birmingham, intimates. The letter, to *My Dear William Patrick* (Willie McGowan) includes:

I might say I am retired from 'Active Service' and which gives me more leisure for prayer and to make atonement for past carelessness in that respect-You know Willie- with 95 hefty boys-clamouring for attention-time for prayer wasn't easy come by, and I'm depending on you, Maureen, Cecilia, Eugene, Margaret and Imelda to give me a helping hand when I come to the 'End of the Road'.[303]

Not quite an apology, but certainly seeming to plead for the context of care demands and constraints to be understood; and, interestingly, needing this from one of those she had cared for, a person whom she respected, and who reciprocated this regard, and who kept in touch with her throughout her life, including when she moved to England.

When Michael Porter read of Sister Attracta's treatment of Paddy after he had secreted the sixpence, what surprised him most was Paddy's obduracy in lying and denying what he had done. Michael could never recollect Attracta hitting him or anyone else:

She didn't need to. A look was enough. I would never have dared do what Paddy did, though I could understand how much the money must have meant to him; to have something of your very own would have been so wonderful. Above all it would be the lying that would have got her goat; and then to lie again and then again. That would have been the thing that maddened her, much more than hiding the sixpence.[304]

Sister John confirmed that: *Attracta ran a tight ship.*[305] Generally those teachers or carers who can exercise control resort less to outbursts of extreme or inconsistent behaviour than those who find control more difficult. Attracta's successor would seem to have fallen in to the latter category, lack of natural control making her generally more punitive according to Willie McCormack.[306]

Yet the same Willie McCormack speaks most highly of a yet later successor, Sister Mary of the Passion. From Willie's and Sister John's testimonies, and from Sister Mary's correspondence with Willie McGowan,[307] a picture emerges of someone well fitted for her senior child care role because of her unusually comprehensive range of appropriate talents: training in child care and development (as an ex Head Teacher): considerable understanding and affection for her charges; personal qualities including empathy, warmth and humour; physical strength and determination; administrative and intellectual abilities; and a capacity to exercise firm but considerate control. Rare, I imagine, are the leaders, carers or Sisters who would possess such a complete range of talents for their work. Sister Mary of the Passion would almost certainly have handled the sixpence incident far more appropriately and in so doing would have retained the respect of the child without losing authority.[308] [309]

There is a further factor, with two components to it, that gives additional insight into Attracta's brutal abuse of Paddy; it is what I would term *anticipatory fearfulness*. This is where a parent, teacher or carer over-reacts to a transgression in order to forestall future repetitions of the offence, hoping that the extremity of the punishment will be remembered by the miscreant, and act as future deterrent. The other component is the religious one, and the particular gloomy, sepulchral, Jansenist, sin-obsessed aspect of Catholicism mentioned earlier that was then so prevalent, especially in Ireland. Paddy describes it thus: *Fear had to be embedded into the hearts and minds of children and the earlier the better. The fear of God, the police, of ghosts, of sin, of thunder, of the Devil who I believe never exists (sic) and never did.*[310] Michael would agree with every word of Paddy's diatribe, except for the Devil element: *We were taught more about fearing God than about loving him.*[311] William McCormack reinforces this: 'I'm sure that this Catholic God the nuns worshipped was not the God of love but the God of fear'.[312]

Protestant catechisms included the admonition from Proverbs: 'The fear of the Lord is the beginning of knowledge, indicating a wider Christian culture of the fear of God at this period'.[313]

1.9.14. Anticipatory Fearfulness

The fear of the boys getting out of control of the Sisters as they got bigger was something I had earlier encountered in social work. A boy, George, was due to leave a Catholic Residential Home at the age of nearly 18 years. The Home, moderate in size, was run by Sisters in a northern English city. George was a big soft lump of a lad, good natured, and very immature for his age. He still attended a facility for children with special educational needs. He could literally fall asleep standing up when doing woodwork. The Catholic Care Society[314] had tried several times to foster him without success, his special needs and rather unprepossessing physical features being factors in these failures. His care as he approached 18 was transferred to the City's Social Services Department as the Sisters recognised that he would need support well beyond 18 years. I was allocated as his social worker and we managed to find him a supported living situation in the city with a family that might be described as a not-quite-fostering family placement.

What struck me in the planning and discussion meetings with the Sisters was their fear of *what he might do* to the other younger boys (he was by far the oldest boy there). George's hero was *The Incredible Hulk*, someone admired by pre-teens. George liked to pretend that he was the Hulk, showing off his muscles to anyone who would take notice. He liked to play rough and tumble games with the younger lads in the home, but there was absolutely no sexual overtone to this. He felt more comfortable with younger children because his mind and interests were those of a much younger child. Some of the Sisters, it seemed to me, were frightened of him, of *what he might do*, to them, not just the younger boys. This anticipatory fearfulness of him physically challenging and defying them was a further realisation that they had passed beyond their ability to handle him. I suspect that not a little of the fear of loss of control, that the Sisters experienced with George, also underlay Attracta's dealings with Paddy. Paddy, elsewhere in his letters, comments upon how Attracta was great in caring for him and the other boys when they were younger but found the older ones much more of a handful.[315] A further factor behind the change was that Attracta was now in charge of the boys, and had much more responsibility, and so, as Shakespeare wrote: 'Uneasy lies the head that wears a crown'.[316]

Paddy Baker records that (with forgivable hyperbole for the statistics, as nuns did then seem to be everywhere in Ireland): *The nuns in those days had little or no idea about child psychology. In the bitter days of unemployment young females were struggling desperately to find employment and thousands of them had no alternative but to become nuns. The same can be said for the boys who because of a poverty stricken land became priests. Next to cattle, Ireland's greatest export were priests and nuns. This...cut the unemployment rate down to about 25%.*[317] Had he developed the point further it might have been more pertinent. When so many took the veil, when it was socially expected and school and clergy encouraged, when it was relatively more easy to enter with numbers expanding, when it was a cleaner, better status job than others available, how much more likely was it that a minority of these would lack the qualities really needed for such demanding work.

1.9.15. Father Flanagan of Boys' Town: Vision

Earlier in this chapter, and that on schooling, the somewhat sin-obsessed, negative and sepulchral climate prevailing in the Catholic Church culture in Ireland was linked to the care of the boys. Yet the very same culture produced a very different response from a Sligo educated priest; a reminder of how individuals respond differently to similar circumstances, and a caution against a crude deterministic approach to history. A caution too, against criticism of arguably dysfunctional aspects of any organisation being taken as damning the whole: criticism is often a mark of affection and respect, as well as a sign of health.

Edward Joseph Flanagan had been born in nearby Leabeg, County Roscommon in 1886, one of a large family of children living on the family farm. He later transferred to the diocesan seminary in Sligo, Summerhill College, to train for the priesthood. Even though he was fulfilling his ambition and was there with his parents' blessing, and had family at home (unlike Michael and Paddy), and was a successful student at Summerhill, avoiding trouble and censure, he hated the place: 'Life at Summerhill was an undeniable shock to him; his introduction to a lock-step existence in which every deviation, even when unintentional, meant reprisal....so strict were the rules that the boys lived in terror of making a mistake',[318] the consequences of which could be expulsion. Dickensian-like Summerhill seems to have acted as a spur to produce the opposite atmosphere in the boy's later life.

After Summerhill Edward Flanagan had followed his family to America, and following a spell in Austria where he was ordained in 1912, he returned to America as a curate in Nebraska. There his experiences of working with poor Irish immigrants, the destitute, and homeless and delinquent boys led him to establish a boys' home in 1917 in Omaha. His work was later known world-wide as a result of the 1938 biographical film about his life and work.[319]

Father Flanagan of Boys Town, as he came to be known, maintained his connections with Sligo, visiting the town regularly including an inspection visit to Nazareth House Boys' Home, Sligo in 1946, when the Home's brass band, under conductor Josie

Cummings, played for him. He expressed his satisfaction with the Home care there, but attracted controversy during and after this visit to Ireland for his criticism of the standards and philosophical underpinnings of much of Irish institutional life. He was especially critical of the penal establishments and Industrial Schools to which children had been committed for the whole of their young lives; including Michael Porter's sister, Sadie. Poverty and family breakdown from loss of mother had led to a deprived 5 year old girl being committed to an institution for those characterised as 'depraved'. Father Flanagan challenged the very notion of children as depraved, most famously expressed in his pithy motto: 'There are no bad boys. There is only bad environment, bad training, bad example, bad thinking'.

The establishment of Boys Town in Nebraska was grounded in this, then revolutionary, concept for treating delinquency. The organisation of the Homes involved the boys, of all colours and creeds, having some degree of say and control over the running of the home, including their own Parliament, designed to prepare them for coping with life outside, and to encourage mutuality and support for others. This was reflected in the 1943 Boys Town logo image of a younger boy carried on his back by an older boy, with the phrase: 'He ain't heavy, mister-he's my brother'.

Father Flanagan's views led to attacks on him by Irish press, Catholic hierarchy and government ministers, especially when, in expressing these views in America, he had committed the ultimate sin for an Irishman abroad: disloyalty.

The priest identified two central changes needed: for the boys love and individual attention; and from the carers a change in attitude:

'It is not enough....to see that what has been called an underprivileged child is given good food, warm clothing and a clean bed. An army commissary can do as much. No! More than food, clothes, and shelter, what these lads have been deprived of is a mother's tenderness, and father's wisdom, and the love of a family. We will never get anywhere in our reform schools and orphan asylums until we compensate for that great loss in such young lives'.

144

'And what does that mean? It means that you will have to develop a new class of social workers, not merely distinguished for their professional training, but, more important, consecrated to the great, the soul-lifting task of bringing tenderness and solicitude and understanding and motherly interest, if you please-a doting interest, if you don't mind-to the little affairs of desolate children'.[320]

Chapter 1.10: Further Glimpses into Care at Nazareth House, Sligo

1.10.1. Routine

When Father Flanagan made his inspection visit to Nazareth House, Sligo, in 1946, he expressed a favourable view of the facilities and approach to the care of the boys at the non-Industrial School, Nazareth House, Sligo. These were based, of course, on only the most cursory of *whitewashed coal* visits.[321] Nevertheless his impressions would seem quite well founded, with some obvious caveats, by the more detailed glimpses into the routine and various operational sections of the Home(s) that follow, and that are peppered throughout this book.

Each boy rose early and was responsible for making their own bed when old enough. Boys dressed and washed in one of a long row of sinks without mirrors, before attending chapel, then breakfast. A short period of play, outside if the weather was fine, was followed by a bell calling the boys to assembly in a large downstairs room. The senior Sister in charge of the boys, Sister Attracta, would address the boys and check that they were presentably dressed for school. Notices of the day would be given before the boys paired off out of the room to school, the signal of dismissal coming from Sister Attracta sharply clapping her hands together.

1.10.2. Regimentation and Control

Bell, whistle, hand clapping: all three methods, especially the handclapping, were used by the Sisters to command attention from the boys, to stop them chattering or to dismiss them. Bell and whistle signalling in schools was common on both sides of the Irish Sea, and for much of the twentieth century. Military style yard assembly, regimented PE exercises, and younger children walking in pairs were also the norm in most schools. At Quay Street School when the Headmaster called the boys to order by the playground wall: *all lined up in rows and with outstretched arm resting on each other's shoulder proceeded at the sound of Brother John's whistle in serpentine fashion to our respective classrooms.*[322]

The need to control large numbers of boisterous children was a major reason behind these methods. The British military tradition may have played some part in determining the degree of regimentation. The handclapping seems more peculiarly a feature of nuns, or perhaps of religious in general, or perhaps more of females and female religious? As a mode of dismissal it leaves a lot to be desired compared to the spoken word: as a form of communication it lacks feeling and respect for those dismissed. It also feels rather like power is becoming a habit and an end in itself, rather than as a necessary element for the welfare and protection of the whole community.

As earlier mentioned a further, seemingly ingrained, *modus operandi* of the Sisters was that: *The Nuns did not like us to make eye contact. It was considered offensive to them.*[323]

The boys had learned never to look a Sister directly in the eyes, and this aversion of gaze often leads to a hangdog demeanour. The boys also knew never to initiate verbal contact, as this would have been construed as insolence. This was not much of a problem as Michael recalls that he would never have thought of speaking to a Sister without first having been spoken to. The nature of any communication with the Sisters was always functional, always initiated by them. Behind every communication with the Sisters that Michael recalls was the unspoken thought-*am I in trouble? or what have I done?*[324] Michael Porter felt that what he called the absolute control exercised by the Sisters was a result of their fears that lessening their control, letting their guard down, would result in the boys taking advantage of this perceived softness. He believed that he and the other boys would indeed have abused any perception of weakness or slackening of control by the Sisters, had they been offered the opportunity.

1.10.3. A Just Environment

In contrast to this absolute control was the striking sense of fairness and justice to be expected from the Sisters. The Sisters would always give you a chance to explain yourself as Michael also recalls. Truthfulness and honesty were hammered into the boys by the Sisters (rarely literally). And, as described previously by

Paddy, the Sisters treated all boys equally, and any goods and treats had to be shared with your neighbours. Michael can still remember the definition of a lie he learned from the Sisters. *A lie is saying anything to others with the intention to deceive.*[325]

So a curate's egg of a place seemed Nazareth House to the Quartet. Like most institutions it shared the earlier mentioned regimentation and compliance-inducing control, with separate, parallel communication systems between Sisters and boys. My impression would be that the extra religious element, especially the ideological, and also the Sisters' habit and gender elements, added an extra degree of distance to that appertaining in secular institutions; certainly the extra sin-sanctioning, guilt-retaining perception of the Sisters by the boys added an additional, ever-present, often unwarranted element of apprehension in them.

The overall impression from reports, Inquiries and constant publicity about merciless, sadistic, even perverted nuns in Ireland seems to be entrenched in public consciousness. Those who argue that this general impression of the wider Catholic Church has been fabricated by enemies of the Church (such as Father Flanagan?) seem to me to be wrong. That undesired, but largely deserved, reputation, has been revealed by Inquiry Reports revealing too many incidents of ill treatment of children by those who were charged with their care, leading one priest author to describe it as: *the Dark Night of the Catholic Church.*[326] The reputation has also been earned by the precedence it too often gave to the clerical or religious, uniformed, officer class, when dealing with abuse and exploitation by church staff. I have met many of those in uniform who have abused their position, and abused the implicit trust afforded them by their status, and I doubt not that some female religious, and more than a handful of bad pennies, were entirely lacking in their care for children.

That is not, however, despite the single instance of Attracta, the general picture that has emerged from these explorations into Nazareth House in the period between the wars, although of course it can never pretend to be a comprehensive survey of everyone's life there. My general assessment of the environment there, one that seems rather *contra mundum,* was that it was a generally a reasoned, egalitarian, truth promoting and a just environment; and one, furthermore, where the Sisters cared for and about their charges despite insufficiently demonstrating this undertow of genuinely felt caring, to the boys themselves.

1.10.4. Veiled Feelings

The central problem was, I think, that just as the Sisters were protected from contamination from the sinful, secular world by their multi-layered, personality-occluding garb, so too did they have a parallel veiling of their feelings of care towards the boys (and indeed generally). In researching this book I have often wished that their faces had more often conveyed to the boys the genuine care that they felt towards their charges. It would be too great a step to say that they saw the boys as family; I do believe that they felt a degree of affiliation towards them, and most certainly had a commitment to their welfare.

1.10.5. Roles and Responsibilities: Reverend Mother and the Quest

Each of the Sisters was allocated a distinct role within Nazareth House, although these might be reallocated periodically as needs changed or Sisters were transferred elsewhere to other Congregation Homes. In addition to their allocated sectional duties in laundry, kitchen etc., they also were involved in other duties and tasks according to need and ability. So, for example, Sister Gabriel, who worked with the babies in the Nursery, also took the older boys for singing and plainchant.

Reverend Mother exercised overall control of the Homes and the spiritual supervision of the Sisters. Hammersmith Headquarters required Reverend mother to carry out daily inspections of all areas of the Home. Hammersmith Sisters also made periodic visits and inspections to the Home, making recommendations for change where necessary. To the boys Reverend Mother was a more distant and shadowy person whose work did not appear to have impinged much on their lives or memories. One reason for this may have been that her preoccupations included ensuring that there was sufficient income to enable the Home to continue to function. Meynell had described the Mother General at Hammersmith's similar concern at the financial precariousness of the various homes within the Congregation.

Fund raising to keep both homes operational was also the responsibility of Reverend Mother at Nazareth House, Sligo, with some supervision and assistance from Hammersmith. An important element of this was still mendicancy with two Sisters having been allocated to this task. The Sisters always went begging alms in pairs, travelling considerable distances around Sligo where they must have been a very familiar part of the local landscape in their distinct habits and wimples. Both Paddy Baker [327] and Michael Porter[328] encountered the Sisters begging in distant areas of County Sligo after the boys had left Nazareth House.

1.10.6. Boys Used as Helpers

The Sister who acted as porter not only carried out general reception duties but also arranged tea and refreshment for visitors, including priests who said the daily masses. She was usually advanced in age, unable to carry out the energetic and demanding work of the other Sisters, or climb the many stone steps in the vast building. This Sister also controlled the cleaning materials store and was responsible for choosing which older boys would be allocated to the particular sections of the Home where the Sisters required additional help in their work.[329]

Although it was the clear policy of the Nazareth Sisters that theirs was not an Industrial school, and so the boys were not to be used as *skivvies*, and this was reinforced by my discussions with current Sisters,[330] this policy was breached so often as to be meaningless. All of the older boys were given tasks to do to assist in the running of the Homes, as indeed they would have done had they been at home with their parents. The dearth of staff available, the large numbers of dependent young and old to be cared for, the immense size of the buildings to be cleaned, and the lack of modern electrical household appliances meant that such help was essential. The Homes could not have operated without it.

The Sister in charge of a section would usually specify which boy she would like to assist her but it was the prerogative of the reception Sister to decide whether to allocate the boy requested or choose another boy. According to one inmate this patronage function could be misused. He describes one very old Sister in charge of reception in the late 1940's and early 50's deliberately sending unsuitable boys to the *nice nuns* i.e. those who were kinder to the boys and who were therefore more popular.[331]

It appears that every older boy also took some part in keeping the washing and toilet facilities clean with this seeming to be a routine daily task rather than a particularly allocated task, according to Michael Porter. His main chore was to clean and polish the long tiled floors and stairs. He remembers the sweet smell of polish and liked the quiet steady rhythm of the work which allowed him time to think and to dream.[332]

1.10.7. Sister Felim and the Laundry

The laundry required great physical strength and stamina. Headed by Sister Felim,[333] she received assistance from both current and former residents of the home. Willie McGowan's placement for chores was in the laundry.[334] The work there, as was the case with women's domestic work, was physically demanding and time consuming. At Nazareth House there was a separate dormitory for all the bed-wetters whose sheets required daily washing and the blankets were heavy, water-retaining wool, most probably those from the Sisters at Foxford in nearby County Mayo. The boys' uniform of heavy denim cloth, and band clothes and outfits for special occasions such as religious processions, had to be kept clean, repaired and stored. There was a constant atmosphere of steam and damp in the laundry which was hardly conducive to the health of those who worked there. When Paddy Baker's older brother James left school he continued for a period living in at Nazareth House while working in the laundry, as a Yardman. His adolescent strength would certainly have been welcomed as Paddy recalled:[335] *Sister Felim ran the Laundry Department. She was also overworked and needed a lot more help than she got........For everything had to be washed by hand on a washing board. The washing was taken out in a wheelbarrow to peg out when it was fine.[336]*

1.10.8. Sister Agata (Agatha) and the Kitchen

The kitchen was run by Sister Agata. When working as her helper Paddy Baker, when working there with her, was both amazed and impressed at how she managed to cook for so many boys on the small, anthracite range. The deficiencies of both cooker and kitchen were recognised by the Sisters as the Home records show. In 1937 the Sisters recorded: *With the help of the Jubilee Fund more improvements were made. It was hoped to continue the remainder of the building. It was not to be so. A new kitchen and laundry were badly needed. The collecting Sisters continue their quest for funds.*

The lack of funds for kitchen and laundry was rectified later that year when in November 1937 a substantial sum of money was received from the estate of the deceased James Mullaney, of Geevagh, County Sligo: This was noted as a God-send with mention of buying an Esse Cooker and a Washing Machine with the money. These were in operation for Christmas.[337]

The hot and heavy kitchen work with Sister Agata had its compensations and was a more plum placement for a boy than some of the others, especially because it allowed the boy helper to filch extra food. Paddy took advantage of this bonus whenever the opportunity presented itself. Though writing when in his seventies he cannot help remembering exactly what it felt like as a child, when describing his favourite depredation on kitchen stocks:

I always got on very well with her (Agata) and sometimes ventured to steal a slice of bacon which we boys never had except at Christmas and Easter. I also used to cut the rhubarb when in season whilst she was preparing the crust as a covering for the dish, this being a dessert only for the nuns. I never could overcome the temptation of lifting the crust carefully aside, and with spoon poised for the attack, devoured as much as I could of the rhubarb and replacing the crust carefully as I could in its original position relished the idea that I too was a partaker of this delicacy. This had to be accomplished in absolute secrecy when Agata absconded into the pantry and I can still see the nuns faces as they sit around the table being served with a smaller portion than was expected. What a villain I must have been in those days.[338]

The *villain's* most important job in the kitchen was preparing the industrial quantities of porridge needed for breakfast. He was aroused early by Attracta, then he went downstairs to light the old anthracite stove, boiling the water and literally shovelling in the porridge from the hundredweight sacks of oats. Stirring the glutenating mash furiously with a broomstick Paddy, most improbably, claimed not to have burned it ever, or to have had complaints from its partakers. The daily salt-seasoned breakfast porridge habit was another relic of Nazareth House that all the Quartet members carried with them life-long, and Paddy loved making it for himself and wife in later years. Indeed the kitchen training came in so useful that he did all the household cookery for the whole of his married life.[339]

1.10.9. Nursery and Singing: Sister Gabriel

Sister Gabriel,[340] the singing teacher, seems to have been young-at-heart, gentle, girlish, thoughtful and kind. She worked with the babies in the Nursery. Paddy speaks fondly of her as does Willie McCormack, the latter remembering that:

'During the day (when in the Nursery or Babies' Section) we were made to put our heads down on the desk in front of us and go to sleep. I remember on one occasion as we were taking our nap we were woken by a violent thunderstorm with lightning flashing and loud thunder claps which came one after the other in quick succession and got louder and louder. All of us children were very frightened. Sister Gabriel tried to calm us down telling us not to be afraid as it was only Jesus and the angels moving the beds around up in heaven. We innocents believed her and the fear left us. It just goes to show how a little kindness and understanding worked'.[341]

1.10.10. Infirmary

Willie McGowan had been in the infirmary at Nazareth House when he had passed out after smoking a whole packet of cigarettes.

Willie McCormack also ended up needing to be tended there after a holiday that went wrong.

Willie McCormack wittily captures the prayer-powered Sisters inflicting prayer on their charges at every opportunity, although I think he has missed the point on this particular occasion, where it looks to me like Rosaries are cleverly used to quieten boisterous boys on a holiday journey:

'We actually had times when we enjoyed ourselves at Nazareth House. Playing football together in the playground was a real pleasure and we could forget about the discipline and regimentation. To be fair to the Nuns they treated us boys to a day at the seaside once a year, and of course it was a great day out for us. The first trip I can remember was a very sunny day...the sun splitting the rocks. We all boarded the bus outside the Home gates and as we moved off on our six mile journey to Rosses Point the Holy Nuns started to give out ten decades of the Rosary for a safe journey there and back. Then we had to offer prayers for our bus driver so as God would guide him safely to our destination. If they, or us, were half normal instead of prayers we would be singing some popular songs of the day to pass the time. Favourite at the time was Gilly, Gilly, Ossenfeffer, Catsanalabogan By The Sea, but we were praying'.

'Anyway we arrived safely thanks be to God and all the Holy Angels up above who were looking down on us sinners and protecting us from all evil....The sun did its job on us as well, we were all burnt alive. Of course having red hair and soft skin (and others of the fair skin Celtic race) I suffered after that day. There was groaning and moaning from most of the children as they were roasted by the sun. I cannot remember if we got any kind of treatment, probably not. I don't know what kind of sleep I was having but I was aware that the Nun was sitting by my bed that night. I was in a very bad state, delirious and in great pain. When I came to in the morning the Nun took the chair she had been sitting on and left the room. I was informed by the other boys that she had been there all night.....She probably had visions of another boy dying in the nuns' care and the quality of their care being questioned by a higher authority'.[342]

To sit at the bedside of a sick boy all night after a full day with boys at the seaside, never leaving him until he seemed recovered, then leaving without fuss to be about her daily work, would seem to reveal a much different explanation and picture of the Sister than that attributed to her by Willie.

1.10.11. Sister Upeta and the Old Ladies' Home

Although the two Nazareth Homes for elderly and boys were adjacent, the boys did not generally mix with the elderly, unless on special occasions, or they had their work chore placement there. It seems that working with the elderly was a less favourable placement, although the energy and strength of the older boys must have been a God-send to the Sisters working there. Willie McCormack illustrated what was done and the necessity of invoking the help of the boys to do this:

'At times I helped Sister Upeta in the Old Ladies Section, sweeping and polishing the floors... I was often offered food when helping out, but the smell of so many old people together put me off, like in a hospital, but they were all very clean. My only problem while working there was emptying the chamber pots for the sick in the infirmary...during this exercise.....I would part with my breakfast as my guts would heave. But someone had to do the job and the nun was on her own looking after all those sick ladies. I would also help the nun lift ladies out of bed while we changed the bed sheets. The more infirm were looked after by the nun herself with the help of another grown up'.[343]

1.10.12. Sister Dymphna, the Old Men's Home and the Dying

A similar glimpse of a Sister working to care for the dying and disabled old men is revealed by the boy helper:

'Sister Dymphna ran the Old Men's Section and sometimes I would be sent to help there, but not often. The place was for dying and disabled old men. Even as a child I could see that this nun was definitely over-worked and could have done with professional help.

She was there seven days a week. I just don't know how that nun coped'.[344]

A particular feature of both Irish and Catholic life is the importance given to a dying person being accompanied at their end by family and by a priest. How this was managed at home in Ireland is revealed in an example from that of my grandmother's brother, Michael Carey, who died at this period in Cloontakilla, in the Barony of Erris, in County Mayo. Coming in from work on his small farm at dusk, never having ailed previously, he seems to have had the peasant's premonition and sense of impending death. He asked his family to: *Light the blest candle and send for the priest,* before retiring to bed. The blest candles lit, the Rosary beads entwined in his fingers, the priest got, he was anointed, shriven, composed and fortified for his journey. He died well before midnight, his family about him, the cottage bedroom window opened to allow for the migration of his soul from his body, from his earthly sojourn and from this world.[345]

This same approach to death was followed at Nazareth House, except that most of the elderly residents had no one to watch with them, and the Sister looking after them had many other tasks to do. The boys were brought across from the Boys' Home to ensure that a dying man was never left alone, but also to pray at his bedside for his immortal soul and that he would be spared the: *day of wrath and enjoy endless rest.* Paddy recalled:

Where we were compelled to visit the dying in groups of four to six boys and pay homage on our knees at the bedside of old men (not the women) who unconscious at the time were waiting to take their last breath. There was always two lighted candles at the head of the bedstead and a handkerchief or two on each side of the pillow. I very soon grasped the reason for this as I watched their motionless bodies taking their last breaths of air. A Sister would enter occasionally and sprinkle holy water. Many times whilst kneeling in prayer at these poor creatures bedsides I was often frightened by the strange noises which exuded from their lifeless bodies....Little white worms would protrude from their mouths and the Sister in charge would take one of the handkerchiefs and wipe their mouths clean until the next invasion occurred.[346]

Many Inquiry Reports into the care of the elderly, handicapped and disabled in care homes and in hospitals throughout the last half century have found major problems of neglect: elderly people dying alone, uncomforted, unseen, unclean and unslaked. Years ago one Inquiry Report criticised, indeed satirised, care provision for only: *tending the orifices.* This was meant to illustrate that only basic feeding, watering and cleaning were provided for the patient or resident, without emotional input or any form of human warmth and respect shown to the elderly person. Abundant recent Reports and Inquiries have concluded that not even that satirised level of caring has been afforded the vulnerable and elderly institutionalised person; this in an age of material plenty, professional and trained staff, and resource levels massively higher than those at Nazareth House.

The above illustration captures the dilemma faced by the Sisters in not having enough hands to help; or enough mouths and minds to pray; or enough Sisters to stay with a dying man constantly. Their use of the boys to pray for an old man to ensure that each dying soul was companioned in his last hours on earth was a practical response to the ever present gulf between the scale of human need and the human resources to deal with this. The boys would almost certainly have been similarly employed round the bedside of a dying relative, had they been at home (as had been the case with Willie McGowan, present at the death of his mother).

Not only were the orifices tended at Nazareth House, but a much better level of respect for the dignity of the elderly person is revealed. This dignity-preserving approach to a dying old man, would seem rooted in the Sisters' belief that the dying soul before them had been created by God in his own image and likeness, despite the often physically declining, malodorous, or otherwise unprepossessing body shell presented to them for help and for care. I doubt very much that the Sisters always managed to do this perfectly, or consistently, or without on occasions losing sight of the soul within. Their faults, failings, fallibilities and varying degrees of compassion, tolerance, love, endurance and aptitude would have been sorely tested in the unremitting nature of the work, and found wanting on occasions too.

Yet the care of the dying men, and Sister Dymphna's tending of them, often alone, always on duty, working unremittingly, seems not to have led to a failure to see the essence of the person before her. Was it her faith that was the wellspring of this compassion and dedication? Was it, too, the reservoir from which she so frequently had to draw to sustain her energy and her hope? This work, done so quietly and so unassumingly, would have been unseen and unrecorded but for a rule infraction that allowed a young boy helper to see what was done.

The foregoing instances help explain why Willie McGowan's daughters, Margaret McGowan Judge[347] and Imelda Fitzsimons,[348] both describe the affection, indeed the love, that their father retained towards the Sisters who reared him in Sligo and later in Mallow, in County Cork.

1.10.13. Ohne Hast, Ohne Rast[349]

The issue of lack of holiday by the Sisters was noted by the boys. They were always there, never away or taking a break unless they became ill, died or were transferred. In modern work terms they put in a double shift every day, seven days a week, every week of every year, without holiday, or visits home. If they went on a journey they always went in pairs, or larger groups. They also had to fit in their prayer and daily worship common to all female religious, before, during and after their care of the boys or elderly had ended. There is one instance documented where Attracta had to lock the large group of older boys in the Playroom while she had to attend to other urgent business and there was no one else available to supervise them. Her letters in retirement reveal the guilt she felt at having neglected her prayers while in Sligo. One would have thought that the considerable amount of deed prayer she accomplished in her life would have satisfied her; apparently not, as she asked Willie McGowan and his family to pray for her past omissions for neglecting her prayers when engaged in her work. If she expected the boys to attain high standards of conduct, she applied the same, or even higher, standards to herself, and recognised her failure to meet these.

Even at night some of the Sisters would still be on duty, asleep in room or cubicle adjacent to the dormitories, or with the babies in the Nursery, or tending to the sick, disabled or the dying. Their work was physically demanding and the large rooms and many staircases made it even more so.

1.10.14. Shy Communication

One can sense this development of a more individualistic approach by the Sisters, although still formal and restrained, when the older boys helping different Sisters with their allotted areas of work: certainly with Willie McGowan, and Paddy's brother, James Baker, and Michael Porter. For the Sister, too, this must have provided some degree of welcome young companionship amidst the constant drudgery, often loneliness, of their work. For Sisters Upeta and Dymphna, constantly working near alone with only the old, sick, disabled and dying, what a mental and spiritual uplift must have been given them by the sight of young, vigorous life in the form of the boy helpers. The following picture of a young Sister and adolescent boy is presented as a glimpse of this 'relationship'.

Michael Porter was found an activity to keep him busy and to make his contribution to the House, after he had left Quay Street school but before he had obtained his first Situation placement outside the Home. This was in a sock-making task that Michael and the Sister shared. A new circular, weighted, sock-making machine had been bought and Michael and the Sister had to fathom out how to use it.[350] Michael, who had inherited his Porter family's practical bent, enjoyed the work, becoming quite proficient at turning heels and adding stripes where needed. Socks were made to order for all the boys in the Home and anyone else who needed them. The socks were identical to the type worn by the boys in the photograph of the Quartet.[351] The process of deciphering instructions, and of resolving difficulties with weights and tensions while knitting, necessitated a closer physical and communicatory relationship between Sister and boy.

Sitting side by side at the table with the softly spoken young Sister, in the multi-purpose workroom, she hand knitting or mending clothes, he machine making socks, fifteen year old Michael recalls a most peaceful, harmonious and contented atmosphere.[352] Michael recalls being painfully shy, hardly even obliquely glancing along to his companion, speaking rarely and sparely, and almost always only in reply. Michael sensed shyness and kindness in the Sister; yet shyer still was he.

The training of the Sisters, the need for them to be chaperoned outside, the distance-maintaining *protective* religious habit, the celibacy, perhaps to a degree the threat that the lay or outside world was perceived to present, are tentatively suggested in the quiet, yet sensitive, side-sitting, supervisory Sister. Yet the calmness, the rarely broken silence, conveyed to Michael memories of quiet achievement and pleasure; of not needing to speak to communicate; above all of being treated kindly and personally and respectfully by the Sister. He sensed that she liked him, that she appreciated and respected him; and he, her.[353]

It is in these allocated helping roles for the older boys that I sense that a less collective approach to their welfare occurred. Working alongside the Sisters allowed each boy to be treated and seen as more of an individual; and to be told, or more probably sense, that they were appreciated. It also shows yet again that beneficial consequences can arise a needs-must breach of rules; a not ideal but practical solution to extreme resource deficits. Had the strict rules been observed then none of this contact would have occurred.

1.10.15. Sister Attracta: Swaddled Emotions

The overall senior child-care Sister for the older boys, Sister Attracta, has a number of additional incidents about her that give further insight into her character, to the culture within Nazareth House, and to the values, attitudes and conduct characteristic of some of the other Sisters.

When Attracta was much older, in the early 1950's when she must have worked for at least three decades in child care at Nazareth House, Sligo, one of the boys found out that it was her Feast Day.

The Sisters celebrated the feast day of the patron Saint whose name they had taken on professing their vows. Saint Attracta was a Sligo born nun from the fifth century who was reported to have received the veil from St Patrick himself. Her feast day is celebrated on 12th August. Attracta loved flowers, geraniums especially, and three of the boys, knowing this, picked flower petals from the gardens of the Home. They then arranged them neatly, strewing them in a pattern of the floor of the large Recreation Assembly Hall. None of the boys had any money to buy her a present so this was the only way they could show their appreciation and wish her a Happy Feast Day. The boys all ranged themselves around the Recreation Hall walls to allow Attracta to see their handiwork as soon as she came into the room. When she finally entered the room the boys immediately carried out their pre-planned round of applause. Taken completely by surprise, red faced Attracta waved for them to stop clapping, reportedly telling the boys: *What a waste of good flowers. Get this mess cleaned up immediately.*

She then left the room, presumably flustered and having forgotten what she had wished to communicate to the boys.[354] What an ungrateful curmudgeon and killjoy she initially appears: certainly so to the boy who remembered this. Yet, based on the different and quite prevalent Catholic culture then, another interpretation of her thinking and feelings about this incident is possible. Here was someone who daily, yearly, steeled herself to be a figure of authority, to enable her to run a *tight ship*, with few crew and many passengers. Her training eschewed personal vanity, self or other approbation, these being *occasions of sin*. Her work she did because she had chosen to do it. It was a duty only in the sense that she had chosen duty. She did what she did because of the calling she believed she had. It required not praise, not appreciation, not plaudits; rather these might diminish the worth of the work by seeming to be done for personal satisfaction, reward or vanity.[355] The clapping by the boys was a most unusual, if not unique, happening in these circumstances. Would this undermine her authority if she did not stop this act of individuality, of spontaneity? The boys must have seen her embarrassment, her red face (interpreted as anger), how flustered and thrown out of kilter she had been. Would they sense her vulnerability caused by the gesture and the flowers? How could they have known that this of all presents, her favourite thing, would have been the very one to move her? Would they know how this gesture had lanced her heart? But she had got out in time without mishap; without breaking down in public; without showing weakness (her emotions); and without having let down her guard.

She would have had to tell Reverend Mother and the other Sisters of this incident because they would have heard the unusual noise and perhaps feared rebellion. She may have been touched by the boys' gesture and treasured this secretly, guiltily, warmed often by its recall. It is even possible that she may have confessed this *sin* to the priest, for the guilty pleasure, the vanity and feeling of love and appreciation that had been shown to her, and that she had relished, when she had only been doing her duty. Would she have shed a tear? I think not, for that would have been an indulgence too far. [356]

When very much older, put out to pasture in the Nazareth House Home in Rednal in Birmingham, Attracta was, as ever, tending her beloved garden and flowers. She was a very large woman, appearing yet larger in the voluminous habit. In her pockets she kept sweets to be given to any of the children who passed by when she was gardening. Her crown laid down, her responsibility and authority stays unlaced, able at last to pray, garden and relax, she could now relate more easily naturally and kindly to the children, and in a more demonstrative manner.

The final, most telling, incident that Paddy recalled when he was still in the Nursery Section, and reveals the genuine level of love and care that many of the Sisters felt about the boys, especially perhaps when the boys were younger and less challenging. It also reinforces the earlier perspective about how they usually kept this feeling well guarded, well veiled from the boys. Furthermore, that the boys understood that this was so. Michael also recognised this and the reason for it: the Sisters' training and discipline, and the emphasis on their denial of self. Yet a glimpse of the tension this must have caused in young, childless women is shown when the self-mortification habit was fractured. This occurred in public and before the Sister's colleagues and her superior. It gives a short, sharp glimpse in a rare instance where the Sisters' normally tightly swaddled emotions were suddenly released in an instinctive response to a child's distress.

Sister Attracta, then much younger, and in charge of the Nursery and babies, had been their erstwhile, surrogate mother, and was preparing to leave Nazareth House. The cry of a child, Paddy Baker, elicited a natural, instinctive, maternal response, despite this apparently being against: *the rules of the house.*

Sister Attracta was the highlight of my life. She was a substitute mother to me and I remember all too well when she departed from us. As was customary in those days when the weather permitted we went for a walk... The news soon spread that Attracta was leaving us, so Miss McGraine gathered her flock near the walnut tree in order that we bid farewell. I was inwardly upset when I saw the other few nuns lining the Porchway outside when Attracta appeared with the Reverend Mother when kisses were exchanged. I could no longer keep my emotions under control so I started screaming. A car was also standing by with the door open and when Attracta heard my screams she also was deeply moved. Ignoring all the rules of the house she ran towards me, held me in her arms and kissed me. Soon after she vanished in the car leaving me still screaming and kicking in the arms of Miss McGraine. This was perhaps the first kiss I have had since I was taken away from my mother. Attracta was replaced by another nun and I wasn't to see her till I reached the age of 5 or 6 or later.[357]

Ignoring all the rules of the house: Paddy has glaringly shown the tension and pain that this unnatural emotional constraint had upon the Sisters.

Paddy's summarises what he felt about his Sister carers and Sister Attracta in particular is the extract below, after Michael Porter's retrospective summary of them. Unsurprisingly both evince mixed views but with a great deal of consistency between them. They were critical of the Sisters' lack of demonstrative love but appreciative of their dedication, diligence and commitment. Michael Porter's reflections today about his care and carers at Nazareth House and Quay Street School are summarised as follows:

The atmosphere was emotionally bleak, but we were treated fairly, justly and equally; information about our families was almost non-existent; our care was regimented but almost inevitably so because of how few Sisters there were to care for us: resources made this a necessity; we were always kept busy with a wide range of activities and stimulation; although we never knew what it was to be bored we did know what it was to be lonely and isolated; teachers caned us, but that was the usual practice at that time; they never caned us without reason, nor went over the top with the cane; the Sisters never punished us physically; the Sisters, Brothers and teachers were, like most adults then, distant from us, but they cared for and about us, and they wanted us to do well, and they worked hard on our behalf.

In 1965 when Paddy had made one of his many post-care visits to Nazareth House, he had searched the grounds for the graves of the Sisters he had known. He looked in vain for the gravestone cross of Attracta because he had not known, or had not asked, where she was buried. (She had not been buried in Sligo):

.....tears flowed from my eyes as I walked just as silently towards the Sisters' burial place where I.....uttered a short prayer for the departed souls who so long ago toiled for us and devoted their lives that we be not naked or starve from hunger as is the fate of so many thousands on earth to-day. I searched the graveyard expecting to find the burial place of Sister Attracta who loved Sligo very much just as she loved all her boys. The memory of her has been so deeply imprinted on my mind.[358]

The memory was indeed deeply imprinted. Although Paddy never forgot Attracta's abusive treatment of him over the sixpenny incident, it does seem that he could recognise that by far the greater portion of her work and commitment had been on his and his fellow Homeboys' behalf. So, although he remembered his abuse, he remembered too the efforts put into care for him by Attracta and the other Sisters. Although the memory of abuse sometimes coloured, occluded or even eclipsed his fonder memories of care at Nazareth House, as had Mr Shine's canings dominated his memories of his schooling, yet he was still able to recognise that the good aspects weighed heavier than the bad.

Chapter 1.11: Travellers to Nazareth

1.11.1. Christmas in Ireland

Christmas was never regarded as important a religious festival as Easter in the general Roman Catholic Church. For both the Sisters of Nazareth and for much of the population of Ireland it was regarded as the most important secular and sacred festival of the year. The Sisters were Sisters of Nazareth, and their special devotion was to the infant Jesus and to his parents, Mary and Joseph. The Holy Family of Nazareth was revered throughout Ireland. This focus on the Holy Family was represented in many aspects of the life on the Sisters: in the care of children that had been chosen as their work; and in their correspondence, where J. M. J. (Jesus, Mary and Joseph) always headed their letters. Even in death it featured: J. M. J. was engraved on their gravestone cross where their adopted religious name, birth surname and birth and death dates were also recorded: birth, life and death on the one memorial.[359]

In rural Ireland, where most of the Sisters had been reared, great preparations were made in the poorest of households for the expected arrival of the Saviour of the world, as a vulnerable, homeless child, born of a virgin. Farm, yard and outhouses were scoured and prepared, cottage whitewashed without, while inside, linen, furniture, floors, pots, pans and delft, were cleaned and shone. Special efforts were made to provide better and more plentiful food and drink. Family returned home if they could. Candles, a rare treat for the very poor, were bought. The custom of leaving all doors open, with candles lit to show the way for *the Travellers to Bethlehem,* was accompanied with a meal being set for three, with a dish of water left on the windowsill for blessing by the Travellers; the lit candles placed to both guide and welcome them. Even the very beasts took part, and their quarters and food were of the best at this time. The commonly held belief was that, at midnight, donkeys and cows would kneel in adoration to the new born Saviour, when they were then possessed of the power of human speech.

For many people in Ireland then, and still some to-day, the Travellers, especially Mary and their swaddled Saviour, were real people who had not only lived on earth, but who trod the Bethlehem path year after year; in need of sustenance, shelter and welcome again on their journey. This powerful peasant sense of duty to show hospitality, especially at Christmas time, and to succour the needy was stressed in Irish Connacht peasant verse:

'Go to Mass unsocked and shoeless,
Doless pride of garb is sin,
Meet-where the three ways meet-the poor,
Bow to him twice and bring him in.

Though thine be the gold in the king's own kist,
Though thy flocks like a mist cover hill and lea,
Refuse to the poor man bed or bread,
And heaven, when dead, thou shalt not see.

Be to the poor man mild and good,
Warm him, clothe him and give him food,
Let alms to the poor be freely given,
For in poor man's shape came Christ from heaven'.[360]

1.11.2. Sisters and Christmas

To the Sisters, *came Christ from heaven* would have been seen as the reason why they entered their Congregation, and the *poor man's shape* would have been represented before them in their boy and elderly charges at Nazareth House. Although the Sisters were never allowed home at Christmas for their own family re-gathering, the memory of this momentous night at home when young would have been with them when cleaning and preparing for The Travellers. If this period was when their vows chafed most, the bustle and excitement of preparations would have eased any discomfort.

1.11.3. A Moment of Grace

Paddy Baker described the Christmas arrangements from a child's perspective. On the eve of Christmas the boys were sent to bed much earlier than usual to enable the Sisters to secretly decorate a room on the ground floor near the chapel, to prepare the chapel and crib for Midnight Mass and to light the window guide-welcoming candles for The Travellers. The boys had to be left unsupervised in their dormitories because the whole small band of Sisters was needed in the short period to make the preparations for Christmas: *We didn't behave like little Angels but had pillow fights leaving a boy at the head of the stairs as sentry. The boy would leave his post and sound the alarm when the nuns were approaching.*[361]

Paddy seems to have believed that the boys' military organisation had misled the Sisters into thinking the boys had been angelically sleeping all the while. I somewhat doubt it, for the noise would have been heard, and the boys' dishevelled appearance, reddened faces and suppressed excited giggles would have been only too evident. It feels more like the boys were granted a very rare period of grace, at least indoors, to act as boys are wont to do.

At about 10 o'clock the boys were given their usual cocoa, or currants for those who were still in the bed-wetters' dormitory. In addition, as a special treat for Christmas, and possibly also to help them survive till the end of Midnight Mass, each boy was given a slice of currant bread, savouring the seasonal treat. Each boy: *picked the last currant from our slice of bread.*[362]

1.11.4. Sacred

For many poor families the candle and electric-lit church, flowers, music and singing, ritual, relative warmth, cleanliness and dryness, wax polished wood and floors, large painted statues represented a magical glimpse of another world compared with the windy, smoky, dark, gloomy, often damp cabins where they spent their lives, with smell of cattle or dung heap ever near. Church was theatre and cinema, the drama-liturgical story of the journey and birth of a child who was God, born of a woman like one of them, always ending in the unveiling of the crib, and carols sung around it.

1.11.5. Secular: Re-Communion with Exiles and Elderly

On Christmas morning any presents sent in by family members were given out to individual children. The boys otherwise received small presents of fruit and nuts. Santa Claus, usually a priest dressed up, distributed a few sweets, at least in later years.

The sacred and secular Christmas celebrations lasted several days. There was always a secular concert organised in the boys' recreation room with the Sisters arranging this and Josie Cummings directing the musical side of the entertainment. The Situation boys also came back for these celebrations over the festive season. For many it was the only home they had known, or could go to at Christmas. Even though some did have homes, such as Willie McGowan, they still came *home* to Nazareth at Christmas.[363] Plays such as the earlier mentioned *Saggart* were put on, with the Situation boys from Father Barry's house contributing to these.

Both the *devil makes work* approach of the Sisters' and Father Flanagan's restated words again come to mind: 'A boy or girl given the proper guidance and direction–kept busy and constructively occupied during their leisure or free time–will prove my statement that there is no such thing as a bad boy or girl'.

Many of the boys who enjoyed the entertainments would have done so in dual roles: observers and participants. The elderly, too, would have looked forward to these entertainments, although only as members of the audience. One can readily imagine how the lights, music, singing, drama and energy of young boys must have both lifted their spirits in the dark nights of their declining years and caused them to wistfully recall their own childhood homes at Christmas time.

1.11.6. No Lonelier Time Than Christmas

Yet to Michael Porter Christmas was the worst time of the year at Nazareth House. He never understood why it was that he seemed to break down then, but it was at Christmas time, and only then, that he cried. Normally he had no problem in containing his emotions but over the few days of Christmas celebrations he often found himself having to run to the toilet, or to find a private corner or cubbyhole, whenever he was suddenly assailed by a bout of tears, fearful that he would be seen crying by one of the other boys. This festive season left him cold, feeling constantly sad; but worst of all was the terrible sense of loneliness and isolation. The whole Christmas period is a blank to Michael Porter other than his memories of isolation; it has never been his favourite time of year, always a period of the year that he has wished would pass quickly.

1.11.7. The Real Message of Christmas

Paddy Baker, with a similar background to Michael, remembers Christmastide very differently: wistfully; with wonder; and with glow-warmth. When in his seventies Paddy replied to correspondence from Willie McGowan who had alluded to his financial struggles especially at Christmas time when rearing a young family. Paddy encouraged him to tell his grandchildren, reared in a more material age, about their experiences at Christmas at Nazareth House. His words to Willie convey the deep, abiding essence of Christmas that he had absorbed when a child at Nazareth[364] and whose recollection seemed to warm and comfort him in his last years of life:

Only a few children ever received a small Christmas stocking from their parents[365] and I never felt a sense of bitterness, or resentment from any of the boys who were less fortunate. We were, after all, a big family not knowing what the future held in store for us. Christmas is after all a fantasy for little children only, just as it was when Jesus was born in Bethlehem. To-day it has, unfortunately, grown into a great enterprise and a very expensive one at that. Christmas has become a world of greed with little or no thought of its background...That was not so in Nazareth when we picked the last currant from our slice of bread. Do you remember it Willie?...May Jesus be your Jesus this Christmas. He is worth more than all the presents that this world can offer.[366]

Chapter 1.12: We Are the Music Makers: Josie Cummings

1.12.1. Music Has Power

'We are the music makers,
And we are the dreamers of dreams,
Wandering by lone sea-breakers,
And sitting by desolate streams;
World-losers and world-forsakers,
On whom the pale moon gleams:
Yet we are the movers and shakers
Of the world for ever, it seems'.[367]

Arthur O'Shaughnessy's *Ode* recognises the power of music to transform mind and emotion and to stimulate imagination. This seems to have been understood by the Nazareth Sisters as music played a central part in the cultural life in all their children's homes. Paddy Baker when in his seventies received a newspaper cutting, from Willie McGowan who was then learning to play the fiddle. The cutting was about Michael Coleman (1891-1945), the fiddle player from Gurteen, in County Sligo, and ex Sligo Feis competitor in 1909 and 1910.[368] This triggered Paddy into a reverie about the relationship between music and life. His description of Coleman's ability through music to reach the soul stands too for many of his Nazareth confreres:

He played his heart off in the execution of his music thereby translating into sound like the sadness of his life. In those bygone years he added a new dimension in musical feelings, a kind of awakening in the hearts of all Irish people at home and abroad that convinced them that music is, in a deep and subtle way, a translation of the soul in its response to all the agonies and ecstasies that the passive parade of life brings with it. [369]

Willie McGowan kept newspapers cuttings of music that stirred and moved him and his grandchildren emulated his brass band playing.[370] Michael Porter in later life, although he could never cry, said two things only could produce a moistening in his right eye:

the sight and smell of a new born baby; and hearing a piece of music performed with depth of feeling.[371] Willie Walsh became a Nazareth House bandmaster at Swansea. Music learned young remained of central significance to all four throughout their lives.

1.12.2. Sligo, Music and Feis

Music, and especially brass band playing, was by far the most important and memorable aspect of the Quartet's recreational and cultural life at Nazareth House. The Nazareth House boys were encouraged-actually probably required-to participate in a wide range of cultural activities: drama; recitation; dancing; plain chant; singing; marching and drill; and brass band music. They also played a range of sports and games.

Michael Porter and the other Quartet members were involved in all, not just some, of this wide cultural curriculum. That they lived in Sligo gave them much more opportunity to practise these skills in competitions because of the remarkable cultural and musical traditions in the town, and especially the annual Feiseanna, which were held every year at Eastertide.

The first Sligo Feis Ceoil (feast of music) had occurred in June 1903[372] and was a rather modest celebration of Irish language, music and culture, lasting only 2 days. By the time of the Silver Jubilee of the Feis in 1927, it had attracted 717 entries. As bands, choirs and groups would have been counted as single entries, the total number of participants would probably have numbered over 1000. (The following twenty five years saw the number of Feis entries doubling to 1,429 by 1953). Yet the population of Sligo Town, even though it was an important port and regional centre, was relatively modest: numbering 10,870 at the beginning of the twentieth century and increasing to 12,565 by the 1936 census.

Even though participants in the Feis were drawn from all of Ireland, the majority came from Connacht, including County Sligo, and a large number from Sligo town itself. The competitions ranged from individual to large group, with sections for all age bands, from very young to adult. Many of the groups entered were from local schools or residential facilities, of which there were many in Sligo town. The Mercy and Ursuline Convents were always centrally represented, and the Nazareth House boys had two bites of the cherry, representing Nazareth House in brass band and Irish dancing, but Quay Street School also entered competitions. Although the aim was to encourage all aspects of spoken, sung and played Irish language and music, English was well represented too, and even English patriotic songs such as the Stanford-Newbolt *Drake's Drum,* were performed (albeit by an adjudicator).

The Feis competitions ranged widely over all types of elocution, music and dancing; the Nazareth House boys also were involved in dramatic productions, but these appear to have been performed within the Home. Regular dramatic productions were put on at Nazareth House by the boys in their later years in care there. A number of these were organised by the Marist Brothers from Quay Street School, others, at Christmas time especially, by the Sisters and by the bandmaster, Josie Cummings. The Marist brothers also entered school teams in the Sligo Feis, so some Nazareth House boys may have had dual representation at the Feis. Like the Sisters of Nazareth, the Marist Brothers appeared to follow the *devil makes work for idle hands* principle. Though not under the control of the local secular Bishop, they responded to work that the Bishop felt needed doing in Sligo, in addition to their normal teaching and educational duties. The immediate proximity to Nazareth House of the Marist Brother's Home in Church Street was a boon for regular rehearsal practices.

1.12.3. Drama and Marist Brothers

The Marist Brother who organised the plays in Nazareth House treated the whole exercise very professionally and conducted proper auditions. The giant multi-purpose playroom at Nazareth House was used both for play rehearsals and for the final performances. The preparations took some time as scenery, costumes and props had to be made, and a proper stage had to be erected. The audience for the performances comprised all the non-participating boys at Nazareth House, the Sisters, the Brothers, some of the local clergy and, most important of all, the residents of the adjacent Home for the elderly. Because the only deficiency in the playroom that was used for the theatre was a lack of microphones, voice projection was a critical requirement for the participants, especially for the leading roles. At school the boys learned a lot of poetry by heart. (Michael can still recite Yeat's *Inisfree*). The boys were also taught plainchant and were used to learning Latin by heart for Mass, Benediction and hymns. They were also encouraged to learn large chunks of religious prose. Michael's memorising and mastering of the, now discontinued, beginning of St. John's Gospel *In the beginning was the Word, and the Word was with God, and the Word was God* contributed to his being chosen for two lead roles in the plays.[373]

The first play performed was *Father John*, a drama, and the second was a dramatic comedy about a burglary. Michael describes himself as *a bit of a devil* and he feels sure that the Sisters would not have chosen him for a part in the play because of this. The Marist Brother, however, approached the task professionally, auditioning for each role, keen to choose those who had clear diction, a retentive memory and a sense of presence and confidence to carry off performing in front of such a large, adult audience. Being *a bit of a devil* was positively a recommendation for such a role, rather than a handicap.

Michael was chosen to play Father John in the first of the plays. Nothing else is remembered by Michael of the *Father John* play, other than it was serious, moral and religious in content and tone, and that *Father John* became his nickname thereafter at Nazareth House. The play may have been about Father John Murphy, the Boolavogue priest involved in the Wexford revolt of 1798. Michael thought that the Marist Brother wrote both plays himself.

Each play was presented in succession, on a single night, so considerable planning, organisation and skill must have been needed to carry this off successfully. It also demanded much from the boys, not least the ability to remember a lot of dialogue but also to be able to switch mood from serious, morally uplifting to tense and comedic. The second play was set in a large country house, well staffed with servants. The plot involved a burglar regularly breaking into the house, never being caught. The householder set a plot to catch the burglar with the cooperation of his staff. Michael's role was that of the maid, Jane, whose job was to catch the burglar red-handed. The maid sat in a chair, hidden by a large coverlet, unseen by the burglar. As the robber went round the room collecting the valuables in his sack he edged nearer to the chair in which, well known to the elderly, expectant audience, sat Jane. Edging nearer, then away from the maid-filled chair, the tension was allowed to build until the burglar, sack filled, sat down in the chair for a rest. Throwing the coverlet round the helpless, captured burglar, Jane leapt up, shouting for help, which quickly arrived. The dénouement brought the house down.

During the performance of the plays Michael could hear the old folks getting carried away as they became engrossed by the performances. Hidden under his coverlet for much of the second play he was able to hear them saying things like *Look out there, be careful* as the burglar approached the chair and *Look at him getting caught,* and he could sense the excitement and tension rising. When the play finished to applause and cheering from the audience, and Michael drank in all the adulation he thought was directed at him, he thought he saw some of the Sisters sat at the back of the room give him a look which indicated: *don't you be getting above yourself.*

Religious and moral themes continued to form the content of some of the plays at Nazareth House. The Summerhill College educated McGuiness brothers, John and Michael, destined for priesthood and religious life, were unsurprisingly chosen for the starring roles in a play entitled, *The Beautiful Hands of a Priest.* It is almost impossible for people today to understand how great a reverence was shown to both priest and to a priest's hands, because Catholics regarded them as instruments in changing bread and wine into the body and blood of Christ. A few stanzas from the poem of the same title (author unknown) convey; a flavour of this reverence; the lifelong social link between pastor and parishioner; and how these both contributed to the concomitant power the priest in Ireland had over his flock:

'At the altar each day we behold them,
And the hands of a king on his throne
Are not equal to them in their greatness;
Their dignity stands all alone

And when we are tempted to wander,
To pathways of shame and of sin,
It's the hand of a priest that will absolve us
Not once, but again and again.

When the hour of death comes upon us,
May our courage and strength be increased,
By seeing raised over us in blessing
The beautiful hands of a priest'.

There may have been more than one play about priestly life. On New Year's Eve, 1936, the older boys prepared a play called *The Saggart. (Saggart* is the Irish name for a priest). At Christmas and New Year in particular the Home musical and dramatic performances were organised by the Sisters for the residents, both young and old, with Josie Cummings, the bandmaster, supplying the music. 'Situation' boys who had left Nazareth House, and who were working and living in Sligo, came back over the holiday period for Mass, to play in Father Barry's recreation house, to reminisce and to be entertained. There is a famous poem, *Soggarth Aroon*, (*priest darling* in English), written by the nineteenth century, Kilkenny born author, John Banim (1798-1842). I think it possible that this play was based on Banim's poem, whose theme, like the earlier poem, includes the lifelong ministering to the poor peasant by his priest. The following stanza from the poem captures both theme and tone:

'Who in the winter's night,
Soggarth aroon.
When the cold blasts did bite,
Soggarth aroon,
Came to my cabin-door,
And on my earthen-floor
Knelt by me, sick and poor,
Soggarth aroon?'

The performances of religious dramas at Christmas in England, especially in the non-conformist, Methodist north of England, were Mendelsshon's *Elijah* and especially Handel's *Messiah*. The three hour *Messiah* was so popular, and so many performances were available in the West Riding of Yorkshire, that a person managed to attend three full performances in a single day. These works do not seem to have featured at all in the cultural or musical training of Catholic working class children, in Ireland or in Britain, having presumably been classified as *protestant*. They would certainly not seem to have been beyond the compass of the Nazareth House boys to perform, given their other accomplishments. That the first performance of Messiah had been in Dublin would only seem to emphasise a Catholic Protestant denominational division in music and hymnology.

1.12.4. Dancing

Irish dancing was taught to the boys by Miss O'Rourke.[374] In 1935 at the Sligo Feis the Nazareth House boys won 1st and 2nd prizes in the Irish Dancing competition, and the same prizes the following year for Irish Figure Dancing.

Illustration 14: Nazareth House Eight Hand Reel. Sligo 1934

The photograph shows the Nazareth House boys' eight hand reel dancing team, which includes Quartet members. The boys were taught to dance in twos, fours, sixes or eights and the competitions usually involved vying against four or five other teams. An important factor in the success of Willie McGowan, Paddy Baker, Willie Walsh and Michael Porter and the other Nazareth House boys in the various competitions they entered, was the confidence they had acquired from their public performances. These were so frequent, covered so many areas of music, drama, dancing and sport, allied to the drill, routine and practices they experienced, that they were able to rely on this bedrock of drilled routine to master competition nerves. Indeed drill, i.e. marching drill, was another area where the Nazareth House boys excelled, winning the drill competition in 1936 at the Sligo Gaelic Athletic Association School Sports Day. (The prize was a Travelling Rug).

1.12.5. Singing

Sister Gabriel conducted voice and singing training with the assistance of Josie Cummings. Paddy Baker joyfully remembered her fun-filled coaching of them. Most of the full repertoire of songs that the boys declaimed were in English; the themes of these were Irish and traditional, religious and patriotic. The Sisters seemed moved by music and took every opportunity to punctuate daily life with it. One of the Nazareth House boys, somewhat older than the Quartet members, *had the most beautiful voice, and he had been entered into a National competition in Dublin and came high reward, if not first.*[375]

This singer was in Michael Porter's age group. The boys could be playing football or other games when a Sister would ask this boy to sing. He would immediately stop what he was doing and 'give out' on command. This often occurred when visitors were shown around the Home or grounds. Even though, or perhaps because, singing and music formed such a central feature of their daily worship with the boys in chapel, the Sisters seemed to feel the need to hear the purity, and perhaps the innocence, that the *lark in the clear air* voice of a young boy brought into their lives. *It was nothing for the Sisters to ask this boy to suddenly sing out;* or indeed any one of the more talented singers such as Paddy Baker, Michael or Willie. This might occur anywhere in the Home and the boy would, *give out at the drop of a hat.* Michael and Paddy regretted that the boy, or they themselves, were expected to sing without being given the note to start with. They also always felt better able to perform when Josie Cummings was present. Josie made the boys feel secure.

The words of Thomas Moore were those that featured most often in the songs they sang; the Irish tenor, John McCormack, was the master whose singing the boys sought to emulate.

1.12.6. Count John McCormack's Visit to Nazareth House and to Sligo

John McCormack (1884-1945) was the most famous and influential Irish singer in the first half or the twentieth century. Few were the emigrant homes in Britain, the United States and other places of widespread Irish migration, that were without his music. Although born in Athlone, he had received the same education as Willie McGowan and Willie Walsh: Marist Brothers schooling (in Athlone where he had been born); followed by secondary education at Summerhill College, Sligo from 1896 to 1902. In 1903, the year the Sligo Feis commenced, McCormack won the gold medal at the Dublin Feis Ceoil. The *count* title, by which he was known, was one of four papal awards made to him for his religious singing, and his most famous performance had been at the 1932 Eucharistic Congress in Dublin, where he sang *Panis Angelicus.*

John McCormack's connections with Sligo resulted in him giving a celebrity concert in Sligo on 15th January, 1936. This very successful concert in the Gaiety Cinema, Sligo, raised funds for the Jubilee Fund for Nazareth House. Michael Porter recalls the 16 or 17 standing ovations that the boys' hero was given at this concert. John McCormack also visited Nazareth House during this visit to Sligo. The visit to Nazareth House appears to have been to select a suitable boy to receive advanced singing and musical training to be funded by Count John McCormack.[376]

Paddy Baker well conveys what this visit was like for the boys who were present:

Like all human creatures he grew old and his voice began to fade. He knew that his life here on earth was now coming to an end and so he decided to visit Sligo and Summerhill (where, when a student there, his eyes were focused on the poor boys of Nazareth House). I was an admirer of John and so when the news spread around that he was coming to visit us, I felt all gooey inside.[377]

The visit of John McCormack took place in the boys' recreation room, but Josie Cummings does not appear to have been present:

John McCormack now appeared in the room accompanied by Reverend Mother and I think two or three others. Sister Attracta then took command and the choir came out to the centre of the floor where we sang for the master. There was big applause ....we returned to our benches hoping that John would now sing for us. This was not on the programme. Attracta called out one boy to sing solo in the centre of the room, which he did, bowing and returning to applause to his seat. Once again Attracta stood up and called out my name. I too had to sing a song but with the sudden demand I was prepared to make a retreat. I was not prepared for this and as Josie was not present I did not know what to sing or for that matter what note to take. So there I was like a pillar of salt before the famous tenor and as silent as a grave. My look caught the angry eyes of Attracta which spurred me into singing something, so I sang the first song that came into my head....I felt ashamed of my performance.[378]

John McCormack and the visitors had a brief discussion by the door before leaving. Later in life Paddy learned from Sister Attracta that he and the other boy had been auditioning before John McCormack, with a view to being chosen for musical training, funded by him:
She told me that I was the chosen one and that I had missed my future career in that I had run away from Nazareth House.[379]
(Paddy absconded some time after the concert, probably in 1936). Paddy's dependency on Josie Cummings, the music and band master just referred to, gives some indication of the influence this man had in the lives of so many residents at Nazareth House.

1.12.7. Development of Nazareth House Brass Band: 1910-1933

The Nazareth House brass band was by far the most important activity for many of the boys, and especially the Quartet members. Music had been a central feature of most Nazareth House Children's Homes, and almost all of them had either a Brass Band or a Ceilidh band. The Sligo Nazareth House brass band had experienced at least three phases of operation in the quarter century of its operation up to the mid 1930's.

The first Nazareth House bandmaster had been Harry Depew.[380] Mr Depew, a carpenter by trade, had been born to an American father and Sligo-born mother in New York, returning with his mother to Sligo after the death of his father. He had a flourishing carpentry shop and business in John Street, Sligo.[381] He had been involved from a young age in local politics, was elected as a councillor and alderman, and in the 1923 General Election had even stood for election to Dáil Éireann, this time as an Independent.[382]

Harry Depew had long-standing involvement in band music and in the Sligo Feis. In the inaugural 1903 Feis he had won first prize in the Bass Solo when in his late twenties. In 1913 he had been the Director of the Hibernian brass and reed band[383] and he continued for many years to run the town band. In the 1930's he was secretary of the Sligo Feis Organising Committee; his wife Mary and daughter, Alice, a music teacher, were also Committee Members involved in organising the Feis.[384] He was Chairman of the Feis Committee for twenty years from 1932 until his death in 1952. His co-members of the Organising Committee were the likes of Countess Markievicz and Lady Gore-Booth.[385] In short he was a notable professional and political Sligonian with a formidable background in brass band music, and the central figure for decades in the organisation of the Feis, including selecting the paid adjudicators and accompanists. I have been unable to determine why Harry Depew ceased to be the bandmaster, and a Mr Ellis took over from him sometime in the 1920's. The polymath nature of Mr Depew and the sheer scale of his interests and commitments would seem to be a not unreasonable factor in his relinquishing the position of conductor of the Nazareth House Band. The building works and the consequent relocation of Homes in the mid 1920's may also have interrupted the band's operation.

The reign of the second bandmaster, Mr Ellis, ended badly with the band folding and the instruments being put into storage. Paddy Baker remembered, when still in the nursery section of the Home, hearing Mr Ellis stamping his foot in rhythm to the melody the boys were trying to play.

1.12.8. From Workhouse Homeboy to Bandmaster: Josie Cummings

Mr Ellis became great friends with the third bandmaster, and the man who was to become the most significant Sligo Nazareth House band master, Joseph Cummings. Joseph, or Josie as he was always called, would have been trained in brass band music by Harry Depew, and also by Mr Ellis. His approach to music and to training the boys was, however, very much of his own crafting, instincts and background.

Illustration 15: Josie Cummings, Nazareth House Bandmaster

Josie Cummings had most probably been an inmate of the Sligo Workhouse as a boy, one of those children that Bishop Clancy had tried to rescue from Workhouse incarceration with adults, by founding Nazareth House, although Josie was not one of the earliest batch moved to the Home in 1910. The 1911 census shows a Sligo town born, Josie Cummings[386] (his name is variously spelled with and without the *g* as one of the 514 inmates of Sligo Workhouse. Aged 7 years he was literate, spoke Irish and English, and was not hospitalised, or noted to be deaf, dumb, blind or an imbecile. No other person of his surname was listed as a Workhouse resident.

The photograph of Josie Cummings shows him at the age of about 50 years with the Swansea Nazareth House Brass Band. This photograph does not show his disability, his hump back, probably as a result of spinal curvature. Josie was of diminutive height and looked very squarely built because of the disproportionately wide appearance that the hump gave to his shoulders. The hump back, most pronounced, may have been the result of normal spine growth working within his stunted, frame. Another photograph of him in the 1950's, with the Sligo Nazareth House Brass Band, gives a clearer picture, reinforced by Michael Porter's recollections, of just how small Josie Cummings was.

This diminutive height, about four and a half feet according to Michael, was to prove crucial to his bandmaster role on one occasion in competition. At the Sligo Feis in the mid 1930's, when all the Quartet boys were playing in the full band, Nazareth House had been competing against the Sligo Town Band of Harry Depew. When the time came for the Nazareth House Band to strike up, they missed their cue because some of the band could not see the diminutive Josie. Michael remembers his feelings as if it were yesterday:

I wanted to die with shame. I knew we had missed our entrance and we would not win and I could see from Josie's face that he knew it too. I felt that we had badly let him down after all the hard work he had put in to get us up to scratch. And we were good, good enough to have beaten them but for the entrance mistake. It was an awful feeling playing on and knowing that from our mistake we couldn't win. If I remember right they only just beat us for first place, even though we had made such a big mistake at the start.[387]

The work that Josie Cummings put into the Nazareth House Brass Band can be gauged from a number of incidents in its history. After Mr Ellis had retired from the band mastership the instruments were

185

put away in storage. The Sisters managed to achieve the revival of the band by training one of their former Homeboys for the post of Band Master. First he was sent for music lessons in Wolf Tone Street in Sligo town[388] and then, when his industry matched his talent the Sisters recorded that: *One of the boys, Josie Cummings, displayed a great talent for music. This talent was developed by sending him to London where he obtained Senior and Higher Grade Musical Certificates.*[389]

Josie's role at Nazareth House had hitherto been as a Yardman, the term for the general manual labourer at the home, who resided in the stable yard upper floor, and who performed those outside, more arduous physical tasks, that were beyond the strength of the Sisters. Many of the Yardmen seem to have had some form of disability, and would therefore have found it particularly difficult to find any work and accommodation in the outside world, when competing against able-bodied men and boys in inter-war, economically stagnant Ireland. The employment of these ex-Nazareth House boys, often lifelong, seems to have been a way of ensuring that some of the more vulnerable 'old boys' were protected, living in familiar surroundings, spared the beggar or Workhouse options that might have been their lot outside.[390] A hunchbacked, diminutive, block-shouldered, ex-Workhouse, ex-Homeboy, who had never lived outside an institutional setting, and was still living as an adult in his former care Home as a Yardman labourer, seems a most unusual selection for training as a bandmaster; one that it is harder to imagine having been made in the secular world.

Josie Cummings began his role as bandmaster after completing his musical studies in May 1933,[391] treating his work seriously and working with fierce diligence to knock the band into shape. Yet his start was disappointing as Paddy Baker remembered:

I also remember when the band started and we took the instruments with their sticking valves out of the cupboard and tried to rejuvenate them by puffing and blowing in ever increasing crescendo (all of us bragging of course) until Joseph Cummings (R.I.P.) drew our attention to a word called diminuendo which had little effect on our ears as we puffed and blowed (sic) completely ignoring the existence of a bandmaster....all the instruments had to be sent to Dublin for repair and polishing. It was then that the band really got started and poor Josie really did his best to get a tune out of us. It was then that we started participating at the local feiseanna where we had to learn to dance under the guidance of Miss O'Rourke and our voices were tuned to that of singing birds with the help of Josie and Sister Gabriel.[392]

Paddy neatly outlines both the control challenges Josie must have faced from a bunch of lively lads, but also the drive of the new bandmaster.

1.12.9. A Natural Teacher

An early intimation of Josie's natural way of relating to children and boys, allied to his musical ability, was recalled by Paddy, and this may well have been a consideration in the Sisters spotting Josie's aptitude for the post. Paddy had been in the Nursery section and had been singing loudly under the table disturbing the other children, probably bored. The Sister in charge took him to the newly built Father Barry's House, still empty but for chair and harmonium. Paddy was offered the chair by the Sister, who brought Josie in and then left, after giving him instructions. Josie began playing a tune and then fitted Latin verses to it, encouraging Paddy to join in, which he did after a while: *I now had to sing solo but stumbled a few times with the Latin which sounded something like as follows; Laudi Deum Angelorum, Sumae Laudis pekatorum, Santa Maria.....and was complimented for my endeavours.*[393]

In summary: a busy nun brings a Pied Piper to harness a bored boy's natural singing talent, with Piper Josie Cummings using the 'sit by Nellie', apprenticeship, learn-by-doing form of teaching. Much later he was given the challenge of teaching another boy, one with no musical knowledge, to become proficient enough to play an instrument in the band in just two weeks after another boy had left:

'I had to play by ear as the bandmaster Joseph Cummings did not know how to read music either. If he did he was not telling us. His method of teaching was easy. He stood behind the chair I was sitting on and hummed the tune in my ear. Bearing in mind he was about four feet six tall his mouth was level with my ear. He was ok and I was able to march with the band at Grange Sports Day'.[394]

The reference to Josie not knowing how to read music was wrong. The boy had confused simple teaching with lack of knowledge; probably also he had assumed that the use by Josie of Tonic Sol-fa[395] to teach the boys music, meant that he could not read musical notation. The Oxford Dictionary gives a clear explanation of Tonic Sol-fa: 'A system of naming the notes of the scale, usually (doh-ray-me-fah-soh-lah-te) used especially to teach singing, with doh as the keynote of all major keys and lah as the keynote of all minor keys'.

Josie Cummings used this to teach all the boys how to recognise musical notation without needing to read musical scores. Paddy Baker regretted that only Tonic Sol-fa was taught, a regret of Willie McGowan too: *The only regret is that Josie Cummings never taught us to read music properly. Instead of tonic sol-fa he should have introduced c, to e, note reading.*[396]

1.12.10. A Natural Communicator

The communicative gap between Sisters and Homeboys has already been outlined; Josie made up for this deficiency to some degree. The brass instruments were kept in a large cupboard in the playroom. Each member was responsible for cleaning and polishing his instrument. When the boys assembled for band practice it was Josie's habit to let the boys chat and generally show off and play about a bit, letting off steam to some degree, before the actual rehearsal began. Michael remembers never feeling so unconstrained when supervised in the large playroom by the Sisters, and welcomed this freer, enjoyable interlude. It was here with Josie Cummings that Michael remembers having the friendliest relationships with his fellow Homeboys, this in part being because of their shared love and task of band music. There was a camaraderie he felt there, but his description of the scene left me feeling that Josie conducted more than the band: his natural human conducting skills were as evident as his musical ones.

After a period Josie would call the band to order, the boys quickly obeying. They respected his authority, perhaps in part because of the period of conversational grace they had been granted. The practice sessions, lasting an hour and a half to two hours each, were always prefaced by targets, with Josie informing the boys about their next performance, venue and competition. He would happily answer the boys' queries about venues, transport, competitors, or other matters. If he did not know something he would promise to find out, and report back.[397]

1.12.11. Coaching the Band

The rehearsals were never marred by stupid or disruptive behaviour; yet Michael never remembers Josie raising his voice, let alone chastising anyone. When conducting, Josie would single out a person to correct a note or other aspect of their performance, yet he never played an instrument to demonstrate technique to them. Everything was done by word or gesture. If a band member was missing Josie never filled in by playing that boy's instrument, leading Michael to query whether Josie could play any brass band instruments himself. Michael remembers feeling warm and respected when Josie spoke to him, either to give advice or answer a question. Michael would never initiate a question to a Sister (unless working individually with her). With Josie he went out of his way to approach him in the playground, confident that Josie would listen and follow up on the query. While these contacts could hardly be described as free-flowing conversations, they were the closest Michael ever got to conversations with an adult figure during his whole career at Nazareth House.[398]

The running of the band involved Josie writing out a card for each band member, in tonic sol-fa. He would do this for each of the fifteen to twenty band members, repeating the process for each new tune he taught them, with each card individually adjusted for the separate instruments. Members of the full band included James Brinton, Donald Farrell, Thomas Scully, and Michael Dirrane, in addition to the Quartet members of Willie McGowan, Paddy Baker, Michael Porter and Willie Walsh.[399] Michael Porter remembers looking out of an upper floor window in the new home building, observing Josie, in his quarters above the stable yard, painstakingly scripting each individual

189

card for his band. As there were anything up to fifty tunes that the full band played, this involved the preparation of up to a thousand cards. The boys had a pouch hung on a shoulder strap which they used to store those cards needed for marching or performing for any particular day. Each card was numbered, and Josie would simply call this number out for the next tune to be played.

Josie ensured that each boy learned to play several brass instruments in order to develop the boy's talents but also to ensure that he had cover for each instrument should sickness or a boy leaving the Home deplete his instrument players. Michael played the cornet, and also the flugelhorn (wing horn) with a pitch lower than a cornet. The different lip sizes caused problems and Michael always felt more confident with the cornet rather than the flugelhorn (also called French horn) that he is featured playing in the Quartet.

The full band comprised a cornet, second cornet and bigger horn instruments such as the euphonium of Willie McGowan, together with a big drum, kettle drum and double bass. When they took part in marching, processions and competitions all around county Sligo, from the age of about ten upwards, the physical demands of carrying the large instruments were considerable for such young, and generally small, boys. They dressed in their band uniform of green jacket, with a crest, and short trousers.[400] They were trained to march in step while playing the music. Michael recalled that the synchronised marching became second nature to them, allowing the boys to concentrate on the task in hand of playing the music. They also had to ignore the distractions to the side of them, whether the crowds who were watching or the street urchins of Sligo.[401] A band, playing and marching, is a magnet for young children and the Nazareth House band was often followed all around the streets of Sligo by groups of young children, some of them schoolfellows from Quay Street. The band boys were trained to look only front, reading and playing the music before them. Michael does not remember any cheek, mockery or abuse being directed to the band, or to the hump-backed conductor leading it, by the children of Sligo. The band and marching experience, and the discipline that this required, came in useful occupationally for many of the boys, as it helped them with entry into the Irish or British Armies when they left Nazareth House.[402]

1.12.12. Extra-Curricular Interests

Music-mad Josie especially loved playing the organ. Michael Porter recollects that Josie could not pass a church without entering to practise his skills on an unfamiliar organ. When out marching it was quite common for the band to stop and Josie to dart inside a new church for some organ playing, with some of his band co-opted into pumping the organ bellows.[403] He was also, especially in his later years, known to dart into public houses, if funds, or former old boys looking him up, supplied the Porter.[404] Several times he had to be rousted out late at night by the Sisters.[405] His suit, he always wore one, usually the same one, was always dusted in snuff, to which he was addicted.[406] One of the Sisters at Nazareth House came from Buncrana in County Donegal where her family owned a snuff mill. She obtained copious free supplies of snuff for Josie which helped him eke out his modest wages.[407]

1.12.13. The Quartet and 1934 Sligo Feis

Any new band conductor would be keen to make his mark, and the way to do this in Connacht was to succeed at the Sligo Feis. Josie set out to do this against considerable odds. He was only appointed in May 1933 and then the instruments had to be returned to Dublin for refurbishment. He had to teach the boys how to read and play music, as well as singing, and probably had only nine or ten months to do this before his first Feis challenge in 1934. As well as training and entering his full band he chose the four best boys to form a Quartet.

The Nazareth House Brass Band Quartet comprising William McGowan (Euphonium), Patrick Baker (Horn), Michael Porter (French Horn) and William Walsh (Cornet) competed in the final of the Sligo Feis Ceoil in St John's Church Hall, on Thursday, 5 April, 1934.[408] The chosen four boys were competing against the adult band of Mr Henry Depew, who was the embodiment of the Feis; old against new, both in age and in experience. Harry Depew's quartet was much older than the Nazareth House boys who were aged 13, 11, 12 and 14 respectively. The competition test allowed each quartet to choose its own test piece. Josie Cummings had selected the Londonderry Air, better known as Danny Boy, as the Nazareth House piece.[409] Although the audience did not decide the outcome of the contest, this being the sole responsibility of the independent adjudicator, Mr Rowley, their response to the music would hardly be without some influence on the judge. Josie's was an inspired choice, as although he was probably unaware of G.K. Chesterton's 'quartet' of lines from 'The Ballad of the White Horse', his choice captured the spirit of Chesterton's script:

'For the Great Gaels of Ireland
Are the men that God made mad,
For all their wars are merry
And all their songs are sad!'[410]

Josie gambled that nothing makes an Irish audience happier than a sad song combined with a great tune and that Danny Boy would deliver both.[411]

Mr Alec Rowley had been appointed as one of the two Independent adjudicators, by the Sligo Feis Committee whose Chairman, was Harry Depew, the conductor of the opposing band, and Josie's former teacher. The remuneration for 4 days work for the adjudicator was 25 guineas plus expenses; a princely sum.[412] One presumes the adjudicator wished for future Feis bookings. It must have been tempting to award the prize to the Depew trained band, but no, Mr Rowley awarded the first prize to the Nazareth House Homeboy Quartet.[413] Mr Rowley gave his reasoning for the result.

'Mr Depew's Quartet had tackled a more difficult piece of music than that of the boys but they were: not always clean in attack and fell down in the quickest pieces. Nazareth House were very note-sure and convincing, and their play was very commendable for boys so young'.

The winning margin was 86 marks to 83. Michael seemed surprised that the result had been so close; he felt that the Nazareth House performance was the best they had ever played. Yet the result may well have hung on a small miracle. In all the practices

Michael Porter had never hit the highest, most difficult, note cleanly because the mouthpiece of his 'second' instrument, the French, or flugelhorn, was larger than his first choice instrument, the cornet. In the final he had managed to play the note purely, the only time he ever remembers having done so.

The adjudicator knew his music. Alec Rowley (1892-1958) was a noted composer, pianist and organist and had performed regularly on the BBC and at the Henry Wood Promenade Concert in London. He taught at the Trinity College of Music in London. Many of the participants at Sligo would have been performing music arranged by him, as he specialised in arranging music for amateurs. After the Father Mathew Feis in Dublin which attracted 2000 competitors and the Sligo Feis which attracted over 1000 entrants, both in 1936, Alec Rowley commented that: 'he found English children more fond of accuracy, while Irish children played with temperament and expression. They did not mind making Mistakes which were not unmusical, and they were apt to reach a higher standard than those who played for safety. People of this kind made the best composers'.

Alec Rowley's comments may well have had in mind the music of the likes of Josie and the Quartet. Josie Cummings seems to have been gifted with a love of music that he used to transcend his physical and social handicaps: doubly gifted, as he was able to nurture this love in the boys he trained.

1.12.14. Music has Charms[414]

The decision to involve the boys in so much music, and the operation of the band in particular, proved to be an inspired move; doubly beneficial to the boys, intellectually and emotionally, and the benefit lasting life-long. Alec Rowley's general observations in his Feis adjudicating role about 'temperament and expression' had been formed by listening to particular musicians, including the Nazareth House Quartet. What emotions had he observed in their playing, what depth of expression? How much had their musical training developed, as well as soothed, 'the savage breast'? To what degree can the playing of these boys be an indicator of emotional development? Could such a performance that had so

193

impressed the eminent and sensitive, Alec Rowley have been produced from children subject only to an emotionally sterile Home and School environment? How much did the music itself, and the camaraderie of the Quartet, help abate to some degree, the sense of isolation and loss of family? Above all, what contribution to the boys' emotional life was made by their bandmaster's firm, respectful and interested treatment of them? How much sustenance did the musical training by Josie Cummings's and the well-named Sister Gabriel give to the emotionally orphaned boys at Nazareth House? Did it serve to nurture their hibernated feelings, keeping them from destruction by the cold of neglect, never quite letting winter root-destruction take hold?

John McCormack expressed very similar sentiments in slightly different words: 'Singing is most of all an expression of something felt, rather than thought-though who can say where thought ends and music begins'.

1.12.15. The Real Reason for Success

The picture on the front cover, taken by Sister Attracta, shows the Quartet boys with their winner's medals pinned to their jerseys. The medals were presented at a later date and each boy also received two shillings and six pence along with his individual winner's medal. William McGowan remembers the Sisters relieving him of his coin on return to Nazareth House.[415] The boys were allowed to keep their individual medals.[416] Photographs of all winning teams at sport or any Feiseanna event were put up on the wall of the boys' recreation room to encourage others to emulate the successes of their fellow Homeboys.

Paddy Baker illustrates the concrete nature of the Sisters' faith in the following vignette:

I remember when the competitions took place and we were dressed in our best, Attracta gave us a spoonful of holy water to drink in the hope that this would produce the desired miracle and award us the first prize. A little sugar in our porridge would have been more beneficial.[417]

PART 2

AFTER NAZARETH:
ADOLESCENCE (1936-1939)

Chapter 2.1: First Forays Outside Nazareth: Michael Porter

'For each age is a dream that is dying,
Or one that is coming to birth'.[418]

2.1.1. Cobbling and Sock-Making

Michael Porter felt neither regret nor excitement after he finished his schooling and awaited the next phase of his life outside leaving Nazareth House. His overwhelming emotion was passivity because he received no information about what was planned for his future.

After a Nazareth Homeboy had completed his schooling the Sisters explored the possibility of him returning to live with his family. Most of the boys still had family living, including a father still alive. The death of a mother combined with family poverty and sickness, seemed to be the commonest constellation of factors behind the boys' entries into care. It seems that many families had 'parked' their son or sons at Nazareth House for the duration of their childhood, reappearing to take them home when their schooldays were done, and where they could begin to make an economic contribution to the family.

Michael left school at the summer of 1936 when he was 14¾ years old. He would have enjoyed his summer holiday free from school work while he waited for the next chapter in his life. His father and family would have been contacted to see if he could go home to live with them. The answer was negative but it seems possible that his father then briefly began to make a contribution to his keep now that his son had left school.[419]

To tide Michael over until he was found a Situation placement outside the Home, he was engaged in learning two new skills; cobbling and sock making. He was trained by an old cobbler who Michael thought was a resident of the adjacent Home. The man, stooped, grey haired and balding, was quietly spoken and very patient. Michael remembers him as a very quiet man; he would have been as he was deaf and dumb.[420] Yet Michael has no recollection of either his muteness or deafness, a further indication of the partiality, even fallibility, of childhood memory.

It seems that the cobbler was yet one more of the disabled, waifs or strays who was, found succour, shelter, work and purpose within the more protective grounds of Nazareth House; an oasis of calm sheltered from the troubled Ireland of civil war earlier referred to.

One aspect of the deaf and dumb cobbler puzzled Willie McGowan: how did he manage to make his confession? As the cobbler could read and was an accomplished writer Willie thought that he may have written down his sins. Yet this still did not explain how the normal interaction between priest and penitent could operate in the darkened confessional. The cobbler's literary competence suggests that he may have had special schooling related to his disability in the past, probably in a Church run institution, possibly also learning his trade there to equip him to make his living in the world.[421]

The cobbler had a large wooden kist (chest) in which he kept all his equipment, and materials, the box big enough to double up as a work bench. In the kist were full skins of un-dyed, tan coloured, animal hide. Each hide varied in thickness, one from another, but also within individual hides. Pig bristles, hemp and wax were also stored there, and Michael and the cobbler worked these together to produce the threads for attaching the new leather sole and heels to the boys' boots, the necessary thickness of hide being cut from the full skin. Strength, dexterity, good eyesight and precision were needed. Michael remembers making mistakes, but being patiently shown the techniques until he had mastered them. He worked a couple of days a week with the cobbler, sitting by the large window in, he thought, the downstairs dining room, looking out of the window to the playing field beyond.[422]

He was also put to making the socks to go with the boots using a circular weighted sock making machine that fitted on to the table top with the young Sister mentioned earlier (in 1.10.14). Michael's native Porter aptitude for matters technical and mechanical, soon had him proficient in sock making, easily able to turn a heel and add stripes to the socks.

In three years of intensive discussions with me Michael had been adamant that he had never heard mention at any time at Nazareth House that he had had a father. Suddenly when I was probing this period of the gap between leaving school and starting his first placement, he remembered a conversation that he had had with a nice softly spoken new Sister.

2.1.2. Shy Sister Mentions Father

Conversation with the Sister was usually limited, he being shy in her presence, she generally working quietly away at her mending and making duties, while keeping an eye on his work, helping if he encountered problems. The Sister said to him: *your father made a contribution to your care.*[423] Michael said not a word in reply and the conversation went no further. So entrenched was his belief that he had no parents, indeed no family at all, that he was unable to process the information. The mentioning of something 'personal' to him was entirely unfamiliar and beyond his ability to comprehend. He left Nazareth House still convinced that he was an orphan, and that he had never been told that he had any family.

Other than that mention by the 'nice Sister' of his father, Michael is clear that the matter of father and family were never raised with him by any of the Sisters. He never thought to ask because he thought that he had no family. It may possibly be that the young Sister broached the matter to check Michael's openness to the matter of talking about his family. It is understandable that his non response was interpreted as him not wanting to talk about the matter of family. Understandable too that the Sisters might not want to hurt him by telling him that his father did not want, or could not take, him home. When he went out into the world, neither on this or on any subsequent placement, was he ever told about father and family. He was allowed to leave Nazareth House, 'unaware' that he had a family, unaware of even where he had originated from. As with Paddy this could have had fateful lifelong consequences for him, resulting in his never having been reconnected with them because of not knowing of their existence.

2.1.3. Communication with Parents, and with Boys After Leaving Care

The Sisters had a comprehensive and efficient tracking system to follow the boys when they left. Furthermore they acted as a conduit to family seeking to find the whereabouts of their sons. Nevertheless the communication from Sisters to boys, and indeed from parents to children, and from adults to children, was lacking: for Michael and for the other Homeboys.

The majority of parents whose sons were resident at Nazareth House made no, or little, financial contribution to their care;[424] the majority of the boys there came from very poor families, and poverty was a factor in their coming into care. Michael's father had already asked the Mercy Sisters at Ballinasloe to keep his daughter there beyond her due leaving date after her 'sentence' expired. This was recorded as: *Father requested Mary would be kept on in Convent after 16th birthday.*[425] It seems reasonable to assume that his father made a similar request to keep Michael at Nazareth House and it may well be that the financial contribution was made at this late date, towards the cost of his care until a placement was found for him. Michael was kept at Nazareth House for over nine months after leaving school, before a first placement was secured for him, and he became, in the Sisters' parlance, a 'Situation boy'.[426]

2.1.4. Sisters' Work-Finding for the Boys

The Sisters' awareness of the need to help secure work and accommodation for the boys would seem to have been somewhat in advance of general practice for the time. The Sisters, rather like their nineteenth century Sisters at Hammersmith, tried to place children with families for their first living and work experience and training outside the Home. They sought to provide a half-way house, a combined work and living situation, where the young person could be sheltered, fed, kept safe and trained while they built up their skills and confidence before a bigger step towards fully independent living. They also provided a back-up refuge taking back the boys after, not unusually, many of their initial placements broke down. The range of placements for the boys put them in competition with the large number of other poor boys and girls in the economically underdeveloped Ireland of the 1930's. The effect of the Anglo-Irish trade war were still being felt, emigration was still high, opportunities of work very limited and wages were very low.

A variety of placements were found for the boys. A number continued working at Nazareth Houses, in Sligo or elsewhere; there was certainly a considerable movement of boys from Sligo to Nazareth House, Mallow, Cork. The home there was only for the elderly and as the Sisters had a large farm and work yards there young male labour from Sligo fulfilled a labour shortage for them. Usually these placements were of months to several years duration until the young man obtained a more permanent or better situation. Some former Homeboys, such as Willie Walsh and Josie Cummings, always gravitated back to the family substitute security of Nazareth House homes throughout Britain and Ireland.

The Sisters' own families of origin were sometimes used for farm placements, seemingly a common practice among religious orders. As well as maintaining that good old tradition of nepotism, this practice had two additional advantages; firstly the benefit of having a known, respectable, presumably good Catholic, family to give both example and supervision to the neophyte in the big world; secondly the Sisters could feel that such families were safe and suitable living situations for young boys. Another group of placements was the lay equivalent of the Sisters' families; 'known' Catholic families who provided hotel, domestic service, farm or shopkeeper work: placements where bed and board were combined.

The Leitrim author, John McGahern, and others, have shown how a number of these children from poor families, not just ex-care ones, were economically and sexually exploited.[427] Placement with known families would at least have given some security of conscience to those placing the boys in the 1930's, when such risk was either not known or barely recognised. Such known placements would still not have prevented the sexual exploitation of the vulnerable ex-care residents, both male and female. Intra-institutional sexual abuse has received enormous public attention. I suspect that a significant minority of ex-care residents and working class children employed as domestics or farm servants, were sexually exploited when on these placements. Those exploitative situations which led to pregnancy then resulted in the child being removed and permanently separated from the 'child' mother.[428]

Where a young person lacks family, and where their living and work situation is in the same place, they feel trapped and unable to escape when the grooming for sexual abuse, or even more direct sexual predation, does take place.

2.1.5. First Steps Outside Nazareth

Michael was sent to a Catholic family well known to the Sisters in Sligo for his first placement when he left Nazareth House for the first time in May, 1937. The home records state that Michael: *Went to Mrs McLaughlin, Marlborough Hotel, Marlborough Street, Dublin–letter to say he arrived safely.*[429]

Some thought seems to have gone in to this choice of first placement for Michael. The McLoughlin family had lived in Sligo before moving to the capital. Their only child, a boy, was the same age as Michael and indeed had been in Michael's class at Quay Street School.[430] That latter fact may have been a consideration in sending Michael to Dublin; placing him with a family known to the Sisters, and having bed and board provided in with his employment indicates the significance given by the Sisters to the boys' welfare, and to creating as soft a landing for them in their first after-care placement as possible.

Michael was not involved in the choice of placement, nor does he recollect any preparation for this. He was provided with an outfit for his first sojourn in the outside world, a new brown serge suit was bought for him, and he was provided with a new cardboard suitcase for his possessions.[431] He remembers nothing of leaving his companions or what was said to him on leaving. He would have been seen by Reverend Mother and Sister Attracta. The former would have given him rosary beads, counselled him to be good, reminded him to say his prayers morning and night and ensure he went to Mass on Sundays, and given him her blessing: that appears to have been the standard procedure when a boy left.

He was accompanied on the walk down Chapel Hill to the railway station and his companion purchased the ticket for him and set him on the train; he cannot recollect who this was. The journey to Dublin, his first time on a train, was marked more by anxiety than by excitement. He was met at Dublin and taken to the hotel which was near O'Connell Street. Michael wrote back to Nazareth House telling the Sisters that he had arrived safely.[432]

2.1.6. First Placement: Dublin Hotel Work

In the hotel he met Mrs McLoughlin, the joint proprietor, but the person who really ran the hotel and who was the power there; her husband appeared a much vaguer figure to Michael. Michael's duties were of the lowest, skivvy-type of domestic service: carrying coal up and ashes down stairs; sweeping and cleaning; general fetching and carrying; and other non skilled tasks that did not involve much interaction with the guests.

The McLoughlin boy, Michael's former Quay Street classmate, was still attending school, and so was absent from the hotel during the day. The boy, whose Christian name Michael cannot remember, had not settled in the capital, or at his new school, and was somewhat lonely, desperate for company of his own age, wanting someone to 'play with'. The boy made overtures to Michael to join him at play in the yard. Even though the boys were 16 or so years of age they still liked playing games that today would be judges as childish. In the early days in Dublin, the boy persuaded Michael to push him around in an old buggy in the very small back yard and both master and servant enjoyed the game. Michael was grateful to have someone of his own age to play with and talk to: glad too to have some relief from the rather demanding and stern Mrs McLoughlin, whose imperious and distant manner towards him constantly emphasised his inferior status.

Mrs McLoughlin stopped the buggy game and forbade Michael from playing with, or even associating with, her son. Henceforth Michael was instructed to avoid the son altogether, even to avoid speaking to him, a difficult enough task when passing each other in stairs or corridors. He was kept very busy at his work, so had little time to mope. When he did he wished himself back at Nazareth House. He knew he was learning various tasks and so felt that he was making a small first step in his eventual aim of complete independence and self-reliance. He knew that he was well short of achieving this just then. He did not feel happy, nor especially unhappy either. Happiness had been playing in the back yard of the hotel with his companion. Michael had no expectation of a right to be happy and so was able to adjust to setbacks more easily than those who expected sunshine to be their lot. It was clear to him that the McLoughlin boy, desperate for a playmate and peer to talk with, was suffering from the banned contact more than he was. Low expectations of happiness equated with less emotional distress after setbacks or disappointment for Michael. The McLoughlin experience had shown that class prejudice had not left Ireland with the British withdrawal.

After a few months working at the hotel Michael was given a large sandwich board, much bigger than him, to carry into town. Mrs McLoughlin instructed Michael to walk up and down with the sandwich board in O'Connell Street, right in the centre of Dublin, during the daytime, when work was slacker in the hotel. The advertisement for the hotel was designed to catch the attention of people travelling from Amiens Street Station to O'Connell Street, which was just around the corner. One day the weather was horrendous, absolutely pouring with rain, and Michael was forlornly plodding up and down, obviously soaked, unprotected by mackintosh or overcoat. A Guard stopped him and began to question him. Michael immediately became wary, thinking his default thought when accosted by any adult: 'what am in trouble for'? The Guard who seemed to sense Michael's fear questioned him about his age, who his employer was, where his work place was, what he was doing there, where he came from? Michael gave staccato answers but sensed that he should not mention Nazareth House, only telling the Guard that he had come to Dublin from Sligo. The Guard had implied in his questions that he knew Michael was not a Dubliner. After the short interview the Guard sent him back to McLoughlin's.[433]

A few days after this incident Mrs McLoughlin called him in to see her. She was angry and curt telling him: *Right, I am asking you to pack your case and belongings and I am sending you back to Sligo.* No explanation was given; none demanded. He received no pay or wages in lieu. He was supplied with a ticket and was taken to the railway station and put on the train to Sligo by Mr McLoughlin.[434]

2.1.7. Back Home to Recover at Nazareth

When Michael returned to Nazareth House he doesn't remember being asked for an explanation of what had gone wrong, why he had left or had he been dismissed. He felt very ashamed to have to face the eyes of the other boys, knowing that they would think him a failure, which indeed he felt himself to be. His strongest emotion was anger at his unjust treatment as he did not feel that he had done anything wrong. He was sure that his dismissal resulted from the conversation with the Guard, and assumed that the McLoughlin's had been taken to task by the Guard for sending him out in such bad weather.

Michael's recollection of not being asked for an explanation of why he had returned to Nazareth House is contradicted by the Sisters' recording: *Michael found the work did not suit him.*[435]

When Michael found out what the Sisters had recorded about this placement he was furious. I tried to explain that the official record might be dressed up to 'spare his blushes', or might be a verbatim account of what he had told them but he remained angered by what he saw as the lack of literal truth in the recording. He was also concerned at how little recording there had been, despite my having repeatedly warned him that sparse, inaccurate or missing care records were common, almost the norm, especially so long ago. I also stressed to him that the greater problem wasn't usually the inaccuracy of recording, more the lack of detail. Michael did feel an understandable sense of powerlessness and said that his first three placements after Nazareth House had influenced his life more than anything since. He said they had all given him a sense of injustice and a desire to fight injustices subsequently in his life. [436]

2.1.8. Second Work Placement: Farming

After his first placement Michael was taken back into the older boys' dormitory until, shortly afterwards, he was given another placement, this time on a farm. He took the bus from Sligo, along he thought a road near the coast, and travelled some ten to twenty miles at most. On alighting in the middle of the countryside (the conductor must have been told where to drop him off by someone from Nazareth House) he was met by a middle-aged farmer who led him to his small farm cottage. There Michael met the woman of the house. He took her to be either the sister or the mother of the farmer, but as no introductions were made he could not be certain of this. The couple, rather like the Sisters of Nazareth, seemed to operate on the principle that the boys did not need to be told very much. The man spoke little, the woman barely a word for the whole duration of his placement there. During his entire stay there, Michael never spoke a single word to the woman.[437]

The cottage was the classic three room, single-storey thatched cabin so typical of Mayo, Sligo and some of the western counties of Ireland. A central living-cum-dining room had the standard huge open fireplace on the side wall abutting one of the two bedrooms that flanked the living room. A large metal crane, side-hung and hinged to swing over the fire, had various cast iron cooking pots hung from it, over the permanently lit turf fire below. The fire was where all cooking, kettle and water boiling in pots for cleaning took place.

Michael's job was to provide manual labour wherever it was required, but very much working with the man, the woman having as little to do with him as possible, never speaking to him at mealtimes. Michael did not feel that this indicated dislike of him; rather that she was content with silence. She spoke little more to the man, to whom she was definitely closely related. The woman managed the milking, the fowl, the baking, cooking and housework.

Michael and the farmer did the more arduous tillage work. Most of his work digging drills for the next year's potato crop, but with spade, not machine drill. This involved turning back the sticky clay soil either side of a furrow and digging the drill holes with spade.

He found it hard physical work, very dirty work too, but most of all, monotonous in the rain. They managed to put in a late, half day shift on the day of his arrival.

After his evening meal, food was plain but plentiful, the farmer showed him into one of the two bedrooms where Michael was left alone to get into bed. He had not gone to sleep and was alarmed when the man came into the room later that night. Michael heard the man undressing and then felt him get into the bed with him, not touching him with his body and turning on his side away from Michael. The man said nothing, and he did nothing. Eyes tight shut, hardly able to breathe, Michael spent the night without sleep. Early the next morning the man rose, dressed and left, Michael quickly following suit. After breakfast they carried on the hard slog all day digging the drills.

Next night there was the same bedtime routine, the same lack of sleep. Michael had been used to his own single, metal frame bed at Nazareth House where he slept on his back with arms crossed on his chest as the Sisters had coached the boys. No other person had ever shared a bed with him or made him feel uncomfortable. The sense of one's own personal space was sacrosanct. Even though the man had done nothing at all untoward to Michael, or sought to make him uncomfortable, having to sleep in the same bed as him made Michael so tense he could not sleep. Again this illustrates the impact of lack of communication from an adult to a child on the child.

Michael thought that the farmer was naturally reticent, possibly shy, and probably unable to relate to a teenager. Living alone with mother or sister in a remote rural area (Michael remembers seeing no other soul when there) would be unlikely to make him verbose. Had he explained the sleeping arrangements to Michael in advance then Michael would have been less alarmed. Silence may have consequences, often unintended, and which are more harmful than actual physical acts. After several nights without sleep Michael could hardly stand up. On Thursday he told the farmer that he would have to leave. He gave no reason for wanting to go. The farmer looked disappointed at the news, but raised no objections.

Michael felt sorry for the farmer whom he thought was probably trying to work out what he might have done wrong. After a short period the man took Michael to the road and put him on the bus to Sligo after paying his fare.

2.1.9. Back to Nazareth Again

Going up the steep bank at Church Hill to Nazareth House an exhausted Michael felt at his lowest ebb. Here he was back at Nazareth House having failed spectacularly, and this time he had given up on the placement. He remembered the shame he had felt when the other Homeboys had seen him come back from Dublin. He had only left Nazareth House on Monday morning and Mother General had reminded him to be sure to attend Sunday Mass. As it was now only Thursday he hadn't stayed there long enough to miss Mass. He felt a sense of total and abject failure.

On this occasion, and now that he was about 16 years old, he was given a room in the accommodation over the yard stables in the courtyard attached to the Home for the elderly. He remembers getting advice from another boy who was living there, an older lad. This youth advised Michael to go to the Labour Exchange in Sligo to get help in finding work locally.[438]

Michael told the manager of Sligo Labour Exchange next morning that he was looking for a combined work and living placement. Mr Dargan, the manager of the Exchange, told Michael that he was looking for a worker at his own house in nearby Rosses Point. The work involved some basic cooking, light domestic chores and care of the cow and few acres of land and tillage around the house. Accommodation was provided. There were two to cater for: himself and Mr Flynn, both of whom worked and ate out during the day and often in the evening. Michael discussed no such matters as terms or conditions, wages, or contract of employment; he was just so elated to have some good news at last. Above all he had sorted out his own work situation. This seemed to him by far the greatest achievement of his life to date.

2.1.10. Third Work Placement: General Domestic Work

Mr Dargan did not offer to drive Michael and his suitcase out to Rosses Point after work. Michael had no money and he did not want the Sisters to query the suitability of his placement. He asked the older ex-Homeboy who had advised him about the Labour Exchange if he could lend him some money. He was given two shillings which enabled him to purchase a bus ticket. As he travelled on the bus to his new, self-obtained, position at Dargan's, the world seemed transformed since yesterday: despair had been replaced by pride; he felt a sense of achievement; and there was hope in his heart at what seemed a future with prospects.[439]

The new work situation was at Rosses Point, some 5 miles or so outside Sligo where Joseph Dargan occupied a large detached house with stable yard. The road to Rosses Point followed the wide estuary of the Garravogue river until it met the open sea. Rosses Point was a desirable seaside living and holiday location that also sported an excellent golf course. On the other side of the wide estuary lay Strandhill where Paddy Baker's mother, Lillian, worked in a hotel.

Born in County Westmeath, after training as a carpenter,[440] Joseph Dargan had joined British Government service, moving to Londonderry where he became a clerk in the newly established Labour Exchange there.[441] Labour Exchanges had been established by the 1909 Act of Parliament, part of a raft of Lloyd George legislative measures designed to prevent working men in Britain shifting their political allegiance from Liberal to Labour. Based on the German social insurance model that Bismarck had introduced, the measures had included unemployment pay and the introduction of Old Age pensions. Although some working class organisations such as trade unions and trade councils had opposed their introduction, this was not the case in Sligo. The Act's initial implementation was limited by finances and some reservations about the efficiency of the measures, and some qualms about the principle of state intervention in relations between employer and employee.

Labour Exchanges were not particularly effective in securing employment, finding jobs for only 25% of the registered unemployed, although this must be set against a lack of jobs available. The first Exchange in Britain had only been opened at the beginning of 1910. Sligo trades council and the Sligo County Council acted quickly to petition the Board of Trade in London to establish a Labour Exchange in Sligo.[442] Sligo North Member of Parliament, Thomas Scanlan, pressed the proposal to have a Sligo based Labour Exchange for the province of Connaught. Mr Buxton, the President of the Board of Trade, replied that: 'It is not possible at present to provide Exchanges in every important area (of Ireland)'.

Local pressure on Parliament from Sligo, including from the Harbour Commissioners, to open a Labour Exchange in the town persisted. The pressure succeeded and by 1912 Alderman Reilly was the clerk of the recently opened Sligo Labour Exchange.

When in Londonderry the unmarried Joseph Dargan had lived in a large boarding house with other clerk and commercial types, in Foyle Street. Neither when living at home with his family in Bishopgate, Mullingar, nor in Londonderry would he have ever had to cook or clean. By his late 50's the slimly built Dargan had used his position as manager of the important Sligo Labour Exchange to obtain a large house. He had neither time, ability or inclination to cook, clean or care for the premises. It is surprising that he had not employed a housekeeper to look after him and his lodger, Milo Flynn, a more heavily built, well known Gaelic footballer,[443] who also worked in Sligo, in the same office as Dargan, his boss. The two men would spend all day at work before returning to the house at Rosses Point. They would park the car at the gate and sound the horn until their minion, Michael, came running to open this and close it after them. They never exchanged a word with him during this encounter. Michael remembers the arrogant and imperious attitude of the two men towards him thus: *They showed no respect to me at all, I was just there on sufferance.*[444]

Michael had a bedroom in the house at first. He would rise at 6 am to ready the fire and prepare breakfast for the men. This was basic fare, usually toast and sometimes egg. The men left for work at about 8 o'clock, usually not returning till 8 or 9 o'clock at night. As Mr Dargan, who was always referred to as 'Joe', and Milo Flynn ate lunch and usually their evening meal in town, Michael was left pretty much with the run of the house, yard and gardens to himself all day. He was not expected to do many domestic chores beyond sweeping, cleaning, bed making and very basic cooking, usually just breakfasts during the working week.

As there were no washing facilities at Dargan's the laundry van came to collect the sheets, shirts and underclothing, sparing Michael this task.[445] Michael's main work responsibilities involved tending the gardens and grounds. He had to maintain the rather rough, overgrown vegetable garden. This was his first experience of gardening and he planted, and harvested, potatoes and cabbage in the walled garden surrounding the house. These arrangements suited him well. He could work as he chose, at his own pace, unsupervised by anyone, free to work out, within the limitations of the men's morning and evening presence, his own work, and play schedule for each day.

Although Michael described his position at Dargan's as a *skivvy* and *general dog's body,* the freedom and independence he had there was ample compensation for the episodic menial role he had to perform on his masters' return. Michael recalls that Joseph Dargan and Milo Flynn's attitude to him, their obvious disdain of him, their limited communication with him, gave him an empathy with the negro slaves in the Confederate States of America. He felt that he had been treated in Ireland the same way as black slaves were treated in America.

Dargan's biggest field wasn't mowed. He had a cow and Michael's job was to look after this, moving it around the field to ensure it could eat the sweetest grass. Michael, who had to milk the cow, had had no experience of cattle, or animals. He tried unsuccessfully to milk it not knowing that it was dried up, and painful for the poor cow. Michael never remembers the cow giving milk. Sometimes Joe Dargan brought milk home from Sligo. More usually Michael bought milk from the Rosses Point public house-cum-shop-cum-store. Ireland was markedly different from Britain in the number of these multi-purpose stores that operated in rural areas. Many also acted as taxi services, undertakers and auctioneers as well. A number of the owners obtained the nickname gombeen men[446] indicating the derision the poor felt for those businessmen who were excessively concerned with economic aggrandisement and usury. Such a person was satirised in Joseph Campbell's poem:

'THE GOMBEEN MAN
Behind a web of bottles, bales,
Tobacco, sugar, coffin nails
The gombeen like a spider sits,
Surfeited; and, for all his wits,
As meagre as the tally-board
On which his usuries are scored.
The mountain people come and go
For wool to weave or seed to sow,
White flour to bake a wedding cake,
Red spirits for a stranger's wake.
No man can call his soul his own
Who has the Devil's spoon on loan.
And so behind his web of bales,
Horse halters, barrels, pucan sails
The gombeen like a spider sits,
Surfeited; and for all his wits,
As poor as one who never knew
The treasure of the early dew'.[447]

A pleasant part of Michael's duties was shopping. He would stroll down to the all-purpose pub shop store in Rosses Point where Joe Dargan had an account. There he would chalk up to the account any food or cleaning materials he needed. This left him plenty of time and freedom to play on his own. When at the public house he would sometimes hear a dog going mad in the stables with distemper. Michael became adept at treating the dog, a medium size blue and white spaniel. The dog would be heard howling, racing round in circles, foaming at the mouth, banging its head off the wall as he approached the pub. To calm it he would either pour water into its ears or, if he could not safely do this without fear of being savaged, catch hold of the dog and dunk it in the rainwater barrel outside. On each of the handful of occasions he did this, the treatment calmed the dog.[448]

Joseph Dargan decided to sell his non-productive cow and told Michael to drive the beast into the Sligo market. There he was to give the beast over to the charge of a jobber, who would sell the cow for him. The jobber would settle up financially with Mr Dargan in person in Sligo. Michael was told the prearranged signal to give with his switch so that the jobber would know Michael and the cow.[449]

Michael had set out in the early morning dark but when light it soon became a very hot day. He had a switch to aid him drive the cow to Sligo. The cow was a placid beast but even so it frequently wandered off into the grass verges to eat. The roads were deserted and the journey in was peaceful until Sligo town. It took hours before the tired pair made the market in Sligo, each mile an Irish mile, and Michael handed the beast over to the jobber. He had to wait and mooch around all day as the jobber tried to offload the beast. Finding no gullible farmers in Sligo, nor philanthropists willing to house a dry old cow in its twilight years, the jobber gave back the cow to the care of Michael. It was at least company on the long road home. Undaunted, after a crash diet of more sweet grass, Mr Dargan felt the cow ready for market again. He instructed Michael to take the cow to market, hope triumphing over experience. The similar journey produced the same outcome, with boy and beast, unwanted alike, meandering wearily back to Rosses Point.

Michael took full advantage of the golf facilities at Rosses Point Golf Club and at Dargan's. The links golf course was one of the premier courses in Ireland. Michael used Dargan's set of golf clubs when his employer was working or otherwise guaranteed to be absent for a long period, which was most of the time. He would clean the clubs afterwards to avoid Mr Dargan finding out they had been used. Neither employer nor Milo Flynn ever saw him play or remarked to him that they knew what he had been up to.[450]

Michael caddied for Joe Dargan at Rosses Point Golf Club. The experience gave the boy a lifelong passion for the game. He felt that he had a natural bent for the game, indeed for any ball game. At first he was able to practise his swings in the large field next to the house, that Dargan rented. Rosses Point Golf Club was just across the road from the house and although he had no right to be on the course, he circumvented this by caddying and then playing with some of the other caddies. He remembered that: *They were all just Belters, hurley players; no technique in those days.*[451]

He also took advantage of his employer's absence to borrow, without permission, the air rifle and lead pellets. He would lie on the wall imagining himself as a dead eye shot. There were many sea birds feeding in the fields but he never managed to hit one.

Although he was the sole domestic worker at Dargan's a local, strongly built, Rosses Point man came in occasionally to carry out heavier or more skilled work in the house and grounds. He spoke naturally and easily to Michael, often telling him entertaining tales and stories as he worked. Michael was somewhat surprised at the man's natural warmth and affability, so different from how Dargan and Flynn related to him. The surprise was because of the accounts he had heard in Rosses Point village of this man. He was reported to have been expecting to be granted the tenancy of a County Council bungalow for his family, his name being next on the waiting list. When the bungalow was allocated to another family instead, he, a member of the IRA, and so with access to guns and explosives, blew up the newly built, empty, property.[452] Michael found it difficult to equate the friendly natural workmate with the supposedly explosive character he was reported to be. Other than this occasional workmate Michael was usually alone at Dargan's.

2.1.11. Visit of Collecting Sisters

One day he was most surprised to find two Sisters from Nazareth House at the door. They were out on the Quest begging for alms to keep the homes running. He invited them in and prepared a pot of tea for them. He cannot remember giving them any money, but would have done so had he had any. He has no recollection of ever having been paid when he was at Dargan's. He may have given the

Sisters food to take back with them but cannot remember this. Initially Michael had insisted that the visit of the Nazareth Sisters to Dargan's was entirely unconnected with his presence there. He had been certain that they did not even know where he lived. Several years later when I still expressed scepticism about his belief that their visit was coincidental he said: *Now that I think of it they must have been coming to check up on how I was doing. Dargan's house was in a big dip, well off the main road. It wasn't the sort of place you would see when passing. You would have to have a reason to visit to know where it was.*

There is a recording note in Nazareth House records that Michael could not understand or believe. It reads: *Visited Nazareth House- spent three days. Went back to Mr Dargan. Gave £3 towards outfit.*[453] This brief recording, written in fountain pen, forms part of a continuation sheet log book kept by the Sisters, detailing the barebones changes of placement of the former Homeboys, under the heading: *Address on leaving and subsequent Reports.* Michael's initial *absolute certainty* that he had never sought nor received any money from Sisters eventually led to him accepting that this had happened.

The contemporaneous Nazareth House records, though brief, stand as a corrective not only to Michael's recollections but also to the narrative he had constructed in his mind, i.e.: *Dargan's placement was entirely my own doing; the Sisters had no idea where I was; I made my own way in the world without any support.* One is then left to speculate. Did the Sisters detect that Michael was not well looked after, that he had no money? Did their visit mollify him, and open up the possibility of brief, restorative visit to Nazareth House? If so, when did this occur? It looks as if the shepherd dog Sisters had gone in search of their lost sheep at Rosses Point.

Shortly after this, without prior notice, Michael was informed by Mr Dargan that he would have to vacate his bedroom as this was needed for the new staff coming to work for him. These, a brother and sister, relatives of Dargan, would now be in charge of the household and Michael would have to move out. He was relocated to a loft room above one of the outhouses in the yard, accessed by an outside staircase. Bed and blankets were provided for him.[454] He had always felt that Dargan and Flynn had treated him as *a lower class of beast*; his exile to the stable room confirmed this low caste status.

2.1.12. Dismissed

The stable living quarters lasted but a few weeks. Michael was peremptorily dismissed without reason and without pay, after many months of unpaid work. Yet again he had to pack his Nazareth House cardboard suitcase and make his way back to Sligo. Immediately he set about finding a job and a bed for the night. He certainly had no intention of going back to face the scrutiny of the boys at Nazareth House after this third failure placement breakdown. *I felt that I had let the Sisters down, and also myself.*[455]

Michael does not recollect ever having been questioned or criticised by the Sisters when he had returned, tail between his legs, from Dublin or the farm, or on his recent three day stay there. Yet they knew of his reasons for returning. They seem to have handled sensitively Michael's bruised feelings and diminished confidence.

2.1.13. Fourth Placement: Hotel Work

Michael immediately found a placement at McGarrigle's Hotel, in Castle Street, Sligo. His limited knowledge of Sligo meant that he had never been in Castle Street previously. He cannot remember how he obtained the placement but was certain he had secured this himself, entirely without help from anyone at Nazareth House. He also believed that the Sisters had not known of his presence there for his entire stay there. Yet again this stands contradicted by the Sisters' recording: *Michael changed his place and is now with Mrs McGarrigale, (sic)Castle Street, Sligo, doing housework. Likes it very well and 'visits' here.*[456]

It is highly likely that he would not have been taken on unless he had a 'character'. None of his previous employers, McLoughlin, the farmer, or Dargan would have supplied this. It must have come from the Sisters. His placement and experience at McLoughlin's in Dublin must, however, have been a great help in obtaining the familiar hotel work.

Michael had not forgotten his dismissal from Dargan's. Still angry, he determined to fight his treatment and went to see a town centre solicitor. He wanted to recover the wages owed to him. An adult stranger in Sligo advised him to commence legal action against Dargan for recovery of money owed. Michael visited a solicitor who took details of Michael's case. After listening to his grievance the solicitor told him that he could not represent him because Mr Dargan was an existing client.

Michael's fourth venture into the world, yet again a half-way house, proved to be a successful placement. Mrs McGarrigle (he assumed her to be a widow as there was no Mr McGarrigle) ran a hotel mostly used by commercial travellers. Many of the guests were regular patrons, and it had a bar but only for the use of residents. Mrs McGarrigle handled Michael firmly, not afraid to correct him when he made a mistake, but with some degree of respect.

This unfamiliar recognition of his worth from an employer transformed his view of his work and his life. He gradually widened the range of tasks he performed, both he and his employer, recognising the progress he was making. The tasks were the usual menial hotel ones: fetching and carrying; cleaning; serving; kitchen work; and greeting arriving and departing guests. This latter role he had never been entrusted with at McLoughlin's in Dublin. He got to know some of the regular guests. His ability to talk to guests and his employer changed from 'only speak when spoken to' to being able to exchange a few sentences with adults. One regular guest, Hughes,[457] had particular dietary requirements because he was Jewish, and Michael was allowed to attend to these and cook special food for him. He made sufficient progress to be allowed to help Mrs McGarrigle in the kitchen. It would be too great a statement to state that he was happy: perhaps more importantly he felt settled, content and pleased with himself.

The hotel was in the centre of town, the premises giving out directly onto the street, so there was plenty of life, bustle and noise. An arched door to the side of the premises led to the back courtyard area and outhouses. Mrs McGarrigle had a small pet dog that Michael played with. When the dog was in season the neighbouring dogs tried to get into the yard area to mate with the bitch. Michael spent time driving them off. One particularly large, persistent and rather fierce dog would not be dissuaded by the buckets of water, kicks and abuse Michael directed towards it, constantly scratching and howling at the yard gate to be let in. *Right you blighter, we'll see how you like this* was Michael's thinking as he made a lasso from a very long piece of rope. Copying the cowboys he made a very large noose with the rope, and with this lasso he managed to capture the dog. Pulling it towards him he had to let go of the rope when the enraged dog made to savage him. The dog ran free off in to the town, rope trailing behind it, never to revisit the premises. Puffed with pride Michael was able to tell Mrs McGarrigle that he had saved her beloved pet dog from the 'Townie' mongrel.

Michael never felt that he knew Sligo when he was at Nazareth House, nor ever after, despite attending school there, sometimes wandering around the shops, having played up and down the streets in the Nazareth House Band and attending other events there. Despite now living in the hotel right in the heart of town, occasionally attending the cinema, going to Mass in the nearby cathedral, he still never felt that he got to know the place. Much of his time was of course spent at work, but he admits himself that he never made friends. Indeed he shunned contact with the Nazareth House boys he regularly saw in town, avoiding any attempt by them to greet him, never initiating contact with them: *I was a loner. I was made a loner at Nazareth House,* he recalls. Sligo, the whole of it not just the grounds of Nazareth House, represented to him 'Homeboy' status. His three failures of placement outside the Home he had attributed in no small measure to having been regarded as nothing by those who knew of his background. Henceforth no one would know his Homeboy past.[458]

Despite my attempts, using video, Internet and photographs to refresh his memory, 'walking him through' Sligo of old, Michael still cannot picture Sligo, or even get a mental map of the shape of it. Contemporaneous postcards of the cathedral elicited absolutely no recognition. Michael stated that his intention had been to: *bury the institution in my head.* He did accept that in some ways:

I was pleased that I had been one of theirs (i.e. the Sisters'), *but I didn't want to think of myself as a Homeboy: it's the opposite of what I wanted. I felt that when I was there I was under scrutiny all the time, and it's an awful experience, as opposed to growing up in a family.*[459]

Chapter 2.2: Looking in on his Family: Michael Porter

2.2.1. A Letter Arrives

Michael left Mrs McGarrigale (sic) and went to an uncle in Dublin.
That recording in the continuation log book at Nazareth House,
Sligo occurs after Michael's fourth placement, the one with Mrs
McGarrigle, had ended.[460]

Michael had been enjoying his work at Mrs McGarrigle's hotel and
was becoming increasingly settled. He felt that he was still learning
and his confidence was slowly building up after what he regarded
as three failed placements. He welcomed the incremental increase
in responsibility that he was given by Mrs. McGarrigle; yet he
never imagined that he would stay there permanently. His aim was
always to get out of Sligo: *I felt that I would always be seen as a
Homeboy until I got away from the nuns.*[461]

A number of guests, many of whom were commercial travellers,
stayed regularly at McGarrigle's and so had their post directed
there. One day Mrs McGarrigle, who managed the post, gave him a
letter that was addressed to him. He was rather alarmed as well as
shocked to see a handwritten letter with his name on the envelope.
Now aged 18 years old this was the first correspondence, either
personal or professional, that Michael had ever received. He took
the letter to his room and read it. The address of the letter writer
was Portrane, County Dublin. The letter writer, a Madge Healy,
née Porter, informed him that she was his aunt and invited Michael
to visit her and her husband at Portrane.[462]

Michael's first thoughts were: *How will I get there?* Then, *can I
afford it?* As he re-read the letter he then thought: *Oh, I've got an
aunt, then.* This entirely pragmatic, tunnel-vision response to the
emotional hand grenade of such a letter starkly illustrates how
Michael's care experiences had produced a cumulative deadening
effect on his natural feelings and thinking. He recollects that the
letter evinced no great curiosity about wider family in him; nor
lateral thinking about whether he had other family members. Nor

did he wonder where had she been all his life, why she had never visited him or whether she might have been able to care for him instead of him being in care. Nor did he ask himself the obvious questions: *Why had she never written before?* and *Why now?* or *What does she want?*

Michael's self-contained, unemotional response reveals his priorities and his functioning at that stage of his development. Physical survival and security, with food and accommodation provided in the same setting: that which he had experienced at Nazareth House was still what he sought; at least in his first years out of care. He was eminently practical, realising that he needed to take graduated steps towards his long-term goal of living fully independently. He knew he still needed the combined bed and board arrangements, and the company and adult supervision. His priorities were absolutely mirrored by Paddy Baker, Willie McGowan and Willie Walsh at the same stage of their lives. Willie McGowan told his daughters that his choice of placements was always determined by: *bed and board, bed and board.*[463]

The final obvious question that Michael had never asked himself about the letter was, *How did she know where I lived?* When initially discussing this with Michael he denied the possibility that the Sisters had been the source of this information to his aunt but could not explain how his aunt had found where he lived. That he had never before in 90 years on this earth wondered how his aunt Madge had traced him well illustrates the compartmentalised, incurious and taken-for-granted nature of his thinking. In initial discussions Michael was angrily adamant that he had found this placement at Mrs McGarrigle's: *entirely my own and the Sisters knew nothing about it and didn't know I was there.*[464]

This denial persisted despite my obtaining the contemporaneous records that had noted that: *Michael was at Mrs McGarrigle's, doing well, likes it there and still visits.*[465] His mind and recollections had entirely reshaped reality, completely eclipsing what had actually occurred. When I later explained to him that Mrs McGarrigle was well known to the Sisters, and was used by them as a half-way house, he accepted that this must have been the route by which his aunt found out his address. It had taken over three years of constant probing by me, with my overt expressions of doubt about his memory, before this miracle had occurred. I suggested to him that 'not a sparrow fell to earth in Sligo' (and probably much further afield) but that the Sisters knew of it.

Madge's letter made no mention of Michael having other relatives. He hesitated before replying to his aunt, unsure that he would be granted time off work or afford the fare to Dublin. Mrs McGarrigle readily granted one day's leave when he told her of his aunt's invitation to visit. As the letter only mentioned a visit, not stopping overnight, he did not ask for more, nor could he have afforded an overnight stay in a Dublin lodging house. Mrs. McGarrigle did not ask intrusive questions of Michael; she probably had no need to do so. I think it likely that she and the Sisters were exchanging intelligence about Michael's background and progress.

The striking feature of Michael's first 18 years of life had been passivity. Other people had arranged his life, had delivered, cared for and moved around the human parcel. But with Dargan's and McGarrigle's, and with the invitation from his aunt Madge, he was beginning to experience making a few decisions himself.

2.2.2. First Visit to a Family Member

The cost of finding the money for a return trip to Dublin was Michael's greatest concern. He also worried because he did not know how far Portrane was from Dublin, or how to get there. Sligo Rovers solved his problem. They had drawn 1-1 in the 1939 FAI cup final against Shelbourne Athletic at Dalymount Park in Dublin, in front of over 30,000 spectators, and the replay was scheduled at the same venue, ten days later. Michael joined one of the day-return cheap excursion trains organised for their large band of supporters, after informing Madge that he would visit.[466]

On Saturday, May 13th 1939,[467] Michael joined the excited Sligo Rovers supporters' train to Dublin, the pre-match banter among the crowd helping to mask his anxiety on the journey. On arrival in Dublin he then had to make enquiries about the bus journey to Portrane. On the bus there he began to panic: *I was so long on the*

223

bus I thought I had gone back to Sligo. He feared that he would miss the scheduled return train and lose his job, and therefore accommodation.[468]

Michael's main motive in the visit was curiosity: he wanted to see what a relative looked like and to find out as much information as possible, including where he originated from. On arrival at Madge Porter's seaside bungalow he was tightly strung. On his super best behaviour the meeting felt more like an interview for a job. He definitely sensed that he was being assessed. Questions were put to him, monosyllabic answers given. Madge's dribbles of pertinent family information, including that Michael's father, her brother, was still alive, produced no emotional or verbal response from him. Be good, listen, be polite, make a good impression, get through this ordeal without showing himself up, were his thoughts. He found the visit very stressful. Although Madge's husband, Pat Healy, was present Pat spoke even less than Michael.

The visit lasted barely an hour, and this included a meal and cup of tea. I suggested to Michael that the interview, must also have been an ordeal for Madge: trying to make conversation with such a closed-up, nervous young man, whose stilted, polite answers never allowed a conversation to develop. He had never previously considered this, so engrossed had he been in his own predicament. He had not warmed to his aunt and felt that there was a distance between them. Throughout the 'interview' with Madge he had in any case only been half listening, so preoccupied was he that he must not miss the excursion train back to Sligo.[469]

On the train home Michael did not think very much about the visit, relieved that his ordeal was over, keen to get back to Sligo. His mental and emotional responses followed his customary pattern: (as when the Sisters had mentioned 'family' or 'father' to him). He did not digest the information that he had a father; or wonder where he lived; or what he was like; or where he had been during all his years in care. He still did not know where in Ireland he had been born, or where Madge had originated from. He assumed she came from Portrane. Nor had he any questions about wider family or past. He returned to the noiseless tenor of his way[470], working with Mrs

McGarrigle. She did not probe him about the visit, for which he was grateful, sensing and respecting his desire for privacy.

Michael did not write to Madge to thank her for the hospitality, but rather concentrated his attention on the practical day to day tasks of his work at the hotel, untroubled by curiosity about his family.

2.2.3. Leaving Sligo: Summer 1939

Some weeks after the visit to his aunt Michael received an invitation from Madge to stay with her at Portrane and to leave Sligo altogether. Despite now being offered an opportunity to fulfil his long-term plan to escape Sligo, and what is more to join a family member, he hesitated. He felt settled and secure with Mrs McGarrigle. He knew his work and enjoyed it. He couldn't see himself doing this work forever but it suited him well for now. His other three placements before this had all failed badly: this was by far the best placement he had experienced. He did not want to let down Mrs McGarrigle, by giving in his notice because she had earned his respect. He decided to ask her advice on the matter. She gave her view that the opportunity to find a family should not be cast aside lightly, and the opportunity might never present itself again. His inclination had been to stay with her; had she in any way suggested this course of action he would have taken it.[471] He took her advice and wrote to his aunt Madge informing her that he would move to stay with her at Portrane.[472]

In May 1939, a few months short of his eighteenth birthday, against the grumbling background of rumours of another war in Europe, Michael left Sligo for good. The wider European crisis concerned him not a whit. His concerns were about what would happen to him: of the uncertainty ahead, after the period of calm, steady settlement he had experienced with Mrs McGarrigle; of what work he would next do; of whether he would get work; of whether, this time, his Dublin experience would prove better than the last. In short his focus was of, and for, himself. He had little money to draw from his work, as he earned only a few shillings per week on top of his bed and board. He had a single basic outfit of decent clothes in which to travel. The rest of his possessions fitted easily into the cardboard suitcase that he had been given by the Sisters when he had set out on his first placement in the world.

In late June 1939 Michael Porter took a single ticket for the train journey from Sligo to Dublin. His intention was to leave Sligo forever. He felt no strong ties or affiliations to the area, town or people. He believed that no one in Sligo would notice, let alone mourn, his departure. He felt a complete loner.

As the train pulled out, Sligo was fading as fast from his thoughts as from his sight. Engrossed in the uncertainty he felt as a result of his fateful decision to move home, he consciously decided to relegate his Homeboy status to the back of his mind. He would refuse to think about it. Each mile out of Sligo that the train travelled made less likely the chance of meeting anyone who could identify him as a Homeboy; or challenge the new identity as a past-less young man that he intended to forge.

Michael consciously decided that he would never broach the subject of his Homeboy past to Madge or to any other family member, even though they knew about this. Any new person that he met would never be told anything of his past care life. His first sixteen or so years of life would cease to exist. He had no conscious cover story yet to replace these blank years. Sufficient unto the moment was to avoid or head off any reference to early years. He felt that he had been pre-judged by the McLoughlins and Joe Dargan as a Homeboy, and that his failures there were as a result of the low view of him they had accordingly formed. He knew that he was as good as anyone else and would prove that he was, if only he were to be given an equal, unprejudiced chance. No-one would again have a pre-formed, low expectation of him.

Leaving Sligo was to be a permanent step to anonymity. He decided never to return there. He has never been back to Sligo since.

2.2.4. Gatekeeper to Family: Aunt Madge

The following paragraph shows Michael Porter's father's siblings[473]. The aunt that Michael moved in with in the June of

1939, Madge Healy, née Porter, was the third eldest of this Porter clan.

Mary (Molly): Born 1892, Married Tom ('Brown') Kelly
Laurence (Larry): Born 1893, Married Margaret Cowan
***Margaret Ann (Madge):** Born 1895, Married Pat Healy
Michael John: Born 1897, Died in childhood
Thomas Anthony: Born 1899, Married Ellen (Nellie) Whelan
***James (Jim):** Born 1902, Married Rose Ledwith
Michael Joseph: Born 1905, Married Margaret Murray
***Francis (Frank):** Born 1907, Married May McLoughlin
****John (Jack):** Born 1910, Married Bridgid Marmion
Josephine: Born 1912, Married Joseph Hannigan

* Lived in the Portrane, and Dublin area in 1939.
** Lived in London and Dublin in 1939.

Madge Porter had moved to the Dublin area from her home in Tynagh village, County Galway, to train as a mental (psychiatric) nurse at Portrane Asylum[474] where she met her husband, Patrick Healy, a fellow mental nurse. Both Madge and Pat Healy were very familiar with institutional life from their work at, what was then called, the Portrane Lunatic Asylum. The building of the Asylum, the largest building ever constructed in Ireland under British rule, had begun in 1896. Situated on a 500 acre peninsular site it housed between 1200 and 1600 inmates, several times larger than Hammersmith and Sligo Nazareth House Homes combined. In effect it was an enclosed, self-contained, partly self-supporting village, with farm, shops, hairdresser and laundry.[475] The Asylum was designed to provide more therapeutic and differentiated care for the various strands of mental illness than had previously been available.[476] Like the Nazareth Homes it was housed in large buildings, and far from the communities from which many of the patients came. Did Madge, when working there, think about her nephew and niece in institutional care in Sligo and Ballinasloe?

Madge and Pat Healy had no children. She had retired from work at Portrane when she married as was the custom then. She, the eldest of the siblings who lived in the Dublin area, became the matriarchal organiser of family gatherings at her beachside bungalow. On Sundays, the Porter clan reunited at Madge's seaside bungalow. Frank Porter and his brother, Jack, shared a flat in Blessington Street, in Dublin, when Jack returned from work as a carpenter in London. Another of Madge's brothers, Jim Porter, lived in staff accommodation in Portrane Asylum, where he was also a psychiatric nurse. So Michael gradually encountered these relatives in the summer months he spent living with his aunt.[477]

Family and indeed other historians will have already spotted the classic pattern of Irish, and indeed, chain migration here described: vanguard or pioneer settler (in this case, Madge Porter) moves; settles elsewhere; communicates with family; often helps arrange or fund their move; and then helps find them work nearby or with them. Irish migrants in particular seem to have needed to reconstitute the family and security networks that they had left behind them at home in their new abode. Paradoxically, in so doing, they often unintentionally depleted the very communities from which they had originated, making life there lonelier, less attractive and therefore more likely to perpetuate the migration outwards of the young, the more able, and the ambitious.[478]

Michael later came to believe that Madge had been responsible, together with the Parish Priest, Father Bowes, for pressing the case for him to be taken into care, probably because she would have been concerned at the hygiene standards at his father's home and the risk of tuberculosis to Michael and Sadie. He thought that her training as a nurse would have made her over-sensitive to the standards of care in his childhood home and that she consequently would have prevailed upon his rather weak and less assertive father to let the children go.[479] Whatever Madge's 'responsibility' was as gatekeeper to Michael's entry into care she was certainly the prime mover and portal of his re-entry into the Porter family. She wrote; she acted; she reconnected Michael with his family. A lost, peripheral, perhaps forgotten family member, Michael Porter, became part of childless Madge's, reconstructed migrant Galwagian family, in the Portrane Dublin area.

It seems likely that Madge's first contact with Michael was intended to assess, perhaps even to vet him. Firstly she would have wanted to observe how he had turned out. Was he clean, presentable and polite? What sort of a person was he? What did he look like? Who did he take after? Was he a Porter or a Cowan? As Madge had been in contact with the Sisters at Nazareth House to obtain Michael's address, she may already have received a report about him from them. She would also be able to evaluate *his* attitude to his lost family. Was he embittered, angry, aggressive? Did he blame them? Finally, and I think most powerful of all, was her desire to meet the young man she had last seen as a child, near a generation ago. To meet him, to welcome him, then to plan the reintroduction of him, in the fullness of time, to his father, and to his sister. To Madge's brief mention of his father's name Michael had made no response. Of his sister, Sadie, he was still unaware. Madge was, I think, 'spying out the lie of the land' for the rest of the family, with the long-term goal of reintegrating Michael into it. Tellingly it was she, not Larry, Michael's father, who made these efforts.

2.2.5. Sea-Side Summer Holiday:1939

Michael stayed with Madge and Pat Healy throughout the summer of 1939. Their double fronted, detached, galvanised-roofed, pebble-dashed bungalow lay at the very end of a long narrow boreen, barely a car width wide. With two bedrooms to the right of the hallway and two reception to the left, Michael had a bedroom to himself, and an expanse of dunes, sand and sea to walk, think and relax. There was only one other property, another bungalow amidst the huge stretch of dunes and strand beyond. There were very few public visitors to the area to disturb the tranquillity. The summer weather was glorious.

Because he was not yet working Michael felt he should help out around the house and in the grounds and garden. There were some odd golf clubs in the bungalow and later when working he bought some second hand ones and made up a mismatched set with these. Rosses point and Dargan's; Portrane and Madge's: little wonder that Michael has had a lifelong obsession with playing golf, with boyhood experiences on two fine Irish coastal golf courses to begin with. His irons had hickory shafts, the woods cane shafts, and he managed to buy a 'pencil' bag in which to house them. He practised golf by himself on the dunes next to Madge's for 5 to 6 hours a day as he had no other commitments.

Later, when working, he could occasionally afford a day visitor's fee to play at the nearby Donabate golf club. The facilities there, having been developed under British rule, including some of the other garrison games, notably hockey and tennis. The facility was a sports and social club where locals and Dubliners enjoyed themselves at their seaside clubhouse There was an old railway carriage and Michael would go in there for a cup of tea. Beyond Pat and Madge's land there was a fence and a field and a very large clubhouse used by *protestants* on holiday who played British games like hockey. The protestants were very friendly and would shout, 'Hello Frank' to him, mistaking him for his uncle.[480]

Michael employed himself drilling holes, cutting grass and erecting the tennis nets. On a large field adjacent to the Healy's bungalow he would cut a swathe of grass to make a clock shaped putting area, twelve feet in diameter. This had the numbers from one to twelve, with the clock marked out in a big circle with whitewash. He inserted a tin pot to the centre clock spindle hole he had dug. There he practised his putting incessantly.

Unlike Michael, his uncle Pat Healy was not a competitive golfer, being content to play out on the dunes. Michael, in contrast, was fiercely competitive and the challenge, skill, precision and mathematical accuracy and certainty of golf made this his perfect soul-compatible sport. Whether playing games in the garden, or on the golf course, Michael always strove to win, to beat others. Playing with others for fun never occurred to him, and would have seemed to him an unwanted, eccentric, legacy of British rule. He played to win, not entirely at all costs, but near enough. Cheating was absolutely out. Rules to him were *absolutely* important, and he felt that the rules, and somewhat complex code involved in golf, was the nearest thing to perfection he had encountered in this world.[481]

I had no problems being on my own, Michael remembers of his time outside in the summer at Portrane. Dargan's experience had taught him to be self-contained. He felt himself to be *very much of a loner, quite content with my own company.* Indeed the greater problem was when he was in company, especially with family members at Portrane, particularly in the summer of 1939 when he had not yet developed what was to prove a life time friendship with his Uncle Frank. With Madge he always felt stiff in her presence: *I didn't overuse her space.*[482] With Madge he had the minimum communication necessary.

When the rest of the family arrived Michael would say very little, content to observe and listen. He never spoke unless spoken to first; even then giving only the barest reply that civility would allow. His ears were, however, attuned donkey-like to the slightest mention of family or history, eagerly drinking in this information, trying to make sense of the past, to fill in his knowledge gaps of his family. Often he could not understand who or what was being referred to. Always he felt an outsider, that he wasn't a real family member, that he was a sham. He was sure that they could see through him: with their X ray eyes they could see through his over-eagerness to help, his excessive politeness, his near ingratiating efforts to be accepted as one of them, to his unworthy soul, to the Homeboy.

Pat Healy was one of a type not at all uncommon in Ireland then, softly spoken and a man of very few words. It was as if he believed that God had apportioned him a stock of only a few hundred words to last him the whole of his life. Once these were used up he would die. Consequently he rarely reached into his haversack for a word, or worse yet, a phrase. Parsimonious of speech though Pat was, he was positively garrulous compared with Michael, when the young man was in his family's presence, at least in those early years of unfamiliarity. With Madge for his lifelong partner Pat possibly felt that his several hundred words was an overly generous allotment, unlike his wife who acted as if she had been granted an inexhaustible supply of words, with directive to use them. She apparently strove valiantly both to fulfil her Maker's instructions to her, and to help her husband Pat keep his word stock, with no little success. Michael, as time elapsed, found that his relationships with his family members grew less stilted, more natural and more satisfying; with his uncles Frank and Tom especially; less so with Madge. Frank was not much older than Michael and so their relationship became more brother-to-brother-like than uncle to nephew.

In those early days, however, whenever Michael felt especially uncomfortable, he would take Pat Healy's greyhound dog for a walk. The greyhound, of championship stock, used to be run at the nearby track at Donabate. It never fulfilled its owner's hopes because of its habit of jumping the fence during the race and running the three or four miles straight home, reportedly at championship winning speed. Michael would drive the dog out of the hen run where it used to jump the wire fence to get at the chickens. Scolding the dog as it followed him around he talked more to it than he ever did to his family members at Portrane. It listened attentively, never disagreed, and trailed after him, a silent, comforting companion.

Chapter 2.3: First Forays Outside Nazareth: Willie McGowan

2.3.1. Leaving Nazareth

Willie McGowan left Nazareth House, Sligo on July 18th, 1937 at the age of 16 years, the day after finishing his Summerhill College education. [483] It does not appear that he passed, or even took, any examinations there, as later he was classified as having only reached 8th standard National Schooling level.[484] So, although Summerhill gave him an excellent classical education, including learning Latin and Greek, he was without any form of certificates with which to pursue a clerical or professional career, had he so sought either of these.

All four boys of the Quartet, as well as most of their contemporaries at Nazareth House, knew that they came from the hewers of wood and drawers of water class. Willie McGowan was now in some respects worse off than Michael Porter and Paddy Baker who had stayed at the National School. Michael knew, and Paddy found out, that like others of their social class and nationality at this period, there would be no feather-bedded, soft white 'hands of a priest' or solicitor existence for them; physical strength, native intelligence, ambition, perseverance and hard work would determine their futures to a large extent.

Willie's scholarship at 13 years of age to Summerhill College, had then prefigured such a different path for him; and one that carried certainty, security, prestige and cleanliness. Aspirations raised, to be so suddenly dashed, he must have felt deeply that he was a failure. Now he was in a cleft stick: raised standards and high aspirations negated by low qualifications to achieve these. He had what both Paddy and Michael dreamed of: family to go home to and a farm to inherit. Yet the latter work option seems not to have matched his raised ambitions.[485]

The departure of Willie from Sligo, so very different to that of Paddy, gives a feeling of the boy's character and demeanour, as noted by Paddy himself.

I also remember the morning you left Nazareth. It was early and we were all still in bed me being in St. Patrick's. I didn't know about your leaving. You were smartly dressed as you went from bed to bed shaking our hands in farewell. I was probably 12 years old at the time and that was the last time I saw you.[486]

The Sisters did not operate a prefect system at Nazareth House, one where older, senior, more responsible boys were given some degree of limited authority and guidance over younger peers. Given the skeleton staff and large number of boys this is somewhat surprising as prefects were an almost universal feature of residential facilities such as Public and Boarding Schools. As a result of what has subsequently emerged about the brutality and sexual exploitation of younger boys by some of these prefects this lack of the arrangement may not have such been a bad thing. Although there was no formal prefect or monitorial system at Nazareth House Michael Porter remembers the older lads generally being asked by the Sisters to help protect and see to younger ones in trouble or in tears.[487]

There is another aspect of the prefect system, more nebulous, but perhaps more important than the supervisory: the prefect acting as an exemplar to the other boys. Willie McGowan seems to have exuded this quality. As Paddy has earlier recalled of Willie: *I had a deep admiration towards you...You were always so cool and collected.*[488] One can imagine Willie, although not officially charged with such a role, quietly resolving disputes and stopping bullying of the more vulnerable lads, but also being followed and copied by impressionable peers.

Paddy's reference to not having known of Willie's departure in advance raises the whole issue of a leaving protocol. In the case of Paddy and Michael there does not seem to have been one, or at least one that involved the other boys. Common to all boys was the Sisters kitting out the leaver in a new suit and outfit and providing him with a new suitcase. There usually followed a meeting with Reverend Mother where the importance of prayers, Mass and the faith were impressed on the boy, then Sister Attracta saw to the final leaving arrangements.

Quietly touring all the dormitories in the early morn, even those of
the bed-wetters in St Patrick's; formal, courteous, dignified, shaking
each and every boy farewell. A glimpse of Willie's personality and
of what leaving must have meant to him. He was leaving the group
of boys with whom he had shared such a formative period of their
lives together; the last nine years shared with strangers, none with
his own siblings. Willie McGowan's ritual farewell of Nazareth
House conveys a miasma of sorrowing; it conveys the impression of
someone truly leaving their family, unlike with Michael, or possibly
Paddy. I am left with the paradoxical question this raises: why was
it that the only one among Paddy, Willie and Michael who had a
family (and indeed regular contact with his father) seems to have
been the very one who regarded the Sisters and fellow Homeboys
as a surrogate family? Indeed not only that, but a boy who chose as
his next step in life, to reject his father's wish for him to take over
the farm, instead opting, after a brief period with his father, to stay
with the Sisters of Nazareth, working for them at their Home in
Mallow, County Cork.

2.3.2. The Only Quartet Boy to Be Taken Home

Willie was one of only a quarter of all the boys at Nazareth House
whose family offered them a home, and in his case work also, after
they left school. His situation was unusual, however, because the
home-bound boys usually did so after their widowed father had
remarried,[489] and Willie's father had never done so. Loss of mother
seems to have been the near universal reason for care admission at
Nazareth House. Michael and Paddy, and probably most of the
other three quarters of boys whose families did not offer to reclaim
them, could not understand Willie rejecting the offer of farm and
home with his father. Michael and Paddy would have given
anything for such an offer. Paddy had been puzzled at Willie's
choice:

*I left Nazareth in 1938 just one year after you. I can't however
understand why you left your father's small holding after you had
been only a short time there. Surely it was your Dad's plan that
you take over the farm and after all, that was the reason for taking
you out of Nazareth. Most fathers wish that their sons follow in*

235

their footsteps and I expect that you didn't wish to do so. You were old enough to make your own decision.[490]

But was he? He was nowhere near the 21 years that was then the age of majority in Ireland. In the 1930's a parent's wish was usually much more than that; it was law, it was enacted in practice. The desire to go, and the drive to see this through, must have come from Willie himself. But what lay behind his choice of Mallow where he worked in farming the career he had rejected with his father?

Willie had both a home and family to return to and work available when he left Nazareth House. Willie had always known about his family and had maintained contact with some members of it, including his father; and his father wanted his eldest son to work with him and eventually to take over the running of the family farm. The fragmentation of Willie's family after the death of his mother has been outlined earlier in Chapter 1.2. His eldest sister, May, had remained in the home area, in Skreen, County Sligo, reared by her maternal, Feeney, grandmother. She also, when older, helped keep house for her widowed father. Willie's two younger sisters, Margaret and Annie Elizabeth (Lily) were still in out-of-home placements. Eugene Michael, two years younger than Willie, had been reared by the Gerraghty family, in nearby Easkey. The baby boy, Thomas, whose birth had led to the death of his mother from septicaemia, was still in St. Michael's Home in Dublin.[491]

2.3.3. Why Not a Priest?

Reflecting on Willie's later career in life, I was surprised that he never became a priest, a career choice a number of his contemporaries and friends had made: he had the educational ability, the faith grounding and loyalty; he had been an altar server; he was a pious boy; he both liked and respected the Sisters and he would have wanted to please them; and there could be few things more likely to please many of them than one of their old boys becoming a priest. He had learned Latin but also Greek at Summerhill College, the acquisition of Greek having been restricted to those destined for the priesthood. He later confirmed to his wife that he had been destined for the priesthood, withdrawing from this ambition in his final year at Summerhill.[492] This would have ended any further chance of education at College as any external funding would have been withdrawn from those not progressing to priesthood. Nor could or would his father have kept him on at Summerhill as he could not have afforded it and would have needed his son's labour on the land. It is not entirely clear whether Willie's leaving of Summerhill related to a change in his desire to be a priest, or the College authorities making that decision, or a combination of both factors.

The deterrent impact of Summerhill College may have been one factor in steering Willie's career path away from priesthood. As outlined earlier Father Edward Flanagan, the founder of *Boy's Town* Homes in the United States, another Summerhill alumnus, had described his distaste for the prevailing harsh, cold and excessively fault-finding regime at Summerhill College.[493] Willie shared these feelings and detailed his dislike of life at Summerhill College in his letters to Paddy Baker.[494]

Michael Porter, despite selective and self-dominated recollections, had been struck by the marked deterioration in Willie's demeanour when he had transferred from Quay Street School to Summerhill College. Willie's unhappiness had been so evident that it showed in his bowed physical posture.[495] Summerhill College, the diocesan seminary, had been staffed by clergy. Their regime would seem to have acted as a disincentive to Willie to emulate them and become a priest. Father Flanagan's description of his teachers actively seeking to find fault would suggest a dual or triple tally stick culture at Summerhill then: the, metaphorical, stick being used to trip up the intending ordinand, to score his transgressions on it, and to retain it as a visible reminder of his faults and failings. I think one factor suggests that the decision was made by Willie to leave, to the displeasure of the clergy there: he did not take (or was prevented from taking?) his leaving examinations.

2.3.4. Rejecting the Family Farm Career

Somewhere, in the nine years spent largely at Nazareth House, when Willie continued to go home on occasions overnight at weekend and to spend summer holidays working the farm with his father, haymaking especially, he had decided that he would not return home permanently to live and work the family holding. He had planned his career in the Quartet playing years; priesthood and a secure and respected career in the Church. Suddenly all was changed with no time to plan an alternative. He was taken home to work the farm with his father in July 1937,[496] having no other alternative available to him; it seems he was, at best, ambivalent about making his life on the farm there permanent.

Between July and December 1937 Willie McGowan sought to find something else to do for the rest of his life rather than live and work on his father's small 10 acre farm. The farm also had the usual share turbary rights that enabled him to cut from the bogs his needed share of peat for heating and cooking.[497] The farm was now owned outright on long mortgage by Michael McGowan, Willie's father. This, like the land acquisition for Michael Porter's family, had resulted from the British Government having bought out most of the largest landholders, reorganising, dividing and redistributing the resultant holdings to the occupying peasant proprietors.[498]

2.3.5. Inheritance and Family

Although Willie was the oldest son, and second eldest child, he had no automatic right to inherit. Primogeniture, the right of the first born to inherit did not apply in law in Ireland; nor did the male have precedence over females in inheritance rights (though custom did strongly favour the male inheriting). In consequence, unlike in the United Kingdom where male primogeniture still applied, Willie's father could gift the land to whomsoever he wished, and to female as well as male. The only legal restriction on this, in practice difficult to enforce, had resulted from the various Land Acts that had turned small tenant into proprietor of their holding: the Acts forbade sub-division.

The practice of sub-division of holdings amongst the children of a single family had in any case withered throughout the nineteenth century in Ireland. The period before the Great Famine (there had been many before and many afterwards, not quite so extreme) had seen extensive sub-division of holdings especially in the west. Prior to the 1840's the then tenant farmer, in an attempt to provide for all his children and keep his clann living close by, might subdivide repeatedly. Some resultant holdings were only an acre or less, the prolific and healthy potato enabling the poor to eke out a subsistence living.

The move away from partible (divisible) to impartible land holdings had rapidly increased after the 1840's famines, the traumatic psychological effects of the Great Famines leading to many household heads reducing the number of dependents on each leased holding to mitigate any future famine harm. The normal outcome of impartible inheritance was a stem family, one in which parents, children, and inheriting son and family, lived together, with the non-inheriting siblings often moving out when old enough and when the inheriting son brought his new bride in to the household.[499] The choice of a sole child to inherit and the system of impartible inheritance had both individual and social consequences. There was a move away from an extended family and clann system, where multiple siblings and their families lived on small, clustered, adjacent holdings, with high population density and intense social interaction and support.

The replacement system, where one child alone inherited the land, meant, in remote, economically undeveloped Ireland, migration or emigration as the destiny for most of the remaining siblings of the inheriting child (or marrying into another farm family for a girl with a dowry). The resulting declining or smaller growing population meant a greater chance of social isolation and depression in the area. The consequent dissatisfaction with life there made more likely that the young, energetic, vibrant and ambitious, and critically those of breeding age, especially women, would migrate, further accelerating the tendency to rural decline.

Michael McGowan's choice of sole inheritor from among his six surviving children involved, therefore, as great, possibly even more, significance for the five who would not inherit.

Willie was the one Michael decided to be the chosen inheritor of the farm, not May, the eldest child.[500] This was despite May, who had been reared in her nearby maternal grandparents' farm having increasingly helped cook and clean for her widowed father as she got older. Although females could inherit, the tendency to leave farm to a male heir (by no means always the eldest) was still very strong in traditional Ireland, where custom, expectation, and example of forebears still exercised a powerful hold.

2.3.6. Reasons for Refusing Farm Life

It was far from uncommon for the eldest male to forego the chance of the family farm. Waiting to inherit could be a long one, with the 'boy' in his fifties or sixties before the formal transfer occurred. Until then the prospective inheritor was subordinate to father still, in the household and in the farm work, dependent too on father for his pocket money. Rural poverty, loneliness and depression, the lack of suitable or sufficient females to court and marry, the tendency to celibacy in Irish society, were some of the factors pushing an inheritor out of Ireland.

The enticing pull of life abroad, of its bright lights, cash income, freedom from parental control, looser social mores, and absence of restrictive clerical sanctioning of courting and love, were some of the factors pulling him away. These inducements were often put before the boy by his emigrant siblings and peers abroad; these earlier emigrants who, on visits home or in their remittance letters, seeking the companionship and comfort of their loved ones at home, painted ever more dazzling pictures to entice him to emigrate.[501]

A critical factor in the decision to migrate was previous experience of life elsewhere, either at home in Ireland or in Britain. When so many of the young of both genders from the west of Ireland had experience of seasonal migration, working in England and Scotland in farm work, this greatly increased their tendency to repeat the experience and make the stay abroad a fixed one.

This experience of life elsewhere would seem to be an important factor in Willie McGowan's apparent dissatisfaction with life in rural Sligo on his father's farm. He was very familiar with his home and with farm work, having come home regularly at weekends and working throughout the summer on harvest work. The farm, alone with his widowed father, must have seemed lonely and rather unsophisticated compared with life at Nazareth House, and with Sligo. Like Paddy Baker and Michael Porter found out, on their Situation placements, life on remote Irish farms could be monotonous and lacking in stimulation to those not used to it, especially perhaps to adolescents. Material circumstances were very different from Nazareth House and Sligo: no electric light, no pavements, no central heating, no running water and no toilets or bathing facilities.[502] There were no lights of town, noise of populace, bustle of fellow Homeboy life or even many people of his own age. The long dark winter ahead of him after Samhain, his life in a cabin with an old widowed father, must have seemed unattractive. Willie, accordingly, made efforts to move out of the farm. A common enough situation: experience of life and opportunities elsewhere making the native dissatisfied with his former home and life there.

2.3.7. A Father's Predicament

Common too, the predicament of Michael McGowan. Rather like Laurence Porter he was a small man, rather quiet, who had liked both a drink in the local shebeen and equally the companionship that this afforded him, especially in the dark winter nights.[503] Now nine years a widower, 47 years old, his six surviving children scattered, what hopes he must have invested in his eldest son, and second child, Willie. Michael McGowan might well have experienced mixed feelings when it seemed that Willie's career at Summerhill might lead on to priesthood: the pride that such an honour would be visited on his poor family; the joy that Willie's dead mother had begotten a priest; but regret too that his plans for himself, and the farm succession, would not now be realised. Now the path to that dream had been reawakened and Willie was back home.

The customary path would have been for father and son to work the farm together until eventually a settlement would be made with another farmer's daughter who would become Willie's wife. The son would now take over the land and Michael would live out his last days cared for by his son and son's family. This, the traditional insurance model of care in old age: the first welfare state: the family.

Yet he would sense the distance between father and son. Not, I think, primarily because of Willie having been 'let go' into care; rather, more because of the nature of the experiences that he had gained in Sligo. Michael would have been impressed by Summerhill College's reputation, its huge, august buildings. It would have intimidated and bemused him too. It was beyond his comprehension and his experience. He would have been threatened, too, by his son's learning and demeanour. He would see, indeed sense, how different Willie had become. Willie who seemed so comfortable with the prosperous, professional, protestant Shaws who had been so good to him and who were still so significant in his life.

Michael McGowan would never have heard of the word alienation. I think, however, that he would have fully understood its meaning as a result of sensing and observing Willie's gradual but persistent loosening of affiliation to family farm, and to his father's hopes and plans and Willie's unwillingness to make it his life's work. Willie had the fierce elemental adherence to the land shared by most rural Irish. He was emotionally attached to the two-roomed thatched cabin where his mother had died. He ever came back to his home, helping at harvest and turf lifting time, and visiting his father.

2.3.8. Letting Go Again

A month after leaving Nazareth House Willie wrote to Reverend Mother in Sligo thanking her and the Sisters for their care of him. He seems also to have visited Nazareth House, Sligo, transported by Bertie Shaw, and he expressed his hopes of finding a nice work place. So after such a short period at home he was reconsidering his future there.[504] He stayed at Nazareth House over the Christmas period to join in the celebrations and meet again his fellow Homeboys, Josie Cummings and the Sisters. Realising his unsettled, unhappy, unfulfilled situation, the Sisters made arrangements for him to obtain a position working on their large farm enterprise, attached to their home for the elderly, in Mallow, County Cork.

Michael McGowan, for a second time, had 'let go' his eldest son. Unlike the first occasion he was acceding to his son's wishes, letting go the caged linnet. Michael McGowan could quite easily have blocked Willie's move to Mallow. The Sisters would never have sanctioned the placement without Michael McGowan's agreement to it. It must have hurt him deeply; it had obliterated his future life plans and security; now old age, alone, in an isolated cabin, was his foreshadowed lot.

Michael McGowan still willed the land and home to Willie, May inheriting the maternal Feeney home and farm. His actions seem to me those of a courageous, selfless and loving father: less because he still willed the holding to his eldest son; more, much more, for letting his son take flight, and with his father's benediction. Without the latter I cannot believe that faithful Willie would have, could have, left home.

2.3.9. Return to the Sisters

Willie McGowan worked at Nazareth House, Mallow for several years. Sister Anthony Joseph, a nun then in her sixties, was the Sister in overall charge of Willie in his farm work. He lived on site, living in farm workers' (Yardmen) quarters. He was one of 5 former Sligo Nazareth boys working at Mallow and there were other ex-Nazareth House boys there too, especially from Derry.[505] The recruitment to Mallow of Situation boys from the rest of Ireland, often on their first work placement after leaving care and school, resulted from the lack of a Children's Home on site in Mallow.[506] Paddy Baker's brother, James, who had first worked in the laundry of Nazareth House, Sligo, after leaving school, and was five years older than Willie, worked there with Willie for some years.[507] So the third member of the Quartet, Willie McGowan, had much more contact with James Baker, the brother that Paddy vainly searched for, than Paddy ever had; not only in the duration of this but also, it seems, in the quality of this contacts. Willie formed a relationship with James Baker that Paddy never managed to do.

Willie settled in well at Mallow, loved the work, the company of boys of his own age and background, and got on famously with Sister Anthony Joseph. Willie wrote often to Sister Attracta and to

Reverend Mother at Nazareth House in Sligo, telling them of his happiness in his new situation. He was able to visit the small town of Mallow regularly with his young peers, and they went on holiday together to Killarney.[508] He always visited Nazareth House when on leave in Sligo and had a stay there in June 1939, during his two week's holiday at home.[509] The looming war, just two months off, was to provide an opportunity for Willie's change of career.

Chapter 2.4: First Forays Outside Nazareth: Willie Walsh

2.4.1. First Placements

Willie Walsh, like Willie McGowan, had received a secondary education at Summerhill College in Sligo. His other circumstances when the time came for him to leave care were, however, much more like those of Michael Porter and Paddy Baker: distinctly unfavourable.

Willie's entry to care resulted in cessation of all contact with his mother: he was effectively an orphan; and a loner, like Michael Porter. With no family contact or support behind him Willie was dependent on the Sisters finding work and accommodation for him in a 'Situation' placement. The Situation term suggests the placing of these Situation boys with a family or small business where they would have some support and supervision as well as living-in with their employer. As many working class school leavers, especially in the west of Ireland, were competing for these placements, what often determined the outcome was personal knowledge and connections.

One of the Sligo Nazareth Sisters hailed from the coastal resort of Bundoran in the neighbouring County of Donegal where her father owned a snuff mill. When Willie left school in July 1937 aged 16 years 9 months[510] the Sisters used their contact network to find him seasonal work at the Imperial Hotel, in Bundoran where he worked as a messenger boy. There seems to have been continuing interest in and oversight of the boys' welfare (as Mother General at Hammersmith had stated in 1889). Miss Flanagan, manageress of the Imperial, wrote to the Sligo Sisters expressing her satisfaction with Willie while he also wrote to inform the Sisters that he was enjoying his placement.[511]

2.4.2. The Pull of Nazareth House and of Sligo

In January 1938 Willie returned to Nazareth House due to the seasonal nature of coastal hotel work and the post-Christmas lull in trade. Nazareth House acted as his home (family substitute) base. In June he returned to the Imperial Hotel working there until the season ended in November. Missing Sligo he then obtained work there at Sheridan's Hotel, reporting to the Sisters his happiness at being back in Sligo. In May 1939 Willie Walsh immediately replaced Michael Porter at Mrs McGarrigle's Hotel in Sligo when Michael left to go to his aunt's in Dublin.[512]

Willie, like Michael before him, settled in well with Mrs McGarrigle, remaining there for over two years. This was longer than his previous three placements combined. He visited Nazareth House regularly including attending Nazareth House for midnight Mass and enjoying the Christmastide celebrations with his fellow Situation boys, as well as recreational activities at Father Barry's recreation hall.

A picture emerges of Willie Walsh gravitating to the familiarity, comfort and security of Nazareth House and Sligo; the polar opposite of Michael Porter's self-repulsion from Nazareth House and from Sligo.

Chapter 2.5: First Forays Outside Nazareth: Paddy Baker

2.5.1. Memory, Motivation and Confusion

Paddy Baker's flight from Nazareth House in fear of Mahon's brutality had lacked any planning. His accounts of his subsequent work placements are, unsurprisingly, somewhat confused, contradictory, misperceived or even actually wrong. This makes it difficult to establish the chronological sequence of his various moves. [513]

Although there is a definite element of 'Little Orphan Annie' in some of Paddy's 'escape from Nazareth' narrative and the other accounts of his early life (something that both Michael and Willie McGowan felt about Paddy's accounts),[514] I think that his central narrative is substantially true, even if it is sometimes embellished and over dramatised, and given to hyperbole. Like Michael Porter, he was trying to recollect what had happened some sixty years previously, without documentary records to assist him, and so it is hardly surprising that he may have been confused or mistaken on some matters, or mixed up the sequence of his early work situations.

2.5.2. Making Sense of Accounts: Memory and Reality

Paddy made his way to Carrowkeel, in County Sligo, some twenty miles journey, the trip lasting several days, with Paddy sleeping rough. He eventually found a bed with a Mrs Donagher on her small farm, with thatched house. Paddy reports that the Sisters sent out one of the Yardmen, Michael Durkin, in the donkey cart to bring Paddy back to Nazareth House. Paddy reported that Mrs Annie Donagher sent the Yardman back empty handed.[515]

Paddy believed that Mrs Donagher had prevented him being returned to Nazareth House, in effect defying the Sisters and indeed the Gardai. This is most unlikely. Mrs Donagher knew Michael Durkin.[516] She had been used by the Sisters previously for a Situation placement for at least one Nazareth House boy, Paddy

McLoughlin.[517] Had the Sisters insisted that Paddy, an absconder and under-age child with no parent available to care for him, returned to Nazareth House, the Guards would have brought him back.

A much more probable explanation was that the Sisters were relieved that Paddy had been found safe and well and that they decided to ratify his desire to stay and work there, under the supervision of one of their Situation families. They sent out the Yardman again after three weeks, presumably to check that Paddy was settled. That he was in a Catholic family would have quelled fears about him being enticed to 'the other side'. It seems rather fortuitous that of all the places to choose Paddy happened to land in a Nazareth House Situation family in a remote farm far from Sligo.

I have made an attempt at sequencing Paddy's placements viz:

1. Working on the Donaghers small dairy farm at Carrowkeel and delivering milk for them in Sligo town. (Although he had gone there after absconding, the farm was used by Nazareth House to place boys there after leaving school).

2. Working for a Bertie Hunter, a protestant farmer, on the farm adjacent to the Donaghers.

3. Working on a Nazareth House Situation farm near Ballina in County Mayo. This was similar to the first farm, Michael Porter, briefly worked at.[518]

4. Working for another Hunter family, relatives of Bertie Hunter, again in farm work, in Cairns, County Sligo.

2.5.3. Annie Donagher's Farm

When Paddy absconded from Nazareth House to live and work at the Donaghers this was the first time he had lived outside Nazareth House since the age of two years. He seems to have been fortunate with his placement, which was of course one that included bed and board. He records being paid a shilling a week and found the work he was expected to do there easy. He was treated well by the Donaghers, and developed a great affection for Annie Donagher. The Donagher farm family: *worked at their leisure and never expected me to do otherwise.*[519] Paddy slept in the dairy annexe on a straw bed where the milk was left to cool. The dairy element of the farm was the mainstay of the family's cash income.

Michael, Willie McGowan and Paddy had experience of farm work after leaving Nazareth House. The term farm conveys a misleading image to non-Irish readers to whom the term 'farm' suggests a picture of hundreds or even thousands of acres, and occupied by generally affluent owners who use hired labour and machinery to do the work. The Irish farm, especially in the west of Ireland, was small in acreage, family occupied and worked, and with generally poor land.[520] The farms lacked machinery: family labour and beasts provided the labour power to work the farm.

Farms in Ireland of less than 30 acres, were classed as small; from 30 to 100 acres as medium; and those over 100 acres as large. In 1841, before the Famine, 93% of the 685,309 land holdings in Ireland had been smaller than 30 acres in size[521]. Even as late as 1901, 66% remained less than 30 acres, and by 1960 half of the farms in the Republic of Ireland were classified as small and 52 % of those in Northern Ireland. Much of the farming was subsistence living, with seasonal migration work in England or Scotland, or remittances from emigrant family members abroad, helping keep the family at home in Ireland financially afloat.

A notable feature of Irish farming was the great degree of pastoral farming and the lesser degree of tillage. This shift from growing crops to 'ranching' had markedly accelerated after the great famines of the 1840's and later 1870's. Freeman described Irish farming as: 'a mixed economy in which most of the farmers have a small arable acreage but a considerable area of pasture and meadow, and depend chiefly for their living on some form of livestock, with occasional cash crops'.[522] The arable element of the farm often went to feed the family or the cattle.

Such were the 'farms' where not three of the Quartet worked but also many other poor ex Homeboys or girls, or other landless rural poor, who were usually classified in the various censuses as: in Ireland, 'farm servant' but in England or Scotland as 'hinds'. The farms lacked electricity or piped water. Oil lamps or even rush lights[523] were used, supplemented by the light from the peat fire at night, and water was drawn from spring well, stream or, in the case of the bigger, more affluent farmers who could roof their premises with corrugated iron, from roof run off into rain water barrels. Fetching and carrying water for humans and cattle was a constant chore, and one that partly induced Paddy to change placements.

The farmhouse in the west was often single story with a thatched, slated or corrugated iron roof: the Donaghers was thatched. A central all purpose kitchen, with one or two bedrooms off either side, with centrally situated huge fireplace on one side wall, was a common arrangement of such 'cabins'.[524] In the fireplace a cast iron crane, on which the cast iron cooking implements were hung, was hinged to enable the cooking equipment to be swung in and out of the flames. Potatoes in their skins were boiled in a large cast iron pot, often cabbage also, with meat or fish available or not to accompany this, depending on the class of the family. Prodigious quantities of potatoes were eaten, some estimates citing an adult male manual worker consuming up to 14 lbs of potatoes per day. Butter was made by the housewife, and buttermilk drunk with the heavily salted potatoes and cabbage. Bread and boxty (poor house bread) were also home baked. Apart from tea, sugar, salt and flour, most of the food consumed was produced on the farm.

This family-member-powered and labour intensive mode of living enabled families to subsist on very little cash income. Where a pig was kept, as was often the case, this gave rise to its description as: 'the gintleman who pays the rent', because the sale of the pig was put to such purpose. Paddy, Michael and their ilk were the 'human machinery' drafted in to work the farms. As Paddy wrote of the small farms on which he worked lifting potatoes: *A farmer in those days could not afford machines for doing such work. Such commodities were a privilege for the rich which were few in number.*[525]

2.5.4. Orphanage Labour

It was common for Orphanages and Children's Homes to supply children to farms such as the Donagher's to supplement the family labour, as an 83 year old bachelor farmer from County Cork recalled:

'At about the time that I was going to school my mother got two nice little girls from the Protestant Orphan Society. She had asked the local clergyman to get them for her and they were about three of four years with us....They were about the same age as me and they did all the work for us. One of them would bring up messages from Cappaghglass, and the other little girl would bring in the water, and she would milk the cows and feed the cows for us, and she would feed the pigs. These two girls used to walk with us every day to school, and they were great company. But when they were sixteen you had to pay them, and my mother let them go'.[526]

In contrast to this example was the type of placement common in England from the reign of Elizabeth 1 until the Poor Law Amendment Act, 1834. During the Napoleonic Wars one of my forebears in England, a yeoman farmer, had apprenticed to him an 8 year old poor boy of the Parish. The Churchwardens and Overseers of the Poor of the Parish, with the consent of the Justices of the Peace, apprenticed the boy to the farmer, with properly signed indenture. The indenture, required the farmer to keep the boy until he reached the Age of Majority and to instruct him

in the Business or Occupation of Husbandman... and allow unto the said Apprentice meet, competent, and sufficient, Meat, Drink, Apparel, Lodging, Washing, and other Things necessary, and fit for an Apprentice.

The Parish benefitted from the arrangement by being relieved of the long-term upkeep of the orphan boy. For the orphan he got the usual essential 'bed and board' that the Nazareth Homeboys 'opted' for after leaving care, but also training as a husbandman (farmer), thereby acquiring an occupational skill for life. What is more the placement of the young boy was with a family. A contrast with the non-family placement of the Quartet Homeboys.[527] Chronological advancement does not always produce improved social arrangements.

2.5.5. Sisters on the Quest

The Donaghers sold milk from their farm in Sligo town. After a few months working with them Paddy was taken by Mr Donagher to learn the milk round, committing the houses on the round first to notebook, then to memory. When out one day he met the Sisters out begging, on the Quest, in their usual pair. Paddy made the telling point: *You never, ever saw a nun on her own in Ireland in those days. They were always in pairs, and there were lots of them about. They seemed to be everywhere, and you would even find them out begging in the middle of nowhere.*[528]

The reason for the nuns always being in pairs in the inter-war and immediate post-war period was the then severity of the restrictions on the Sisters' movements, and lives in general. In the days before the Second Vatican Council in the mid 1960's the Sisters were never allowed out alone. They always had to be chaperoned by another Sister, even when travelling long distances or abroad: even when going home on holiday.[529] When Paddy encountered the pair from Nazareth House he gave the Sisters a shilling:

They recognised me immediately and showed me no ill feeling and enquired about my health. We parted on good terms for I knew it was their duty to report me to the Rev. Mother. Actually the shilling was given in the form of a bribe in order that the hounds would no longer follow my tail (sic). It would be disastrous for me if they reported me to the police.[530]

No report was made and Paddy continued working at Donaghers and began to re-visit Nazareth House where he found that: *Attracta showed no ill feelings towards me for having absconded in the darkness.*[531]

2.5.6. Dressed for Mass

Once the milk round had been committed to memory, and Paddy no longer feared 'recapture' by the sisters, he was trusted by the Donaghers with delivering the milk in Sligo town. The problem was that he had no clothes other than the shorts and shirt that he had been wearing when he had absconded, had no shoes and was not earning sufficient to buy a coat. He improvised:

Whilst in Donaghers I stole an old coat from the donkey's back...washed it in a stream. Donaghers made no protest as they saw me wearing the garment but burst out laughing...there were no buttons on the article so Mr Donagher made a rope out of straw and tied it round my waist.....The coat almost reached the ground and my arms were well hidden half way up the sleeves[532].

Barefoot, attired in shorts, shirt, and capacious overcoat held together with sugawn rope belt, but well protected from rain, Paddy was able to deliver milk to Sligo:

With this form of clothing I delivered the milk to the customers in Sligo and every Sunday after delivery I tied the donkey to a telegraph pole outside the cathedral and....stood outside the door to hear Mass. ..... The great thing is that despite all the hardships I had to endure, they were the happiest days of my life. I would not have changed them for all the money on earth.[533]

2.5.7. First Hunter Farm Placement

Michael Porter and Paddy Baker were effectively orphans in their first Situation placements after Nazareth House. As such they responded to a little kindness and attention, especially from a mother substitute. In Paddy's case Annie Donagher became someone to whom he remained grateful and devoted all his life. His poor material circumstances were immaterial compared with his craving for some warmth and kindness.

As with the sixpence the devil tempted Paddy again; again his adversary knew the boy's weak spot; again it was money. A farmer, in a holding adjacent to the Donaghers, had watched Paddy working for his neighbour, obviously impressed with the lad's work; conscious too perhaps by how little he cost to employ. This farmer, a Bertie Hunter, a protestant, had sacked his farm servant and was short of labour. His oldest son was still at school and not yet able to help his father during the week. Bertie Hunter approached Paddy when the boy was doing the job he least liked for the Donaghers: drawing water from a well in Hunter's field, during a prolonged spell of dry weather. The offer of an extra two 'sixpences' a week in wages proved irresistible to the boy and *I sneaked away in the night and made my way to Hunters.*[534]

Paddy was put to sleep in a wooden settle bed in the corner alcove next the ever burning turf fire, while the Hunters and their elderly parents slept upstairs. His bed was cushioned by two straw-filled potato sacks, topped by two, not very clean, grey blankets. The fleas welcomed the newcomer warmly, even penetrating his mouth and nostrils: *I realised it was pointless of me complaining and anyway, one was thankful for a job, food and shelter in those days. I now regretted leaving the Donaghers. I shed many tears each night as I lay there with the fleas and my thoughts went back to Nazareth and the clean beds.*[535]

Paddy performed the full range of farm tasks when working for the Hunters including helping hand milk the 14-16 cows, aided by the rest of the family, who included their children, two girls and three boys, the eldest boy not quite ready to leave school. The bed straw was replaced, temporarily resolving the flea problem, which soon returned. Having mentioned that he used to help with the laundry at Nazareth House Paddy was put to do the family's weekly laundry one day a week in the outside yard. He began to complain about the fleas and as Hunter's son had now left school Paddy was effectively dismissed but he was found another place with a relative of Bertie Hunter, nearby in Cairns.

2.5.8. Farm Placement Near Ballina

Paddy's third half-way house placement was again as a farm hand at a Situation[536] placement organised by Nazareth House. As he reported that unlike Willie McGowan he had, not being given the opportunity to say farewell to his fellow Homeboys this suggests that he had returned to Nazareth House in between placements but entirely forgotten this.[537] Attracta got him to bid farewell to the Yardmen and he was collected by the farmer for whom he was to work, looking back to the boys lined up in the playground as he walked down the drive. He and the farmer then took the bus for Ballina in County Mayo, near where the farm was located.[538]

The farmer and his elderly mother lived alone in the remote cottage, with no other property in sight. Paddy had his own bed in a small room: *I cried nearly the whole night. I never felt lonely in Nazareth and now I felt imprisoned on a farm with an old mother and her son.*[539] The old lady had few words, mostly to do with farm work, and the son the same. The isolation, fear inducing quietness and lack of conversation and absence of young, vibrant life that were the features of the farm, left him lost, bereft of the play, companionship, bustle, and clamour of people-filled Nazareth House. The placement was in winter time and Paddy struggled, to the dismay of the farmer, to carry the heavy bales of hay to the cattle through the snow covered fields. On Sundays the farmer and he footed it to Mass, some two miles distant, his employer carrying out his promise to Reverend Mother that he would ensure that Paddy said his morning and evening prayers, and attend weekly Mass.[540] Paddy thought life unfair at this period, especially when he had to deposit sixpence, half his weekly wage, in the Church collection each week.

2.5.9. Second Hunter Farm Placement in Cairns

The next farm Paddy worked in was for this Hunter and his sister in Cairns, near a holy well close to Lough Gill. Paddy, who was about 16 years old at this time, had became inflamed by love for the sister, a slim, blond, unmarried 'girl'. His romantic reveries about him and her were rudely shattered when an old farmer came a courting the girl, sitting on the bench by the fire, cradling her in his arms and kissing her. Regretfully, Paddy recognised the reality of the respective situations of old suitor and young would-be swain: *the problem was that he had a farm and lots of money and in addition was no doubt more mature than a 16 year old. His name was Oldfield and he looked dirty and unshaven when he visited her.....After a very short courtship they married in the protestant Church in Sligo.*[541]

An almost classic description of rural Irish marriage 'bargains', where the elderly bachelor's material wherewithal overcomes the disadvantages of his age, appearance, hygiene and wooing techniques.

255

The marriage choice of the Hunter girl proved to have mixed outcomes: the blessings of children but marital unhappiness. On a visit to Ireland after the war Paddy had visited both his former love and her farmer brother. Having borrowed a bicycle from Nazareth House Paddy cycled to see what had become of his old flame. On entering the farmyard he was greeted by seven lovely red or blond haired children. They showed no regret when they answered his query about their father's whereabouts by telling him of his death some months previously. They told him that their mother was milking in the shed. He saw her bent over a cow, half hiding her wrinkled face and grey hair when the children called to her and she caught sight of Paddy. He turned away and cycled back to her brother's farm without saying a word to her. Mr Hunter, her brother, told Paddy that the marriage had been a mistake, and that his sister had been beaten by Mr Oldfield for not wanting to have more than seven children, when she had only wanted three.[542]

2.5.10. Meeting with Brother James

Paddy had been working out in the fields scratching out potatoes, which Mr Hunter had earlier ploughed up. Protected by his home-made, potato-sack knee pads against the wet soggy earth, Paddy was making his way along the seemingly endless drills when he saw a well dressed stranger jump the stone wall and make towards him across the field. Thinking that the man could only want to speak to Mr Hunter, and keeping his head down in case his boss thought him slacking Paddy ignored the stranger, until he was just in front of him. Looking up Paddy asked him who he was. *I'm your brother....don't you know me?*[543] When Paddy glanced up he saw his brother James above him but did not offer a handshake because of his mud encrusted hands. The boys arranged to meet in a Sligo cafe much later that day, in the evening, because Paddy feared losing his job if he spent any time talking to his brother. James went off almost immediately and Paddy answered his employer's query as to the identity of the stranger.

Paddy had arranged the meeting with James in the late evening because he still had to finish the evening milking which began at six o'clock and then deliver the milk churn to Sligo town, some five miles distant. He reports leaving more milk in the cows' udders than in the bucket that night in his haste not to miss his appointment with his brother. The old jennet harnessed to the cart could not be hurried with the milk churn on the road to Sligo and Paddy became fearful that he would miss his brother who had to catch a late train to return to his Irish Army barracks in Athlone.

When Paddy found the rendezvous cafe James treated him to bacon and eggs. James, on just a day's army leave, had earlier in the day gone to Nazareth House in Sligo expecting to find Paddy there. The Yardman, Paddy Brannigan, had told James of his brother's whereabouts working for Mr Hunter in Cairns[544] but by the time James had found Paddy most of his day's army leave had elapsed. Sitting in the cafe Paddy recalls:

The minutes of his watch...appeared to be ticking faster as his conversation centred round my future. He wasn't particularly worried about his own as he felt secure in the Irish Army.[545] He wanted to take me with him and having asked me how old I was I couldn't give him an answer.[546] However he did leave me his address and asked me to write him whenever I could. There was no mention of either our Father or Mother and as Attracta had told me a few years back that my parents were dead, questions about such were at least to me superfluous...The time had come for us to part and once again having embraced each other and bid farewell we started off in different directions. I was never to see him again for he disappeared as quickly as he had come.[547]

2.5.11. Communication, Misunderstanding and Inaccurate Assumptions

Although James Baker, Paddy's half brother, was some seven years older than his younger brother, he would not have had any memory of him when they were young. James was born in 1916 and at the age of three years had been admitted to Nazareth House in 1919. He had never lived with Paddy and his mother and would not have seen, or even known about, his younger half-brother who was born in January 1923, and admitted to Nazareth House, in 1925 when James was eight or nine years of age. Earlier in the book the brief meeting between the boys and the man Paddy took to be a putative father was outlined. No further formal contact between the brothers seems to have occurred after that. Paddy remembers James working in Nazareth House laundry after James had left school, and that James had given him the money for the broken window and his fateful sixpence when James was working in Rose Hill Nursing Home. Despite this, less than two years previously, he had not recognised James when he called at Hunter's farm.

These previously mentioned errors, inconsistencies, information gaps and misunderstandings made by Paddy and Michael Porter, and the sometimes episodic or blank memories of the boys, and the seeming lack of attempts by them to connect or understand these, can easily lead to doubt or disbelief of the rest of their accounts. This would, I think, be wrong. It is better to understand and to accept that the memories of informants, especially after so many years, may not be wholly logical, consistent or integrated. Indeed if they were to be, then it would raise more suspicions as to the veracity of their recollections.

Of much greater significance, however, is not what a person does or does not know; rather it is what a person assumes. Paddy assumed that James would have a distinct memory of his younger brother, even though he had been removed into care before Paddy was born. The Sisters assumed that Michael remembered that he has a father, sister and other family living in Galway. The assumptions, although wrong, are regarded as fact by the person concerned. These erroneous facts then form part of the person's memory and understanding, sometimes causing the person to lay blame at the wrong door. Sometimes it is best to simply acknowledge that accounts may never be wholly logical, integrated, consistent and accurate, but still to try to tease out the most accurate and truthful account that memory, other records and the limitations of individual authors will allow.

2.5.12. Still at the Hunter's Farm on the Outbreak of War in 1939

On the outbreak of the Second World War, September 3rd 1939, Paddy was still stuck in a menial, low-paid farm servant post working at the (second) Hunter farm, in Cairns, County Sligo.[548]

He did not like his work and he had no prospects and no family.
The Second World War, unwelcome as it was to most people,[549]
proved a boon for Paddy Baker, opening up for him opportunities of
employment that enabled him to leave behind rural farm labouring,
and to travel, and to make a career for himself: always, though,
keeping in mind the pre-requisite for any work: bed and board
included.

Chapter 2.6. Summary and Discussion

2.6.1. Family Collapse and Loss of Mother

Jack Common's autobiographical novel, *Kiddar's Luck (1951)* describes how the accident of birth influences subsequent life chances:

'There were plenty of golden opportunities going that night. In palace and mansion flat, in hall and manor and new centrally heated 'Cottage', the wealthy, talented and beautiful lay coupled-welcome wombs were ten-a-penny, must have been. What do you think I picked on, me and my genes, that is? Missing lush Sussex, the Surrey soft spots, affluent Mayfair and gold-filled Golders Green, fat Norfolk rectories, the Dukeries, and many a solid Yorkshire village, to name only some obvious marks, I came upon the frost-rimed roofs of a working-class suburb in Newcastle-upon-Tyne, and in the back bedroom of an upstairs flat in a street parallel with the railway line, on which a halted engine whistled to be let through the junction, I chose my future parents. There it was done.....I at once came under the minus-sign which society had already placed upon my parent'.[550]

The Quartet's early life experiences were far more disadvantageous than those of Jack Common. Common's parents were married, his father had a job as a railway locomotive fireman, and he enjoyed a stable, though drink-scarred upbringing within his family and community. All the Quartet boys originated from subsistence-living families in Connacht in the period around Irish Independence. Emigrants sought to escape their economically underdeveloped country that was blighted by poverty, high unemployment and persistent migration; and, as migrants had complained, there was nothing for them at home.

The straitened family circumstances of the Quartet 'compromised', or made 'critical', the care of the children; they did not in themselves cause the boys to be 'let go' into care. Loss of mother was what tipped all four families into 'collapse' and caused the children to spend their lives in care: poverty weakened the family unit; maternal loss broke it up.

At the time there was generally a lack of awareness of the enormous importance of the child's attachment to parents and to their emotional and individual needs. 'Loss' of parent, most commonly the mother, was also the prime reason why the Quartet's contemporaries entered care.[551] Consumption, and death in childbirth, were the major causes of maternal deaths; illegitimacy was the other major reason why children lost their mother. The social death that illegitimacy then represented often resulted in a mother 'letting go' her child, often following powerful family, church and social pressures.

Although the mothers of Willie Walsh and Paddy and James Baker were still alive during the boys' childhoods they were lost to their sons as surely as those whose mothers had died. The mothers' felt a socially reinforced sense of sin, shame, and stigma as a result of their unmarried parenthood resulted in them handing over their sons to institutional carers, often leaving no trail for their searching sons to follow. Illegitimacy often resulted in permanent separation of mothers from children. For those children whose mothers were still alive this loss must have been all the harder to understand and accept; and to explain to themselves why the mothers did not seek them out subsequently. Certainly Paddy Baker never ventured this question, nor did Willie McCormack explore why his father, who abandoned the family, never sought contact with his children; pain enough to deal with without venturing into this explosive area of life.[552]

Willie McGowan's laments in later life about his childhood were two-fold: irreplaceable loss of his mother and the subsequent loss of family life and of meaningful sibling contact throughout his childhood. Yet his greatest loss, that of his mother, was at least understandable. He had seen her dying and dead; he knew that for a fact; it was reality; it could be accepted; it had to be endured. Worse still was the plight of Paddy Baker and Willie Walsh grieving a lost mother but with the loved and needed mother still alive, but dead to them. How could they, how can anyone, make sense of that and so come to terms with it? For the illegitimate child in particular there was the knowledge that their life need not have been as it was.

'Loss of mother: children's lives fundamentally altered': that could well have been the title of this book, for it captures the central problem that affected the Quartet throughout their lives.

2.6.2. Care Life at Nazareth House in the 1920's and 1930's: Resource Shortage

The Poor Sisters of Nazareth was a London based Congregation of nuns. They ran two adjacent Nazareth House Homes in Sligo for boys and for elderly. The Sisters were mendicants whose begging Sisters went out in pairs on 'the Quest', seeking food and funds. This, together with fund raising committees, brought in much of the resources needed to keep the homes operational.

The Homes, both for boys and the elderly, were grossly understaffed, even by the standards of the 1920's. A comparison with staffing standards required today shows that Nazareth House, Sligo, had between 10% and 20% of the staff required to provide safe and appropriate care. This produced a greater degree of regimentation than that which was already common in society and care a century ago. It also explains why the older boys were used as supplementary workers to some degree, helping in kitchen, laundry, cleaning and in manual tasks in the elderly care home. This breached the policies of the Nazareth Congregation but was done so routinely as to render the policy redundant.

The chores did not cause any major problems for the Quartet: Michael Porter certainly understood why help was needed and did not resent his floor polishing chore or even helping to clean the communal toilets. Paradoxically, the rule infraction practice of placing older boys as helpers alongside a Sister in laundry, kitchen or elderly home proved often beneficial. It was then that the boy, corralled from the herd, could work quietly alongside a single Sister, obtaining limited, but greatly valued individual attention and appreciation. Individual attention was not provided otherwise. Care was communal, egalitarian and very just but lacking in any form of development of each boy as an individual person distinct from his peers.

Several factors contributed to the lack of individual attention and emotional neglect of the boys: overwhelmingly the resource deficiencies; secondly a more general lack of awareness of the emotional needs of children in society then; and finally, insufficient emotional intelligence on the part of the Sisters, linked to their lack of specific training for residential care work. The Sisters generally exercised a degree of emotional constraint in their care of the boys: this emotional swaddling derived from their religious formation which emphasised qualities of self-denial and self-mortification.

2.6.3. Care Life at Nazareth House in the 1920's and 1930's: Schooling and Music

The provision of schooling from the age of 7 years in the Marist Brothers' School in Quay Street, Sligo had several significant benefits for the Homeboys. They had contact with Sligo town; they encountered a cross section of other boys to mix and play with; and they had adult males to relate to rather than their Sister carers. Schooling, though marked by the caning that was routine then, was generally enjoyed by the boys, and found to be educationally beneficial.

A number of the talented Homeboys, including two of the Quartet, achieved secondary education at Summerhill College, a diocesan seminary. Secondary educational opportunities for such Catholic children almost invariably involved denominational education. Secondary education for working class children was then rare in Ireland, available only to about one in twenty children. It is very doubtful that the boys would have achieved this had they remained at home with their families. Paradoxically their care status advanced some of them educationally. The Sisters were ambitious for the boys and refused to accept that their care status should lower their ambitions. Sister Attracta encouraged the Homeboys to aim for priesthood rather than the lower status of a religious Brother.[553]

Nazareth House provided a wide range of recreational and cultural activities, including drama, poetry and recitations, dancing, a range of sports, and marching and brass band music. There was a strong emphasis on the Gaelic element in this acculturation of the boys. All Nazareth House Homes provided musical training opportunities for the children in care. The Sligo Nazareth House Home featured a brass band virtually from its inception in 1910. By the 1930's the lack of a conductor had caused the band to fold. In order to re-start the band the Sisters sent off to London one of their ex-Homeboys to be trained as bandmaster and conductor.[554] This bandmaster, Josie Cummings, was a distinctive physical figure and personality. In physique he was diminutive, block-bodied and hunchbacked. He had been an ex-workhouse, inmate and ex-Nazareth House Homeboy. Addicted to snuff, to music, to organ playing and to the dark stuff when he could get it, he proved to be a gifted bandmaster able to coax the best out of the boys. Josie's primary employment was as a Yardman labourer at Nazareth House. He was one of the many ex-workhouse, ex-Homeboy 'waifs and strays', many of them physically disabled, who were found home and work in Nazareth House settings. He, like many other Yardmen, lived all his life in a Nazareth House environment.

From scratch Josie taught the boys music from using Tonic Sol-fa. The brass band provided camaraderie, stimulation, uniform and pride, and also involved many trips in and around Sligo when the band played at events. The home's location in Sligo was fortuitous because Sligo town had developed a notable feast of Gaelic culture and music at its annual Feiseanna. After only nine months of Josie's coaching the Brass Quartet achieved first place in the 1934 Sligo Feis.[555] The full brass band and Quartet enjoyed further successes at the Sligo Feis in subsequent years, one of a number of competitive successes in sport and music the boys enjoyed during the 1930's.

2.6.4. Care Life at Nazareth House in the 1920's and 1930's: Communication with Family

Although not strictly an orphanage Nazareth House tended to operate as such. Family contact did occur for some boys, such as Willie McGowan: for most others it did not, with their families parking the boys there until the boys were old enough to go out to work. A major problem was the failure of the Sisters to discuss family with the boys, leading some to believe themselves orphans when they still had parents alive. No letters home were written or received by most of the Quartet members. The Sisters appear to have not appreciated that boys forgot that they had families. Boys such as Michael Porter thought that all his peers were orphans. He erroneously believed himself to be one and no-one actively disabused him of this belief, because they did not know that he had forgotten that he had a family, and because no-one troubled to talk to him about his family. When a young Sister spoke briefly to him after he had left school and mentioned his father, Michael avoided the subject, unable to comprehend what the Sister was talking about.

2.6.5. Care Life at Nazareth House in the 1920's and 1930's: Communication and Control

In all inquiry reports into organisations, including abuse within them, one factor always emerges as the most significant deficiency: communication. This includes both failure to communicate and misunderstandings between people about what was meant and understood. This was also the case with Nazareth House, Sligo. The reasons were the same as those that led to the emotional bleakness: primarily, resources; secondly, societal understanding: and finally, insufficient sensitivity and understanding on the part of the Sisters. These communication deficiencies contributed to some of the boys' constructing inaccurate or partial perspectives of their life there and incorporating these into their skewed memory narrative of childhood care thereafter.

Many inquiry reports have detailed abusive care. Boys appear at particular risk of abuse in institutions: 'Two thirds of the abused were boys and two thirds of the abuse was sexual'.[556] The picture of Catholic Church personnel exploiting children sexually and physically has been a significant feature of media attention in the last few decades. This appears to be the dominant image of children cared for by religious in Ireland in the twentieth century. It is not, in general, one borne out by this study; indeed much of the evidence suggests committed care by the Poor Sisters of Nazareth, notwithstanding some exceptions.

The care provided at Nazareth House has not thrown up any instances of sexual exploitation or abuse of the boys in the inter-war period. Research has identified how endemic the nature of peer on peer sexual exploitation and abuse has been in male residential institutions: 'Possibly half the total of abuse reported in institutions is peer abuse'.[557] Despite little understanding of this problem in society at that time it does appear that the Sisters attitude to modesty in physical matters afforded some degree of preventive vigilance to head off any sexual contact between the boys. I very much doubt that, despite their efforts, such exploitation did not occur.

Physical abuse, indeed severe physical abuse, has emerged on two occasions at Nazareth House. The first was the bare-bottom, bloodied beating by the senior child care Sister of Paddy Baker, where she locked the door when she abused him (suggestive of secrecy and possibly shame). The second was the sadistic, regular, but brief-lived beating of the boys by an ex-prison warder, who had been brought in to teach the boys physical instructions. When the instructor's activities were uncovered he was summarily dismissed.

These instances appear exceptional. Michael Porter never recollected the Sisters abusing or physically punishing him or his peers[558]: *a look would have been enough to control us,* as he recalled.[559] Despite being a large and physically imposing woman, made even more so by the large, enveloping habit, the senior child care Sister and her Sister colleagues struggled with their control of the boys as the boys grew bigger. The 'anticipatory fearfulness' about losing control of the boys was, I believe, a factor in the exceptional (but probably not unique) beating of Paddy.

2.6.6. Care Life at Nazareth House in the 1920's and 1930's: Carers' Commitment

My impression of the Sisters 'care of their pupils' is that it was marked by commitment, diligence and dogged perseverance but lacking in emotional sensitivity. Their work was always appreciated by Willie McGowan and Willie Walsh, and came to be by Paddy Baker and Michael Porter later in life. The bold statement by the Mother General in the nineteenth century that they never lost sight of one of their charges throughout their after-care life proved very largely true.[560] The constant background of financial insecurity seems not to have prevented the Sisters responding to the human need presented to them: this included outdoor relief and counselling to some of the elderly poor of Sligo.

The unrelenting and resource-deficient pressure of tending the elderly, some of them incontinent, decrepit and dying, was met by remarkably dedicated care by some Sisters, according to one informant.[561] The Sisters' efforts narrowed but could not close the large gap between the scale of need and the level of human resources to meet this: physical care and safety, unsurprisingly, were their priorities. Given this extreme resource mismatch it is hardly surprising that tempers may have been strained or mistakes made: indeed I was somewhat surprised that so few instances of overt abuse have emerged. Kipling's words are worth remembering: 'For the Colonel's Lady an' Judy O'Grady are sisters under their skins'.[562] Inside the habit were people of flesh and blood, not plaster saints.

The care provision at Nazareth House could be summarised as: materially good, with sound, safe and clean physical care with nutritionally balanced and adequate, if Spartan, food; remarkable in the range of cultural, recreational and sporting activities provided for the boys; somewhat heavy in the religious routines the boys were subject to; and emotionally bleak, save for some esteem building from cultural, sporting and musical activities.

2.6.7. Leaving Care: The Whole Cohort of Boys

When the boys' schooling and care careers had ended only a quarter of them were rehabilitated home to their families. The boys who were reunited with their families as a result almost always of their fathers remarrying and obtaining work, usually abroad.

The remaining three quarters of the boys were not taken back by their families, even though many still had parents and extended families alive. These very young boys had, therefore, to tackle the next stage of their life without a home base, family support, guidance or encouragement. The failure to maintain links between family and the care home during the boys' period in care had greatly weakened the ties of the surviving parents to their sons in care, with the fathers now habituated to managing without their offspring.

The Sisters of Nazareth had thus to find occupational opportunities and living situations for the three quarters of their charges who could not return home. The 14 to 16 year old boys then faced competition for work against adult males in a very poor country with high adult male unemployment. The need for 'sheltered', semi-supportive placements that combined bed and board was recognised by the Sisters. They used their extensive network of contacts, including sometimes their own relatives, to secure such first step placements for the boys. Quite often these broke down, and more than once, as happened with several Quartet members. The boys were then taken back in at Nazareth House to lick their wounds and recover until another placement was secured for them.

A significant minority of the boys had their first experience of work in one of the Nazareth House homes in Ireland. In these homes they worked in laundries, farms or in other manual jobs as Yardmen. Some ex-Homeboys who had physical disabilities that prevented them competing for work in the outside world became Yardmen labourers all their lives, working, living and often dying there.

That the Sisters saw their responsibilities to their boys as lasting long after they had left Nazareth House is shown in their post-care continued interest and oversight of them. They knew where almost all the boys had moved to and continued to track them throughout their lives. Nazareth House became a back-up and a bolt-hole for the boys when their placements failed in the immediate post-care years. Showing considerable foresight for the 1930's the Sisters had had constructed a detached youth club cum old boys' meeting-up centre in the grounds of Nazareth House. Named 'Father Barry's house' after its benefactor, this was used by those boys on placement in Sligo town, and by old boys returning for the Christmas celebrations.[563]

All four Quartet boys spent their first few years after care in bed and board placements in Ireland, but only one remained living in Ireland after the Second World War. It was the ambition of many of the boys to join the army. There they hoped to find the uniform, comradeship and a combined living and work environment (bed and board). Above all they gravitated to the army because of their instinct that it would supply the security and predictability they craved. The experience that the boys had gained at Nazareth House in drill and marching, and in band and musical training, helped many of them secure their ambition of an army career. The outbreak of the Second World War in September 1939 greatly assisted those who had left Nazareth House in the years immediately after 1937 obtain army posts, after marking time in other work until an army post was available to them.

2.6.8. Roles of Church and State in Provision of Care

The parish priest was the gatekeeper to care, especially so where admission was voluntary. He exercised several roles in this process: he enjoyed influence with the family in the decision making for out-of-home placement; he had privileged access to the religious care homes; and he funnelled children into Catholic Church homes, thus enabling them to keep operating. While religious and denominational aspects were major factors influencing a priest's choice of placement, they were significant considerations for the families too. The priorities for the child recue model of care were to secure a safe, clean, healthy physical placement where the children's moral, religious, and educational needs could be met.

The wishes of the children were not taken into account nor were their emotional needs understood. Family fragmentation occurred routinely. The needs of siblings to be kept together was barely appreciated, if even comprehended at all. Even had the attachment and emotional needs of the children been understood it is most unlikely that this would have altered the placements of the children: children were sent to wherever there were places available. While resource availability determined the care destination for the child in most cases, gender separation added a significant further fragmentary feature to sibling cohesion. The aforementioned points in this chapter applied to state child care too throughout Britain and Ireland for much of the twentieth century. The general Catholic ethos of gender separation in church-run residential settings meant that brothers and sisters were rarely placed together. Willie McGowan's family dispersal classically illustrates the underpinning reality of how decisions were made.

The placement decisions would not seem to have been made from callousness or cruelty; rather they reflected what adult carers and clerics deemed to be in the best interests of the child, at that time, and in that culture. What constitutes the best interests is interpreted differently at different periods of time, and in different cultures of the same time epoch. Irish Catholic society constructed its view of child needs differently in the first part of the twentieth century compared with how it perceives these today.

Care for Catholic children in inter-war Ireland almost invariably meant church care with the children accommodated in a home managed and staffed by religious. The British Imperial government had allowed and even encouraged the Catholic Church in Ireland to manage and staff many state functions such as workhouses, industrial schools, national schools and children's homes. It had sought to encourage the Catholic Church to provide a controlling and buffering force against secessionist and revolutionary violent nationalists; this moderating influence was generally provided by churchmen.

This increasing church encroachment into state welfare and educational provision greatly aided the Catholic Church's enormous increase in power and more than doubling of personnel in the century before the boys came to Nazareth House.[564] During the late nineteenth and early twentieth century the number of clergy and religious more than doubled at a period when the population had halved. Liam Swords' description of Achonry Diocese during this epoch is apposite: *A Dominant Church.*[565] One might have said 'domineering', 'arrogant' or 'overweening' on occasions. Certainly,

271

after independence in 1922, when the British Imperial writ ran no more, the country continued to be dominated by the other imperious power: and one whose writ ran in both the secular and in the ideological field, and throughout the whole of society. Is a second form of 'independence', one without a violent sudden end, now being worked out in Ireland nearly a century later?

As a significant caveat to the above, the context in which the Church hierarchy found itself must be mentioned. The Irish Catholic Church had to deal with the vast bulk of the population, including most of those who were starkly poor; a very different situation to the more comfortable Church of Ireland's ruling class membership or that of the Quakers. The clergy were faced with the problems of how to 'civilise' or socialise or give a moral framework to those working in jobs that did not lift the heart and mind and often depressed the soul. It is always easier to have benign attitudes when comfortably off.

The vast scale of Catholic provision of care, both building new homes and funding operational costs, was significantly underpinned by charitable donations, including those provided in kind. The power that Bishop Clancy of Elphin undoubtedly wielded in his diocese was used to good effect reflecting Liam Sword's contention, at least in the Bishop's case, that: 'the paternalism practised by priests and others was largely benevolent'.[566] Bishop Clancy's establishment of care provision for young and old at Nazareth House, Sligo, was a significant improvement on the workhouse care it replaced indicating that the problem is less that of power *per se*; more how power is used. The Irish State welcomed the Catholic Church's central care role which relieved it of a significant portion of the overall costs of care provision, for both children and elderly; and in the last few decades the state has been able to avoid much of the blame when abuse of residents emerged from Inquiry reports and investigations into care homes.

The state had no involvement in the care of the Quartet, or indeed of many of their contemporaries at Nazareth House. Children were generally placed in the Home for their whole childhood, rarely being removed. However, there was a positive aspect to this: it avoided the predicament of many children in state care, especially in the United Kingdom, where children were often passed around like parcels, with placement breakdown leading to frequent geographical and school changes.

The Quartet members were not visited by social workers, nor linked to their families of origin, nor was any advice or support given to the Sisters when issues or problems arose:

'If a society damns its institutions as reflecting its evil and uncaring self and therefore doesn't provide them with enough resources, it becomes a self-fulfilling prophecy that under-funded institutions will attract individuals who are less well trained and less motivated, less caring and less responsible, and less healthy'.[567]

Church and state alike left the Sisters to get on with their work unconcerned as to how they were managing, or whether they had the resources for their work. Bishop Edward Daly recently acknowledged this in his evidence to the Hart Inquiry:[568] 'Care of children is very challenging for anybody at any time. The sisters were out in the rain, wind, snow, begging for money. I was as guilty as everyone else of taking them for granted'.

The well-intentioned policy of the Nazareth Congregation to provide for the large scale human need was not matched by adequate personnel and resources to meet these. Nor did the Congregation's leaders exert pressure on the Irish state or on the Church hierarchy to provide additional funds and support. Compliance was the order of the day. The Sisters got on with their demanding work nonetheless: it was not only the boys who were abandoned.

The words of Bishop Daly: 'grossly overworked and underfunded',[569] match my own view of the situation that the Sisters at Nazareth House, Sligo, found themselves in when caring for their boys in the 1920's and 1930's; indeed for the care of the elderly too.

Michael Porter in adulthood worked in Northumberland as an underground coal miner on shift work for over a decade. The system in that coalfield used to involve the miners drawing lots for their 'cavil' (workplace underground) because the underground geology made some sections of the mine much harder to work than others. A miner would talk of having a 'bad cavil'. In this intensely physical and often dangerous work miners admired their fellow pitmen who worked hardest underground. Their highest praise, reserved for a miner who worked exceptionally and unrelentingly for the whole of his time at the coalface, was: 'he put in a shift'.

The coal mining analogy has repeatedly come to mind when examining the work of the Sisters at Nazareth House in Sligo. Many Sisters had bad cavils but none had a lottery draw to relieve them of these; nor did they cavil (complain) about their work situations. And, to borrow the words of the Northumberland miner: 'they put in a shift'.

In Chapter 1.3 the bold claim was made by the Mother General of the Nazareth Congregation at Hammersmith about their after-care contact with their children:

'We never lose sight of one of them ...we keep up a correspondence with them, and when they have holidays they come and see us'.[570]

This research, including that contained in the sequel volume covering the Quartet's adult lives, largely demonstrates that the Sligo Nazareth Sisters did maintain an interest in, contact with and a commitment to, their former boys. This 'pastoral' approach stands in marked contrast to the after-care stance of much state care provision in Britain and Ireland during most of the twentieth century.

Chapter 2.7. Summary of the Quartet's Circumstances at the Outbreak of War

2.7.1 When Britain declared war on Germany on September 3rd, 1939, Michael Porter was a month short of his eighteenth birthday. He had left his hotel post in Sligo some few months earlier to live temporarily with his Healy aunt and uncle in Donabate, near Dublin. He was in the process of moving out into bed and board accommodation at the Mater hospital in Dublin to work as a radiographer's assistant, a post found for him by his nurse aunt. He had also met a couple of his father's brothers after a care career where he had believed himself to be an orphan. He had ceased all contact with Nazareth House and intended never to refer to his sojourn there to anyone he met, or indeed to his newly met relatives. His new work was a step up from his earlier posts but he was still insecure and relations with his new found family were still uncertain and fragile.

2.7.2. Willie Walsh was two months short of his nineteenth birthday in September 1939. After hotel work in Bundoran, County Donegal, and Sheridan's hotel in Sligo Willie had immediately stepped into the hotel worker post that Michael Porter had vacated at McGarrigle's hotel in Sligo.[571] He was very pleased to be back in Sligo, close to the security of his childhood home at Nazareth House. He had regularly written to the Sisters from Bundoran and visited them every Christmas as well as making use of Father Barry's Situation boys' youth club at Nazareth House. Willie had no family contact and, although he had received a secondary education at Summerhill College, Sligo, this lack of family, together with his illegitimacy and the general poverty and high unemployment in Eire, meant that his future life prospects were unlikely to match his innate ability.

2.7.3. Willie Walsh's fellow Nazareth House and Summerhill College companion, Willie McGowan was eighteen years five months at the outbreak of war. After Nazareth House he had been taken home to work with his father as the future inheritor of the small family farm in County Sligo. He was in touch with some of his large family of siblings, their living situations scattered after the early death of their mother. Willie chose to leave his home to work as a Yardman on the Nazareth House large farm in Mallow, County Cork, together with other former Nazareth Homeboys, including Paddy Baker's brother, James. He enjoyed the life and companionship at Mallow, regularly wrote and visited Nazareth House, Sligo, and had an ambition to follow the path trodden by James Baker and other Nazareth House boys and enlist in the Irish Army, as a bandsman. His family situation and educational background left him the most advantaged of the Quartet members.

2.7.4. The least well situated person in the Quartet, and indeed the most vulnerable of them, was the youngest member, Paddy Baker, who was aged just sixteen years and eight months in September 1939. After running away from Nazareth House Paddy had worked in a number of fairly dreary farm 'servant' placements and was unhappily employed at a farm in County Sligo. He had recently had a fleeting visit by his brother, James, who had joined the Irish Army, but otherwise had no family contact, wrongly believing his mother to be dead. He was lonely and lacked peer companionship: indeed he was somewhat of a loner, although unlike Michael Porter, he seems not to have 'chosen' to be so. He maintained limited contact with the Sisters at Nazareth House, and with the Yardmen there. Indeed he visited Nazareth House on the day war was declared, September 3rd 1939. There he listened to Chamberlain's announcement of war clustered round the newly acquired wireless set with the Sisters and the Yardmen. Paddy's future life and career prospects were bleak, a fact he well recognised and indeed recorded.[572]

2.7.5. The essential requirements for many former institutional care residents, bed and board combined, continued to feature in the lives of all the Quartet for some years after they had left care: security was all. Three of them also enjoyed companionship from their peers in their living situations, and the fourth actively sought to regain this.

The Second World War damaged or devastated many people's lives. However, for the Quartet, it opened up opportunities that had not been available to them in peacetime, and war significantly affected the direction of their future lives.

The sentiment-Give me the child.....(until the age of seven).....and I'll give you the man-has been variously attributed to the Jesuits or behaviourists.[573] The Quartet's early years were formed by Nazareth Sister carers and shaped by Marist Brother educators. Whether and how this early moulding continued to underpin their adult lives will be explored in the concluding volume: *The Quartet: After-Care Lives of Irish Catholic Homeboys*.

Bibliography of Primary Sources

'It's amazing what a lot there is in an old man's head when somebody else starts him talking and puts questions to him........'[574]

This list of primary sources contains all those primary documents used in Volumes I and II of the Quartet. Only a couple of these sources is in the public domain. All others were either created or sourced during research into the lives of the Quartet.

The two volumes are not 'padded out' with extensive secondary sources. The key secondary sources that were used are referenced *en passant* as endnotes and are not repeated here.

Aloysius Joseph (Sister of Nazareth, Mallow). *Correspondence to William McGowan.*

Anthony Joseph (Sister of Nazareth, Mallow). *Correspondence to William McGowan.*

Anthony Joseph (Sister of Nazareth, Mallow). *Personal diary.*

Attracta (Sister of Nazareth). *Correspondence and photographs sent to William McGowan* (1960's).

Baker, Patrick Joseph. (October 1969) *Correspondence from John P. Downs.*

Baker, Patrick Joseph. (1994-1997) *Correspondence to William McGowan.*

Baker, Patrick Joseph. *Photographic records of his visits to Sligo.*

Bernadine (Sister of Nazareth, Sligo, formerly Reverend Mother). *Discussions with author* (2012-2013).

Bohan, Rev. Seamus, Parish priest, Tynagh. *Parish BMD records.*

Columbo (Reverend Mother, Nazareth House, Wavertree, Liverpool). *Correspondence to William McGowan.*

Dirrane, Michael. *Records of care career at Nazareth House, Sligo.*

Fitzsimons, Imelda. *Discussions with author re William McGowan.*

Fitzsimons, Imelda. *Correspondence, emails and photographs re William McGowan to author.*

Gertrude (Sister of Nazareth, Northampton and Sligo, and Reverend Mother, Belfast). *Correspondence to Willie McGowan.*

Gertrude (Sister of Nazareth, Sligo, (*see above*). *Discussions with author* (2012-2015).

John (Sister of Nazareth, Sligo). *Correspondence to John Michael Murphy.*

John (Sister of Nazareth, Sligo). *Correspondence to Michael Laurence Porter.*

John (Sister of Nazareth, Sligo). *Oral information.*

John (Sister of Nazareth, Sligo). *Discussions with author (2012-2016).*

John (Sister of Nazareth, Sligo). Unpublished booklet: *Some Details from Records of Events in Nazareth House, Sligo* (1910-1941).

Judge, Henry. *Discussions with author.*

Malachy Joseph (Sister of Nazareth, Mallow). *Correspondence to William McGowan.*

Margaret (Sister of Nazareth, Sligo current Reverend Mother) *Discussions with author* (2014-2015)

Mary of the Passion (Reverend Mother, Sisters of Nazareth, Sligo). *Correspondence to William McGowan and family.*

Mary of the Passion (Sister of Nazareth) (a.k.a. 'Pres'). *Discussions with author* (2014-2015).

Mater Hospital, Dublin. *Testimonial regarding Michael Laurence Porter* (13.05.1942).

McCormack, William (Bill). (Undated). *An Angel Held My Hand.* Internet uploaded account of the author's experiences at Nazareth House, Sligo: 1943-1952.

Mercy Sisters. *Care career records of Mary Bridgid (Sadie) Porter.*

McGowan-Judge, Margaret. *Discussions with author re William McGowan.*

McGowan-Judge, Margaret. *Correspondence, emails, parish records and photographs re William McGowan supplied to author.*

McGowan (nee O'Connor), Mary Theresa (Maureen). *Correspondence with parents on honeymoon.*

McGowan, William. *Nazareth House, Sligo. Care career records.*

McGowan, William. *Nazareth House, Sligo. Care career records: continuation (post-care) records.*

McGowan, William. *Correspondence from Patrick Baker's step-daughter* (March 1997).

McGowan, William. *Correspondence to Mother Veronica (Nazareth House, Sligo).*

McGowan, William. *Family photograph collection.*

McGowan, William. *Irish Army Career records.*

McGowan, William. *Miscellaneous correspondence and documents.*

McGuinness, Father Dominic, O.F.M., Capuchin. *Correspondence to William McGowan.*

Murphy, John Michael. (1983) *Housing, Class and Politics in a Company Town: Ashington, 1896-1939.* M.A. Thesis: University of Durham.

Murphy, John Michael. (1987) *Northern Child Care Group.* Unpublished group-work findings.

Murphy, John Michael. (1987-1989) *Four brothers training case study and video.*

Murphy, John Michael (1998) *Has the child protection delegate role improved how the catholic church deals with allegations of child sexual exploitation by clergy/religious in the study diocese?*

281

(Confidential). M.A. Thesis: University of Northumbria at Newcastle.

Murphy, John Michael. (2014) *Memory research exercise.* (Unpublished research). Mid- Northumberland: University of the Third Age Genealogy Group.

Murphy, John Michael. *Author's correspondence on behalf of Michael and Sadie Porter with Nazareth and Mercy Sisters* (2012-2015).

National Registration Identity Card, Michael Porter.

National Registration Identity Card, Noreen Porter.

National Service Hostels Corporation Limited. *Documentation regarding Michael Laurence Porter.*

National Service Hostels Corporation Limited. *Testimonial and letter regarding Noreen Hay* (12.4.1945).

Nazareth Home Nursing Home, Sligo. *Undated booklet.*

Nazareth House, Sligo Records. *First Holy Communion dates of Quartet and certain contemporaries.*

Nazareth House, Sligo. *Details of cohort of boys who entered 1925-1932 and their destination and subsequent careers after discharge* (Quartet's contemporaries).

Nazareth House, Sligo. *Letter on file from Father Bernard M. Bowes, Parish Priest, Tynagh, County Galway.*

Nazareth Sisters, Sligo. *Author's discussions with.*

O'Connor (nee Porter), Joan. *Oral information re Porter family.*

O' Neill, Geraldine (Ger). *Oral information re Porter family history.*

O'Neill (nee Porter), Josephine. *Oral information re Porter family.*

O'Shea, (nee Cowan),Theresa. *Oral records clarifying Porter/Cowan family history.*

Osbourne (nee Porter), Josephine. *Oral information re Porter family* (2014).

Osmond, Father Matthew, OP. (Mattie Slevin). *Correspondence to William McGowan.*

Porter, Ellen (Nellie). *Correspondence to Michael Laurence Porter.*

Porter, Michael (Junior). *Interviews/discussions with author* (2013-2016).

Porter, Michael Laurence. *Co-operative Insurance record and round book: Newbiggin-by-the-Sea and North Seaton.*

Porter, Michael Laurence. *Correspondence with Irish relatives.*

Porter, Michael Laurence. *Family photographs.*

Porter, Michael Laurence. *Genealogical and family history documents.*

Porter, Michael Laurence. *Interviews with author* (2012-2016).

Porter, Michael Laurence. *Irish and United Kingdom visas and documentation authorising wartime. work, movement and alien registration and reporting to police.*

Porter, Michael Laurence. *Mater Hospital reference and testimonial.*

Porter, Michael Laurence. *Miscellaneous correspondence and documents.*

Porter, Michael Laurence. Nazareth House, Sligo. *Care career records.*

Porter, Michael Laurence. Nazareth House, Sligo. *Continuation record book (post-care events and contacts).*

Porter, Sadie. *Miscellaneous correspondence, documents and photographs.*

Postcard letter from Patrick Joseph Baker's step-daughter informing Willie McGowan of her father's death. (Undated. Received, March, 1997).

Praxedes (Sister of Nazareth, Mallow). *Correspondence to William Patrick McGowan.*

Royal Hotel, Mallow. *Correspondence to William Patrick McGowan.*

Scully, Thomas. Records of care career at Nazareth House, Sligo.

Superintendent Registrar, Sligo. Letter to Patrick Baker (22.02.1996).

Stanislaus (Sister of Nazareth, Mallow). Correspondence to William Patrick McGowan.

Towell (nee Porter), Marie. Oral information re Porter family.

Walsh, William. Care career records, Nazareth House, Sligo.

Walsh, William. Continuation record book (post-care events and contacts).

Endnotes

[1] The detail given to each of the four boys' lives varies considerably according to the documentary material available.

[2] Thomson, David (1991). *Woodbrook.* London: Vintage. Pg. 175. (First published by Barrie and Jenkins, London), (1974)

[3] Murphy, John Michael (1998) *Has the child protection delegate role improved how the catholic church deals with allegations of child sexual exploitation by clergy/religious in the study diocese?* (Confidential). M.A. Thesis: University of Northumbria at Newcastle.

[4] Murphy, John Michael. (1987) *Northern Child Care Group.* Unpublished group-work findings.

[5] Murphy, John Michael. (1987-1989) *Four brothers training case study and video.*

[6] Opie, Iona and Peter (1977). *The Oxford Dictionary of Nursery Rhymes.* Oxford University Press. Pg.ix.

[7] 'Feast (or festival) of music'

[8] Details of the Pollexfens, Yeats's mother's merchant family, whose home it was, can be found in the early section of volume 1 of: *W.B. Yeats: A life* (1977): Foster, R F. Oxford: At the University Press.

[9] 'In our day it was a solid house, big rooms-about 14 bedrooms, stone kitchen offices and a glorious laundry smelling of soap full of white steam and a clean coke fire with rows of irons heating at it. Our grandmother's store-room like a village shop - a place with windows & fireplace-shelves & drawers and a delicious smell of coffee - the house was of blue grey limestone-the local stone-60 acres of land round it-a very fine view of Ben Bulben from the front of the house'.

Foster, R F. (1977) *W.B. Yeats: A life.* Oxford: University Press. Vol. 1. p. 19

This description by Susan Mary ('Lily') Yeats (1866-1949), the younger sister of W.B. Yeats, was of their childhood home, *Merville,* in Sligo.

[10] John (Sister of Nazareth, Sligo). Unpublished booklet: *Some Details from Records of Events in Nazareth House, Sligo. 1910-1941.* The small stone-walled estate was by then much smaller than the original 60 acres because the Sisters did not want farmland to manage. The house was cradled between the hills of Knocknarea and Ben Bulben and, as the name *Merville* suggests, had a view of the sea.

[11] John (Sister of Nazareth, Sligo). *Oral information.*

[12] Porter, Michael Laurence. *Nazareth House, Sligo. Records of entry to care.*

[13] Nazareth House, Sligo. *Letter on file from Father Bernard M. Bowes, Parish Priest, Tynagh, County Galway.*

[14] Three different dates of birth are given for Michael Laurence Porter in Nazareth House, Tynagh RC Church; and civil registration. Michael uses his civil registration date of 3rd October as his date of birth.

The 'grandmother' reference is wrong: she was actually the 'godmother' of Michael. The godmother's address is also wrong.

'Clerking' errors in admission-to-institution records seem remarkably common. Even state records cannot be relied on to be factually correct.

Errors may have been made because of wrongly supplied or wrongly recorded information; or both.

Unfamiliarity with different accents often leads to correctly supplied facts being misheard and wrongly recorded. This latter accent issue is evident in errors in English census and other records about Irish migrants e.g. the very common recording of 'i' for 'e' ('Dinnis' for 'Dennis').

[15] The 'religious' recording of baptism, communion, confirmation, burial and marriage impediment checking contrasts with the paucity of care career recording, but does provide useful marker information for the individual person's life history.

[16] Porter, Michael Laurence. *Interviews with author* (2012-2016).

[17] Ibid.

[18] Ibid.

Both were transitory references. One, oblique, referred to 'family'; the other, more direct, mentioned 'your father'.

[19] It is dealt with more directly in the chapter about memory in Book 2.

[20] Michael Porter uses his civil registration date of birth and that is the one used throughout this book.

[21] Census and BMD records.

[22] The rent the tenant had paid was replaced by a government mortgage repayable, in the case of transfers made under the 1903 Act, over 68.5 years. The majority of the new owners paid less in mortgage than their former rent, usually the mortgage being a half to two thirds of their former rent. The Earl of Westmeath, a major local landowner in the Tynagh area, had 12,000 acres in Galway transferred to his former tenants via the Board.

[23] Freeman, T.W. (1969). *Ireland: A General and Regional Geography*. Compiled from data in pp. 177-179.

[24] Guinnane, Timothy W. (1997) *The Vanishing Irish: households, migration and the rural economy in Ireland, 1850-1914*. Princeton, New Jersey: Princeton University press. p. 117.

The following section dealing with tuberculosis is largely based on Chapter 4 of this book and not further referenced unless directly quoting from it.

[25] The family were then living in the less healthy Gatehouse. Patrick Porter, born in Pallas Gatelodge, Tynagh, 13.04.1918; died Pallas Gatelodge, 18.07.1918. Civil registration records.

[26] Porter, Michael Laurence. *Interviews with author* (2012-2016). Sadie informed Michael that she had been the first family member born in the new house.

[27] Ibid.

[28] Nazareth House records do not contain details of any medical inspection or treatment of Michael, although this did occur on at least one occasion. Admission to care should also feature a medical inspection of the child.

[29] Mercy Sisters. *Care career records of Mary Bridget (Sadie) Porter.*

[30] Onomatopoeically described as 'hockling' in North East England.

[31] 'Pregnancy was known to be one of the stresses that could exacerbate active tuberculosis or even precipitate the onset of illness in a woman who had been exposed to the bacillus'. Quoted in: Guinnane, Timothy W. (1997) *The Vanishing Irish: households, migration and the rural economy in Ireland, 1850-1914*. Princeton, New Jersey: Princeton University Press. p. 120.

[32] Compiled from BMD and other official records, Porter/Cowan documents, and interviews and information from Michael Porter and a number of his relatives.

[33] Michael Laurence Porter. Nazareth House, Sligo. *Care career records.*

[34] 1911 census of Ireland.

[35] Porter, Michael Laurence. *Interviews with author* (2012-2016).

[36] Mercy Sisters. *Care career records of Mary Bridgid (Sadie) Porter.*

[37] Porter, Michael Laurence. *Interviews with author* (2012-2016).

[38] Murphy, John Michael. (1987) *Northern Child Care Group*-unpublished group-work findings.

[39] Ibid.

[40] Baker, Patrick Joseph. (1994-1997) *Correspondence to William McGowan.*

[41] 1900 United States census. Burr Oak Township, Lincoln, Missouri, United States. NARA microfilm publication T623.

[42] 1911 census of Ireland.

[43] 1. Baker, Patrick Joseph. (October 1969) *Correspondence from John P. Downs.*
2. Baker, Patrick Joseph. (1994-1997) *Correspondence to William McGowan.*

[44] Information from: i) 1911 census of Ireland; ii) Baker, Patrick Joseph. 1994-1997 *Correspondence to William McGowan.*; iii) Baker, Patrick Joseph. (October 1969) *Correspondence from John P. Downs.* iv) Nazareth House, Sligo. *Details of cohort of boys who entered 1925-1932 and their destination and subsequent careers after discharge (Quartet's contemporaries).*

[45] *The Catholic Encyclopedia* (1913). New York: The Encyclopedia Press. Volume 7, p. 650. Data is drawn from a statistical table collated from 2 separate sources, in an article by John A. Ryan.

[46] Baker, Patrick Joseph. Information supplied to Paddy Baker by Josie Cummings in 1965 as outlined in (1994-1997) *Correspondence to William McGowan.*

[47] *The Catholic Encyclopedia* (1913). New York: The Encyclopedia Press. Vol. 7, p. 653. Article by John A. Ryan. A very useful source document for Catholic thinking at this period, especially as it can be accessed now online. (It can be found in the parent site, *Catholic Online*). The fifteen volumes of this work were first printed between 1907-1912.

The stated aim of the huge work was: '.... to present its readers with the full body of Catholic teaching, the Encyclopedia contains not only precise statements of what the Church has defined, but also an impartial record of different views of acknowledged authority on all disputed questions, national, political or factional. In the determination of the truth the most recent and acknowledged scientific methods are employed, and the results of the latest research in theology, philosophy, history, apologetics, archaeology, and other sciences are given careful consideration': The Catholic Encyclopedia (1913), op. cit., Vol 1, p. vi.

[48] John (Sister of Nazareth, Sligo). *Discussions with author* (2012-2016).

[49] McGowan-Judge, Margaret. *Discussions with author re William McGowan.*

[50] McGahern, John (2005). *Memoir.* London: Faber and Faber.

[51] Compiled from BMD and parish records, *and interviews and information from Margaret McGowan-Judge and Imelda Fitzsimons.*

[52] 1.Fitzsimons, Imelda. *Discussions with author re William McGowan.* 2.McGowan-Judge, Margaret. *Discussions with author re William McGowan.*

[53] McGowan, William. *Nazareth House, Sligo. Care career records.* Willie McGowan's admission records contain similar errors to Michael and Sadie Porter's. His mother's name is given as Eileen (Celia or Cecilia) and 'Gerrib' townland was rendered 'Greeba'.

[54] 1.Nazareth House, Sligo. *Details of cohort of boys who entered 1925-1932 and their destination and subsequent careers after discharge (Quartet's contemporaries).* 2. Information from Sister John, Sligo. 3.McGowan-Judge, Margaret. *Discussions with author re William McGowan.* 4.Fitzsimons, Imelda. *Discussions with author re William McGowan.*

[55] Porter, Michael Laurence. *Interviews with author* (2012-2016). Michael's aunt was stunned when he contradicted her belief of how care had been beneficial for him.

[56] 1.Nazareth House, Sligo. *Details of cohort of boys who entered 1925-1932 and their destination and subsequent careers after discharge (Quartet's contemporaries).* 2. John (Sister of Nazareth, Sligo). *Oral information.*

[57] In an example of the *de facto* power of religious leaders to exercise temporal power he had already managed to obtain agreement to allow his 3 female nominees to be elected unopposed as Sligo workhouse Inspectors. His reasoning, that women were better able than men to assess the moral and practical care needed in institutions and rectify any problems, shows that he was prepared to wield power to some enlightened end.

[58] Such concerns were features of all three local workhouses at Boyle, Sligo and Carrick-on-Shannon. Indeed the Carrick workhouse case was so serious, involving accusations against Captain Wynne, the workhouse Inspector, that it was investigated by a committee of the House of Lords.

See for example a detailed account of the Carrick- on-Shannon Workhouse case described in: Thomson, David (1991). *Woodbrook.* London: Vintage. pp. 156-172.

[59] John (Sister of Nazareth, Sligo). Unpublished booklet: *Some Details from Records of Events in Nazareth House, Sligo. 1910-1941.* Only male children were to be cared for, separate provision being available elsewhere for females run by other religious orders or congregations.

[60] *Ibid.*

[61] 1911 census of Ireland.

[62] Baker, Patrick Joseph. (1994-1997) *Correspondence to William McGowan.*

[63] It was part of an explosion of new Religious Orders/Congregations in the Roman Catholic Church in the nineteenth century.

[64] *Nazareth: The Poor Sisters of.* Article. Archivist, PO Box, 386, Camberwell, Vic 3124.

[65] The Poor Sisters of Nazareth became an offshoot of the Little Sisters of the Poor, then an independent Congregation of nuns. Both had been founded by Bretons. The little Sisters only cared for the elderly whereas the Nazareth sisters cared for young and old. Both Congregations/Orders were founded by Bretons and both employed begging to raise alms for the poor. See: Milcent, Paul (1982): *Jeanne Jurgan; Foundress of the Little Sisters of the Poor.* London: Catholic Truth Society.

[66] Many Catholic and other denominational organisations involved in such work used 'rescue' in their titles. This habit continued well into the late 20th century in the United Kingdom where many diocesan societies were know as 'The Rescue Society' or 'Catholic Rescue'.

[67] The title of the Congregation was not inappropriate in the early days at least. Victoire Larmeniers who died on 16th June, 1878, in Nazareth House Hammersmith had her will probated on 5th November that year: 'Personal Estate under £5'.

[68] 1901 census of England.

[69] The outline of the functioning of Nazareth House, Hammersmith in the late 19th and early 20th Century, is principally drawn from drawn from: *The Illustrated London News* and *The Tablet.*; census analysis; and T*he Poor Sisters of Nazareth, An Illustrated Record of Life At Nazareth House, Hammersmith.* Meynell, Alice (1889). London, Burns and Oates; Article: *Nazareth, The Poor Sisters of.* Archivist, Po Box, 386, Camberwell, Viv 3124.

[70] *The Illustrated London News.* March 28, 1891, p.417.

[71] Booth, General. (1890-October) *In Darkest England and The Way Out.* London:, The Salvation Army. Booth listed some statistics for London alone: 51,000 in Workhouses and asylums; 33,000 homeless; 390,000 starving; and almost 1 million who were very poor. Coloured frontispiece chart (unpaginated).

The population of London was 5.5 million in 1891. The 'dark' implies the hidden and the unknown.

[72] Stanley, Henry M. (1890- June) *In Darkest Africa.* London: Sampson, Low, Marston, Searle and Rivington. 2 vols.

[73] See for example: Metcalfe, Camillus. (2014) *For God's Sake: The Hidden Life of Irish Nuns.pp.* 38-39.

[74] The spiritual underpinning of the habit was the example of obedience that the Sisters were meant to emulate: their Saviour: 'He humbled himself, becoming obedient unto death, even to the death of the cross'. *Douay Rheims Catholic Bible.* Philippians 2: 8.

[75] Metcalfe, Camillus. (2014): *For God's Sake: The Hidden Life of Irish Nuns.* pp. 32, 52, 53, and 64.

[76] Schmid, Max, S.J. (1932) *The Sister in Charge*. New York: Benziger Brothers. Translated from the German by Speicher, Norman F, (O. M Cap.).

[77] Ibid., 153.

[78] Ibid., 155.

[79] Metcalfe, Camillus. (2014): *For God's Sake: The Hidden Life of Irish Nuns.* pp. 38-39.

[80] I had thought that each Sister chose her new name and that appears to be the case more recently. In December 2014 Sister Gertrude of Nazareth House, Sligo, 89 years old, informed me that in her day the name was chosen for her; there was no question of the Sister being allowed such licence. Another example, perhaps, of the crushing degree of control and conformity exercised by some religious Orders and Congregations then.

[81] Meynell, Alice. (1889) *The Poor Sisters of Nazareth, An Illustrated Record of Life At Nazareth House, Hammersmith.*: London: Burns and Oates. p. 30.

[82] Ibid., 15-16.

[83] Ibid., 16-17.

[84] Ibid., 27-28.

[85] Ibid., 21-22.

[86] Ibid., 39-40.

[87] A particular concern was for the girls to be able to earn a living and not be drawn into prostitution. Booth calculated that there were 30,00 prostitutes in London plus many others who 'secretly increase their earnings by this shame', out of a population of 5.5 million. General Booth (1890): *In Darkest England and The Way Out*. London, The Salvation Army. Coloured frontispiece chart (unpaginated).

[88] Meynell, Alice. (1889) *The Poor Sisters of Nazareth, An Illustrated Record of Life At Nazareth House, Hammersmith.*: London: Burns and Oates. p. 40.

[89] Nazareth House, Sligo. *Details of cohort of boys who entered 1925-1932 and their destination and subsequent careers after discharge (Quartet's contemporaries).*

[90] The Yardman term was used as the work title for the few adult males, all seemingly ex-Homeboys of Nazareth House, who had been given board, lodging and modest wages in return for carrying out the range of heavy manual work around the home and grounds. The term probably originated from the men's primary workplace having been the courtyard, stables and outhouses around the old Yeats home, and/or from their living quarters having been above the stable block.

[91] Baker, Patrick Joseph. (1994-1997) *Correspondence to William McGowan.*

[92] Ibid.

[93] Ibid.

[94] Ibid.

[95] Ibid.

[96] Ibid.

[97] Ibid.

[98] The policy of age group separation was standard practice in state homes, too, but the resource pressures were also less in these homes. As the Nazareth Homes were staffed by the same Congregation of Sisters and under overall control of Reverend Mother greater flexibility might have been expected.

[99] Baker, Patrick Joseph. (1994-1997) *Correspondence to William McGowan.*

[100] McCormack, William (Bill). (Undated). *An Angel Held My Hand.* Internet uploaded account of the author's experiences at Nazareth House, Sligo: 1943-1952.

[101] Baker, Patrick Joseph. (1994-1997) *Correspondence to William McGowan.*

[102] Leo X111, Pope. Extract from *Rerum Novarum.* Quoted in: Eyre, W. H. (Rev.) (1895) *The Pope and the people; Select letters and Addresses on Social Questions.* London: Art Book Co. The Condition of the Working Classes, 1.7.

[103] Author's son.

[104] McCormack, William (Bill). (Undated). *An Angel Held My Hand.* Internet uploaded account of the author's experiences at Nazareth House, Sligo: 1943-1952.

[105] Baker, Patrick Joseph. (1994-1997) *Correspondence to William McGowan.*

[106] 'Boys go bad; girls go mad': a phrase used to describe the greater tendency of males to express trauma angrily and outwards whereas females are more likely to internalise their distress.

[107] Baker, Patrick Joseph. (1994-1997) *Correspondence to William McGowan*

[108] 1. John (Sister of Nazareth, Sligo). Unpublished booklet: *Some Details from Records of Events in Nazareth House, Sligo. 1910-1941* and 2. Baker, Patrick. (1994-1997) *Correspondence to William McGowan.*

[109] Michael Porter was the 296th boy when he arrived in August, 1926.

[110] John (Sister of Nazareth, Sligo). Discussions with author, 2012-2016.

[111] Ibid.

[112] 1. McGowan-Judge, Margaret. *Discussions with author re William McGowan* and
2. Fitzsimons, Imelda. *Discussions with author re William McGowan.*

[113] John (Sister of Nazareth, Sligo). Unpublished booklet: *Some Details from Records of Events in Nazareth House, Sligo. 1910-1941.*

[114] 1911 census of Ireland.

[115] John (Sister of Nazareth, Sligo). *Discussions with author* (2012-2016).

[116] Porter, Michael Laurence. *Interviews with author* (2012-2016).

[117] Attracta (Sister of Nazareth). *Correspondence and photographs sent to William McGowan* (1960's).

[118] This was commented on by both Paddy Baker and William McCormack.

[119] 1. Porter, Michael Laurence. *Interviews with author* (2012-2016). 2. Baker, Patrick Joseph. (1994-1997) *Correspondence to William McGowan.* 3. McGowan-Judge, Margaret. *Discussions with author re William McGowan.* 4. Fitzsimons, Imelda. *Discussions with author re William McGowan.*

[120] 1. Baker, Patrick Joseph. (1994-1997) *Correspondence to William McGowan.* 2. McCormack, William (Bill). (Undated). *An Angel Held My Hand.* Internet uploaded account of the author's experiences at Nazareth House, Sligo: 1943-1952.

[121] Porter, Michael Laurence. *Interviews with author* (2012-2016).

[122] Baker, Patrick Joseph. (1994-1997) *Correspondence to William McGowan*

[123] John (Sister of Nazareth, Sligo). *Discussions with author* (2012-2016).

[124] Porter, Michael Laurence. *Interviews with author* (2012-2016).

[125] McGowan-Judge, Margaret. *Discussions with author re William McGowan.*

[126] John (Sister of Nazareth, Sligo). *Discussions with author* (2012-2016).

[127] Baker, Patrick Joseph. (1994-1997) *Correspondence to William McGowan.*

[128] 1. Ibid. 2. Porter, Michael Laurence. *Interviews with author* (2012-2016).

[129] John (Sister of Nazareth, Sligo). *Discussions with author* (2012-2016).

[130] McCormack, William (Bill). (Undated). *An Angel Held My Hand.* Internet uploaded account of the author's experiences at Nazareth House, Sligo: 1943-1952.

[131] Baker, Patrick Joseph. (1994-1997) *Correspondence to William McGowan.*

[132] Rowntree, Seebohm (1901): *Poverty: A Study Of Town Life.* London: Macmillan.

[133] Booth, Charles. (1902-1903) *Life and Labour of the People in London*. London: Macmillan, 17 vols.

[134] General Booth. (1890) *In Darkest England and The Way Out*. London: The Salvation Army.

[135] Rowntree, Seebohm. (1901) *Poverty: A Study Of Town Life*. London: Macmillan. 24.7% of the children who lived in the poorest areas died before the age of 1 year compared to 9.4% of the servant keeping class.

[136] Ibid., 216-221. 26.5% of recruits in York, Sheffield and Leeds were rejected as medically unfit for army service between 1897-1901. Of the remainder who had been accepted some 29% had only been taken on as 'specials' i.e. not fit but capable of being fed and exercised to reach an acceptable minimum standard of fitness. Taking these into account meant that 47.5% of recruits were unfit for service when they first attempted to enlist.

[137] And also much more likely to be killed than those in the ranks during World War 1.

[138] Related to the overwhelmingly rural and non-industrial nature of Irish society.

[139] Almeric, William Fitz Roy, Sir. (1905) *Report of the Inter-departmental Committee on Physical Deterioration*. London: Darling and Son (for H. M. Stationery Office).

[140] See the sequel volume to this book, *The Quartet: After-Care Lives of Irish Catholic Homeboys* where Michael Porter when in England saw the same principles of differing nutritional needs leading to higher ration and food allowances for those involved in heavy manual work.

[141] Although it appeared that his firm stood to gain by the increased sales of cocoa, Rowntree's character would suggest that financial gain was not the primary reason for the inclusion of cocoa in the diets. (Other rival firms, often also owned by Quakers, also produced cocoa).

[142] Rowntree, Seebohm. (1901) *Poverty: A Study Of Town Life*. London: Macmillan. p. 101.

[143] See the chapter on Memory Mining in the sequel volume to this book, *The Quartet: After-Care Lives of Irish Catholic Homeboys* .

[144] Fitzsimons, Imelda. *Discussions with author re William McGowan*.

[145] Willie McGowan, Paddy Baker and Michael Porter.

[146] *The Times*, London: December 20th, 1890. Front page.

[147] Newspapers throughout England, Wales and Ireland carried reports of the activities of the Nazareth Congregation's fund raising committees, including boxing events. They also carried illustrations of the charitable activities of the Sisters.

[148] John (Sister of Nazareth, Sligo). Unpublished booklet: *Some Details from Records of Events in Nazareth House, Sligo. 1910-1941.*

[149] Ibid.

[150] Ibid.

[151] I remember carrying a radiogram from north east England to Aughoos in remote north west Mayo in 1963 where electricity had not long been installed.

[152] Baker, Patrick Joseph. (1994-1997) *Correspondence to William McGowan.*

[153] McCormack, William (Bill). (Undated). *An Angel Held My Hand. Internet uploaded account of the author's experiences at Nazareth House, Sligo: 1943-1952.*

[154] Porter, Michael Laurence. *Interviews with author* (2012-2016).

[155] Article by Brother Zephiriny in *The Catholic Encyclopedia* (1913). New York: The Encyclopedia Press. Vol. 9. p. 749

[156] John (Sister of Nazareth, Sligo). Unpublished booklet: *Some Details from Records of Events in Nazareth House, Sligo. 1910-1941.*

[157] Baker, Patrick Joseph. *Photographic records of his visits to Sligo.* Paddy Baker was aware of the location of the Marist monastery.

[158] Baker, Patrick Joseph. (1994-1997) *Correspondence to William McGowan.*

[159] The extensively reported cases can still be accessed by Internet search.

[160] Baker, Patrick Joseph. (1994-1997) *Correspondence to William McGowan.*

[161] Ibid.

[162] McCormack, William (Bill). (Undated). *An Angel Held My Hand. Internet uploaded account of the author's experiences at Nazareth House, Sligo: 1943-1952.* Such punishments were far from restricted to Sligo or even Ireland. Although common in state schools too in the United Kingdom, and indeed in public schools, it would be my impression that Catholic schools were more punitive because of the extra dimension of sin scouring. Some of the physical punishment would also seem to have had a sexual undercurrent to it.

[163] Baker, Patrick Joseph. (1994-1997) *Correspondence to William McGowan.*

[164] Porter, Michael Laurence. *Interviews with author* (2012-2016).

[165] John (Sister of Nazareth, Sligo). *Discussions with author* (2012-2016).

[166] Porter, Michael Laurence. *Interviews with author* (2012-2016).

[167] Ibid.

[168] Baker, Patrick Joseph. (1994-1997) *Correspondence to William McGowan.*

[169] *The Times,* London: 21.10.1912. Pg. 9. Obituary of Bishop John Clancy, Roman Catholic Bishop of Elphin.

[170] *The Tablet,* London: 06.09.1902. Pg. 23. Michael Davitt accused Bishop Clancy of using moral law to vindicate English property rights in the De Freyne evictions.

[171] McCarthy, Michael, J.F. (1914) *Priests and People in Ireland.* London:, Simpkin, Marshall, Hamilton and Kent.

[172] Of the four countries that comprised the then British Isles one country stood out for the educational opportunities it gave to poor children: Scotland. In that country there had been a long standing tradition of providing bursaries and scholarships to able pupils to enable them to progress, not only to secondary education, but also on to the universities. Fees and basic accommodation costs at university were met for the 'bag o' meal' students. These were so-called because many of the poor students from rural areas carried a sack of oatmeal with them from their homes at the beginning of term-time. Salted oatmeal porridge, the standard breakfast fare at Nazareth House, Sligo, was the meal many a poor Scottish undergraduate ate, morning, noon and night.

[173] Fletcher, George (Ed.) (1922), *Connaught.* Cambridge: University Press. p.132. The guide book, *Connaught,* described the college as: 'the Important Summerhill College', also stating that: 'while the National Schools of Ireland are, in principle, undenominational in character, the secondary schools are frankly denominational'. The 'in principle' caveat above confirms that much elementary education was in reality strongly denominational in Ireland, and secondary education even more so. That it was so was a result of the Catholic Bishops' opposition to mixed education, in both England and Ireland, and of their determination to control the religious ethos of their schools. The tenor of this is contained in the address of Dr. Healy, Coadjutor Bishop of Clonfert, when he gave the sermon at the opening of the College of the Immaculate Conception in its new premises in Summerhill in 1892:

'We will have none of their mixed education; we will have none of their bribes; we will not barter our freedom; we want no Godless schools and colleges. If they will not give us Christian schools and colleges then we will build them ourselves, and maintain them, too, and they will be our own, and we mean to have religion first, and everything else in the second place'. The 'they' referred to above was the protestant government of Great Britain, the would-be suitor of the Catholic Bishops, whose blandishments and inducements were so contemptuously and confidently rebuffed by the Catholic hierarchy. An interesting confirmation of the degree of *de facto* power the Catholic Bishops felt and exercised in pre-independence Ireland.

[174] Porter, Michael Laurence. *Interviews with author* (2012-2016).

[175] Ibid.

[176] Ibid.

[177] Ibid.

[178] Ibid.

[179] Oral information from family members can be a useful supplement or corrective to official records.. I had originally recorded that the McGowans were not native Irish speakers after searching the 1911 census returns which did not state that they were speakers of Irish. Being familiar with the area they lived in and knowing that a good proportion of the natives there then spoke Irish, I decided to double check. Willie McGowan's daughters confirmed that their grandparents were Irish speakers. 1. McGowan-Judge, Margaret. *Discussions with author re William McGowan*. 2. Fitzsimons, Imelda. *Discussions with author re William McGowan*. The lesson to be drawn: do not assume a negative because a positive is not stated.

[180] Recent attempts to revive it proved fruitless as it felt to him that he was learning an unknown, foreign language. He had been taught Irish using Gaelic script and where lenition was represented by the overdot. The abandonment of these in modern standardised Irish proved too unfamiliar to him.

[181] Porter, Michael Laurence. *Interviews with author* (2012-2016).

[182] Propulsion by prayer perhaps?

[183] Baker, Patrick Joseph. (1994-1997) *Correspondence to William McGowan*.

[184] 1. Fitzsimons, Imelda. *Discussions with author re William McGowan*. 2. McGowan-Judge, Margaret. *Discussions with author re William McGowan*.

[185] Baker, Patrick Joseph. (1994-1997) *Correspondence to William McGowan*.

[186] Porter, Michael Laurence. *Interviews with author* (2012-2016).

[187] Ibid.

[188] [188] Schmid, Max, S.J. (1932): *The Sister in Charge*. New York: Benziger Brothers. Translated from the German by Speicher, Norman F, (O. M Cap.). p. 120.

[189] John (Sister of Nazareth, Sligo). *Discussions with author* (2012-2016).

[190] McCormack, William (Bill). (Undated). *An Angel Held My Hand*. Internet uploaded account of the author's experiences at Nazareth House, Sligo: 1943-1952.

[191] They are even seen in England as in those at Ushaw College, the Diocesan seminary in County Durham, a legacy of the many Irish men who trained for the priesthood there.

[192] Porter, Michael Laurence. *Interviews with author* (2012-2016).

[193] It really was so named. A rather redundant adjective one would have thought. Now known as the Pontifical Urban University. I rather prefer the directness of the original.

[194] McGowan, William. *Correspondence to Mother Veronica* (Nazareth House, Sligo).

A nice touch was the evident pride that Willie McGowan felt at his friend's achievement: something he related to a later Reverend Mother at Nazareth House, Sligo, in case she had been unaware of this.

[195] Baker, Patrick Joseph. (1994-1997) *Correspondence to William McGowan.*

[196] Ibid.

[197] Porter, Michael Laurence. *Interviews with author* (2012-2016).

[198] Ibid.

[199] Pounds, shillings and pence.

[200] Baker, Patrick Joseph. (1994-1997) *Correspondence to William McGowan*

[201] Porter, Michael Laurence. *Interviews with author* (2012-2016).

[202] Ibid.

[203] Ibid.

[204] Ibid.

[205] 1. John (Sister of Nazareth, Sligo). Unpublished booklet: *Some Details from Records of Events in Nazareth House, Sligo. 1910-1941.* 2. 1911 *census of Ireland.*

[206] 1911 *census of Ireland.*

[207] The boys were presumably dependent Independents.

[208] John (Sister of Nazareth, Sligo). Unpublished booklet: *Some Details from Records of Events in Nazareth House, Sligo. 1910-1941.*

[209] Ibid.

[210] Baker, Patrick Joseph. (1994-1997) *Correspondence to William McGowan.*

[211] John (Sister of Nazareth, Sligo). Unpublished booklet: *Some Details from Records of Events in Nazareth House, Sligo. 1910-1941.*

[212] Ibid.

[213] Ibid.

[214] Ibid.

[215] 1. BMD records. 2. John (Sister of Nazareth, Sligo). Unpublished booklet: *Some Details from Records of Events in Nazareth House, Sligo. 1910-1941.*

[216] Baker, Patrick Joseph. (1994-1997) *Correspondence to William McGowan.*

[217] Porter, Michael Laurence. *Interviews with author* (2012-2016).

[218] Ibid.

[219] 1. John (Sister of Nazareth, Sligo). Unpublished booklet: *Some Details from Records of Events in Nazareth House, Sligo. 1910-1941.* 2. Porter, Michael Laurence. *Interviews with author* (2012-2016).

[220] John (Sister of Nazareth, Sligo). Unpublished booklet: *Some Details from Records of Events in Nazareth House, Sligo. 1910-1941.*

[221] Porter, Michael Laurence. *Interviews with author* (2012-2016).

[222] Ibid.

[223] Ibid.

[224] John (Sister of Nazareth, Sligo). *Discussions with author* (2012-2016).

[225] Nazareth House, Sligo. *Details of cohort of boys who entered 1925-1932 and their destination and subsequent careers after discharge (Quartet's contemporaries).*

[226] Porter, Michael Laurence. *Interviews with author* (2012-2016).

[227] 1. Nazareth House, Sligo. *Details of cohort of boys who entered 1925-1932 and their destination and subsequent careers after discharge (Quartet's contemporaries).* 2. John (Sister of Nazareth, Sligo). *Discussions with author* (2012-2016).

[228] Porter, Michael Laurence. *Interviews with author* (2012-2016).

[229] John (Sister of Nazareth, Sligo). *Discussions with author* (2012-2016).

[230] Porter, Michael Laurence. *Interviews with author* (2012-2016).

[231] Ibid.

[232] John (Sister of Nazareth, Sligo). *Discussions with author* (2012-2016).

[233] Porter, Michael Laurence. *Interviews with author* (2012-2016).

[234] Ibid.

[235] Ibid.

[236] Utting, William (Sir). (1997) *People Like Us: The Report of the Review of the Safeguards for Children Living Away from Home.* London: The Stationery Office for The Department of Health. p. 99.

[237] 1. Baker, Patrick Joseph. (1994-1997) *Correspondence to William McGowan.* 2. McCormack, William (Bill). (Undated). *An Angel Held My Hand.* Internet uploaded account of the author's experiences at Nazareth House, Sligo: 1943-1952. 3. Porter, Michael Laurence. *Interviews with author* (2012-2016).

[238] Nazareth House, Sligo. *Details of cohort of boys who entered 1925-1932 and their destination and subsequent careers after discharge (Quartet's contemporaries).*

[239] Baker, Patrick Joseph. (1994-1997) *Correspondence to William McGowan.*

[240] That was the sole visit Paddy ever had from the unknown man.

[241] Baker, Patrick Joseph. (1994-1997) *Correspondence to William McGowan.*

[242] *The Irish Catholic Directory and Almanack for 1920.* Dublin: James Duffy. p. 294.

[243] McCormack, William (Bill). (Undated). *An Angel Held My Hand.* Internet uploaded account of the author's experiences at Nazareth House, Sligo: 1943-1952.

[244] 1. McGowan-Judge, Margaret. *Discussions with author re William McGowan.* 2. Fitzsimons, Imelda. *Discussions with author re William McGowan.*

[245] 1. McGowan-Judge, Margaret. *Discussions with author re William McGowan.* 2. Fitzsimons, Imelda. *Discussions with author re William McGowan.*

[246] 1. Nazareth House, Sligo. *Details of cohort of boys who entered 1925-1932 and their destination and subsequent careers after discharge (Quartet's contemporaries.* 2. Porter, Michael Laurence. *Interviews with author* (2012-2016).

[247] It might be more accurate to state that Michael does not remember any other references rather than there were none. It took some 3 years of constant probing with Michael before he remembered that someone had mentioned the name father to him. Previously he had been adamant that this had never occurred.

[248] Porter, Michael Laurence. *Interviews with author* (2012-2016).

[249] Ibid.

[250] Although Michael did not know to which Order or Congregation of nuns these Sisters belonged he did know from their habits that they were not Nazareth Sisters.

[251] Compare this with the 'The Child Pilot' section of Memory Mining in: *The Quartet: After-Care Lives of Irish Catholic Homeboys.*

[252] Porter, Michael Laurence. *Interviews with author* (2012-2016).

[253] Calculated from: Nazareth House, Sligo. *Details of cohort of boys who entered 1925-1932 and their destination and subsequent careers after discharge (Quartet's contemporaries).*

[254] Baker, Patrick Joseph. (1994-1997) *Correspondence to William McGowan.*

[255] Porter, Michael Laurence. *Interviews with author* (2012-2016).

[256] Lecky, William Edward Hartpole. (1899) *The Map of Life.* London: Longmans, Green and Co. p. 328.

[257] Cohen, Stanley and Taylor, Laurie. (1972) *Psychological Survival: The Experience of Long-Term Imprisonment.* London: Penguin Books.

[258] Ibid., 71-72.

[259] Baker, Patrick Joseph. (1994-1997) *Correspondence to William McGowan.* As the foundation stone reads:

THIS STONE WAS LAID BY

THE MOST REVEREND B. COYNE D.D

NOVEMBER 21ST 1921

Paddy has extracted his desired fact while ignoring the significance of the rest of the information.

[260] See another blending of fact and fiction in a child's memory in 'The Child Pilot' section of Memory Mining in: *The Quartet: After-Care Lives of Irish Catholic Homeboys.*

[261] Porter, Michael Laurence. *Interviews with author* (2012-2016).

[262] Ibid.

[263] Ibid.

[264] Porter, Michael (Junior) *Discussions with author* (December 2014).

[265] There is no confirmatory evidence about this man who may not have been Paddy's father as it seems that Paddy and James Baker had different fathers.

[266] This, I assume, was in response to Paddy raising the issue of a mother with her as it does not seem that otherwise the Sisters broached the matter of family with the boys.

[267] Baker, Patrick Joseph. (1994-1997) *Correspondence to William McGowan.*

[268] Ibid.

[269] Not knowing his mother was alive meant that Paddy did not search for her in his early years after leaving care. When he did begin the search it was too late.

[270] A repeated theme in this book.

[271] For most of the Nazareth boys including the Quartet this meant not being Protestant or English.

[272] See question 370 of the Penny Catechism: *After your night prayers what should you do?* After my night prayers I should observe due modesty in going to bed; occupy myself with the thoughts of death; and endeavour to compose myself to rest at the foot of the Cross, and give my last thoughts to my crucified Saviour. Online version available at: www.proecclesia.com/penny%20catechism/index.

[273] Online version available at: www.proecclesia.com/penny%20catechism/index.

[274] Porter, Michael Laurence. *Interviews with author* (2012-2016).

[275] The Second Vatican Council of the 1960's removed the *Dies Irae* from the Requiem Mass.

[276] *Dies Irae:* Wikipedia. The Latin original and 2 different translations are given there.

[277] Matthew 16:26.

[278] An old classic text on institutional care that still resonates today is: Goffman, Erving (1968) *Asylums: Essays on the Social Situation of Mental Patients and Other Inmates.* United Kingdom: Penguin Books.

[279] 1. McCormack, William (Bill). (Undated). *An Angel Held My Hand.* Internet uploaded account of the author's experiences at Nazareth House, Sligo: 1943-1952. 2. See also the gaze aversion in the training of some sisters referred to in Chapter 1.3.

[280] Father Edward Flanagan of Boys Town. Quoted in: Oursler, Fulton & Oursler, Will. (1949) *Father Flanagan of Boys Town.* New York: Doubleday and Company.

[281] Utting, William (Sir). (1997):*People Like Us: The Report of the Review of the Safeguards for Children Living Away from Home.* London: The Stationery Office for The Department of Health. p. 7.

[282] Maslow, Abraham. (1943) *A Theory of Human Motivation in Psychological Review.* American Psychological Association.

[283] Despite Father Flanagan's dismissal of this basic provision in 1.9.15 later.

[284] Meynell, Alice. (1889) *The Poor Sisters of Nazareth, An Illustrated Record of Life At Nazareth House, Hammersmith.* London: Burns and Oates.

[285] A more detailed summary of evolving understanding of abuse is outlined in: Murphy, J. M. and Welbury, R. R. (1998) *The Dental Practitioner's Role in*

Protecting Children From Abuse. 1. The Child protection System. London: British Dental Journal. Vol. 184. No. 1. January 10, 1998.

[286] John (Sister of Nazareth, Sligo). Unpublished booklet: *Some Details from Records of Events in Nazareth House, Sligo. 1910-1941.*

[287] Meynell, Alice. (1889) *The Poor Sisters of Nazareth, An Illustrated Record of Life At Nazareth House, Hammersmith.* London: Burns and Oates.

[288] And indeed manifested this much more towards them when they had left Nazareth House, or worked as Yardmen or when the boys revisited the Home in adulthood.

[289] Detailed in chapters 1.7 and 1.12.

[290] Baker, Patrick Joseph. (1994-1997*) Correspondence to William McGowan.*

[291] Porter, Michael Laurence. *Interviews with author* (2012-2016).

[292] Baker, Patrick Joseph. (1994-1997*) Correspondence to William McGowan.*

[293] Porter, Michael Laurence. *Interviews with author* (2012-2016).

[294] Baker, Patrick Joseph. (1994-1997*) Correspondence to William McGowan.*

[295] Ibid.

[296] It has been my experience that uniformed organisations tend to have a greater degree of affiliation among their members, a greater degree of separation from the 'outside world' and a greater tendency to support and defend any co-member who is in trouble or charged with abuse; this includes the police.

[297] Murphy, John Michael. (1998). *Has the child protection delegate role improved how the Catholic church deals with child sexual exploitation by clergy/religious in the study diocese?* M.A. thesis: University of Northumbria at Newcastle. (The thesis is protected by confidentiality arrangements).

[298] My own view is: probably not.

[299] Porter, Michael Laurence. *Interviews with author* (2012-2016).

[300] Ibid.

[301] Ibid.

[302] Paddy's brother, James Baker, later told him that was what had occurred.

[303] Attracta (Sister of Nazareth). *Correspondence and photographs sent to William McGowan (1960's).*

[304] Porter, Michael Laurence. *Interviews with author* (2012-2016).

[305] John (Sister of Nazareth, Sligo). *Discussions with author* (2012-2016).

[306] McCormack, William (Bill). (Undated). *An Angel Held My Hand*. Internet uploaded account of the author's experiences at Nazareth House, Sligo: 1943-1952.

[307] Mary of the Passion (Reverend Mother, Sisters of Nazareth, Sligo). *Correspondence to William McGowan and family.*

[308] William McCormack describes just such caring handling of a difficult incident by Sister Mary.

[309] McCormack, William (Bill). (Undated). *An Angel Held My Hand*. Internet uploaded account of the author's experiences at Nazareth House, Sligo: 1943-1952.

[310] Baker, Patrick Joseph. (1994-1997) *Correspondence to William McGowan.*

[311] Porter, Michael Laurence. *Interviews with author* (2012-2016).

[312] McCormack, William (Bill). (Undated). *An Angel Held My Hand*. Internet uploaded account of the author's experiences at Nazareth House, Sligo: 1943-1952.

[313] The Shorter Catechism Agreed Upon By The Assembly of Divines at Westminster. Glasgow: W.R. Holmes. Undated (probably Edwardian). Front cover.

[314] Formerly known as The Catholic Rescue Society.

[315] Baker, Patrick Joseph. (1994-1997) *Correspondence to William McGowan.*

[316] Shakespeare, William. Henry IV Part 11. Act 111, Scene 1.

[317] Baker, Patrick Joseph. (1994-1997) *Correspondence to William McGowan.*

[318] Oursler, Fulton & Oursler, Will. (1949): *Father Flanagan of Boys Town.* New York: Doubleday and Company. p. 35.

[319] *Boys Town* (1938), starring Spencer Tracy and Mickey Rooney.

[320] Oursler, Fulton & Oursler, Will. (1949) *Father Flanagan of Boys Town.* New York: Doubleday and Company. p. 6.

[321] When Royal visits were due at some British coal mines the tidy up operation included whitewashing some of the surface coal.

[322] Baker, Patrick Joseph. *Photographic records of his visits to Sligo.* Photograph with recording on rear of last remnants of Quay Street School wall.

[323] McCormack, William (Bill). (Undated). *An Angel Held My Hand*. Internet uploaded account of the author's experiences at Nazareth House, Sligo: 1943-1952

[324] This he remembers was because he usually had plenty of, as yet undiscovered, boyish misdemeanours on his conscience.

[325] Porter, Michael Laurence. *Interviews with author* (2012-2016).

[326] Geary, Brendan and Greer, Joanne Marie. (1911) *The Dark night of the Catholic Church*. Stowmarket: Kevin Mayhew.

[327] Baker, Patrick Joseph. (1994-1997) *Correspondence to William McGowan.*

[328] Porter, Michael Laurence. *Interviews with author* (2012-2016).

[329] McCormack, William (Bill). (Undated). *An Angel Held My Hand*. Internet uploaded account of the author's experiences at Nazareth House, Sligo: 1943-1952.

[330] John (Sister of Nazareth, Sligo). *Discussions with author* (2012-2016).

[331] McCormack, William (Bill). (Undated). *An Angel Held My Hand*. Internet uploaded account of the author's experiences at Nazareth House, Sligo: 1943-1952.

Ibid.

[332] Porter, Michael Laurence. *Interviews with author* (2012-2016).

[333] Baker, Patrick Joseph. (1994) *Photographic records of his visits to Sligo*. Paddy photographed Sister Felim's memorial cross. Sister St. Felim (McCaul) died on 13th June, 1970.

[334] McGowan-Judge, Margaret. *Discussions with author re William McGowan.*

[335] Baker, Patrick Joseph. (1994-1997) *Correspondence to William McGowan.*

[336] A wet place is Sligo.

[337] John (Sister of Nazareth, Sligo). Unpublished booklet: *Some Details from Records of Events in Nazareth House, Sligo. 1910-1941.*

[338] Baker, Patrick Joseph. (1994-1997) *Correspondence to William McGowan.*

[339] Ibid.

[340] Baker, Patrick Joseph. (1994) *Photographic records of his visits to Sligo*. Paddy photographed Sister Gabriel's memorial cross. Sister Gabriel Philip (Doherty) died on 21st April, 1945.

[341] McCormack, William (Bill). (Undated). *An Angel Held My Hand*. Internet uploaded account of the author's experiences at Nazareth House, Sligo: 1943-1952.

[342] Ibid.

[343] Ibid.

[344] Ibid.

[345] Information supplied to the author by Michael Carey's daughter-in-law, Norah Carey (nee Lally), of Cloontakilla, Bangor Erris, County Mayo.

[346] Baker, Patrick Joseph. (1994-1997) *Correspondence to William McGowan.*

[347] McGowan-Judge, Margaret. *Discussions with author re William McGowan.*

[348] Fitzsimons, Imelda. *Discussions with author re William McGowan.*

[349] Meynell, Alice. (1889) T*he Poor Sisters of Nazareth, An Illustrated Record of Life At Nazareth House, Hammersmith.*: London: Burns and Oates. The quotation is taken from Johann Wolfgang von Goethe (1749-1842). 'Without haste, without rest'.

[350] Porter, Michael Laurence. *Interviews with author* (2012-2016).

[351] Ibid.

[352] The Sister had a small group of young children to supervise also. The children would have been unwitting chaperones for the Sister.

[353] Porter, Michael Laurence. *Interviews with author* (2012-2016).

[354] McCormack, William (Bill). (Undated*). An Angel Held My Hand.* Internet uploaded account of the author's experiences at Nazareth House, Sligo: 1943-1952.

[355] Arguably another form of vanity in itself.

[356] I would pay good money to be able to see Sister Attracta's reaction to anyone taking a 'selfie' today.

[357] Baker, Patrick Joseph. (1994-1997) *Correspondence to William McGowan.*

[358] Ibid.

[359] Baker, Patrick Joseph. *Photographic records of his visits to Sligo.* Paddy took photographs of many of the Sisters' graves on his visits to Nazareth House in later life.

[360] Hyde, Douglas. (1906). *The Religious Songs of Connacht.* London:. T Fisher Unwin. p. 375

[361] Baker, Patrick Joseph. (1994-1997) *Correspondence to William McGowan.*

[362] Ibid.

[363] This tradition is still maintained to this day, especially at Hammersmith, where old boys re-gather at Christmas.

[364] As he and Willie McGowan always called their care home.

[365] So Paddy was aware that a few boys did have parents, unlike Michael Porter.

[366] Baker, Patrick Joseph. (1994-1997) *Correspondence to William McGowan.*

[367] O'Shaughnessy, Arthur. (1874): Ode: In *Music and Moonlight:*. London: Chatto and Windus. 1874. p.1.

[368] Coleman never managed the first place of the Quartet, however: achieving joint third place on both occasions.

[369] Baker, Patrick Joseph. (1994-1997) *Correspondence to William McGowan.*

[370] Fitzsimons, Imelda. *Discussions with author re William McGowan.*

[371] Porter, Michael Laurence. *Interviews with author* (2012-2016).

[372] *Sligo Feis Ceoil,* (1953) Golden Jubilee Year publication.

[373] The beginning of St John's Gospel was always known by Catholics as *The Last Gospel* because of its appearance at the end of Mass, until its discontinuance after the Second Vatican Council in the mid 1960's.

[374] Baker, Patrick Joseph. (1994-1997) *Correspondence to William McGowan.*

[375] Porter, Michael Laurence. *Interviews with author* (2012-2016).

[376] Baker, Patrick Joseph. (1994-1997) Correspondence to Willie McGowan.

[377] Ibid.

[378] Ibid.

[379] Ibid.

[380] John (Sister of Nazareth, Sligo). Unpublished booklet: *Some Details from Records of Events in Nazareth House, Sligo. 1910-1941.*

[381] 1. 1901 and 1911 censuses of Ireland and 1880 United States census. 2. Wheatley, Michael (2005). *Nationalism and the Irish Party: Provincial Ireland, 1906-1916.* Oxford: Oxford University Press. p. 144.

[382] *ElectionsIreland.org.* 1923 General Election: Leitrim Sligo. Mr. Depew received 1.6% of the votes coming 13th on a slate of 18 candidates.

[383] Wheatley, Michael. (2005) *Nationalism and the Irish Party: Provincial Ireland, 1906-1916.* Oxford: Oxford University Press. p. 144.

[384] 1. Sligo Feis Minute Books. 2. *Sligo Feis Ceoil, 1953.* Golden Jubilee Year publication. pp. 9 and 11 (the latter page regretting his recent death). 3. Sligo Bands (uncited extract). pp. 122-123.

[385] Sligo Feis Minute Books.

[386] 1. 1911 census of Ireland. 2. John (Sister of Nazareth, Sligo). *Discussions with author* (2012-2016).

[387] Porter, Michael Laurence. *Interviews with author* (2012-2016).

[388] Baker, Patrick Joseph. (1994-1997) *Correspondence to William McGowan.*

[389] John (Sister of Nazareth, Sligo). Unpublished booklet: *Some Details from Records of Events in Nazareth House, Sligo. 1910-1941.* (I assume that he would have been accommodated at Nazareth House, Hammersmith, during this training. The Sisters always referred to the inmates, or former inmates, as 'boys', 'old boys' or even 'pupils').

[390] Michael Porter referred to most of the Yardmen having disabilities including one with a most severe deformity of the leg.

[391] 1. Sligo Bands (uncited extract). p. 123. 2. John (Sister of Nazareth, Sligo). Unpublished booklet: *Some Details from Records of Events in Nazareth House, Sligo. 1910-1941.*

[392] Baker, Patrick Joseph. (1994-1997) *Correspondence to William McGowan.*

[393] Ibid. I have not altered Paddy's phonetic rendering of what he heard.

[394] McCormack, William (Bill). (Undated). *An Angel Held My Hand.* Internet uploaded account of the author's experiences at Nazareth House, Sligo: 1943-1952.

[395] The Tonic Sol-fa system of music teaching was developed in the mid nineteenth century by a Yorkshire Congregational minister, John Curwen, based on a mediaeval Benedictine monk's work and, later, Sarah Ann Glover's Norwich sol-fa system. It is best remembered from Julie Andrews' song in the film: *The Sound of Music.*

[396] Baker, Patrick Joseph. (1994-1997) *Correspondence to William McGowan.*

[397] Porter, Michael Laurence. *Interviews with author* (2012-2016).

[398] Ibid.

[399] Baker, Patrick Joseph. (1994-1997) *Correspondence to William McGowan.* Paddy listed these from a photograph sent to him by Willie McGowan.

[400] Sligo Bands (uncited extract). p. 123.

[401] Porter, Michael Laurence. *Interviews with author* (2012-2016).

[402] John (Sister of Nazareth, Sligo). *Discussions with author* (2012-2016). They did not usually join as bandsmen but it seems that the musical and marching training and the discipline gave added weight to their application for an army post.

[403] Porter, Michael Laurence.) *Interviews with author* (2012-2016

[404] Baker, Patrick Joseph. (1994-1997) *Correspondence to William McGowan.*

[405] John (Sister of Nazareth, Sligo). *Discussions with author* (2012-2016). Sister John said that: 'Josie had the Sisters' hearts scalded'.

[406] 1. Baker, Patrick Joseph. (1994-1997) *Correspondence to William McGowan*. 2. John (Sister of Nazareth, Sligo). *Discussions with author* (2012-2016).

[407] John (Sister of Nazareth, Sligo). *Discussions with author* (2012-2016).

[408] *The Sligo Champion.* Saturday, April 7th, 1934. p. 12.

[409] Porter, Michael Laurence. *Interviews with author* (2012-2016). (*The Sligo Champion* extract does not give the tune played).

[410] Chesterton, G. K. (1911) *The Ballad of the White Horse.* Book 2. (Accessed on Project Gutenberg Ebook).

[411] Lady Dufferin's: *An Irish Emigrant's Lament,* beats it for misery, however.

[412] Sligo Feis Minute Books.

[413] Take a bow, Mr Rowley, wherever you are, you good, honest, foolish man. I suspect that Mr Depew was not too unhappy that his former protégés had won, and Mr Rowley's integrity would not have had detrimental financial consequences for him.

[414] 'Music has charms to soothe a savage breast'. First line of William Congreve's play: *The Mourning Bride (1697).*

[415] McGowan-Judge, Margaret. *Discussions with author re William McGowan.*

[416] Winners and place medals from the 1930's still come up for sale periodically on Ebay.

[417] Baker, Patrick Joseph. (1994-1997) *Correspondence to William McGowan*

[418] O'Shaughnessy, Arthur. (1874) Ode: In *Music and Moonlight:* London: Chatto and Windus. p.2.

[419] Porter, Michael Laurence. *Interviews with author* (2012-2016).

[420] 1. McGowan-Judge, Margaret. *Discussions with author re William McGowan.* 2. John (Sister of Nazareth, Sligo). *Discussions with author* (2012-2016). 3. Fitzsimons, Imelda. *Discussions with author re William McGowan.* All of the above knew about the 'dummy' (as the boys then referred to anyone who was deaf and dumb) cobbler at Nazareth House.

[421] 1. McGowan-Judge, Margaret. *Discussions with author re William McGowan.* 2. Fitzsimons, Imelda. *Discussions with author re William McGowan.*

Many cobblers in Ireland seem to have been deaf and dumb then. Michael's cousin in Dublin, Ger O'Neill (nee Porter) remembers her local cobbler being deaf and dumb.

[422] Porter, Michael Laurence. *Interviews with author* (2012-2016).

[423] It was only after three years of intense discussions, with Michael having been adamant that no mention of either parent had ever been made to him at Nazareth House, that he remembered this incident. Not remembering does not mean that something did not happen.

[424] John (Sister of Nazareth, Sligo). *Discussions with author* (2012-2016). Many could not have afforded to do so.

[425] Mercy Sisters. *Care career records of Mary Bridgid (Sadie) Porter.*

[426] John (Sister of Nazareth, Sligo). *Discussions with author* (2012-2016).

[427] McGahern, John. (2005) *Memoir.* London: Faber and Faber. John McGahern's sister was sexually exploited by the draper in whose house she lived while being trained as a draper's assistant.

[428] One of Willie McGowan's sisters was also exploited in this way and the resulting child taken away from her. (McGowan-Judge, Margaret. *Discussions with author re William McGowan.* 2. Fitzsimons, Imelda. *Discussions with author re William McGowan).* Paddy Baker's mother also fell into this category of vulnerable person.

[429] Porter, Michael Laurence. Nazareth House, Sligo. *Care career records.*

[430] Porter, Michael Laurence. *Interviews with author* (2012-2016).

[431] 1. Porter, Michael Laurence. Nazareth House, Sligo. *Care career records.* 2. Porter, Michael Laurence. *Interviews with author* (2012-2016).

[432] Porter, Michael Laurence. Nazareth House, Sligo. *Care career records.* This is recorded on file but Michael retains no record of writing this letter: indeed he is adamant that he never ever wrote back to the Sisters after first leaving Nazareth House.

[433] Porter, Michael Laurence.) *Interviews with author* (2012-2016.

[434] Ibid.

[435] Porter, Michael Laurence. Nazareth House, Sligo. *Care career records.* Was he homesick?

[436] Over a period of years I noticed an enormous change in Michael's response to new information. In the earlier period 'absolutely' or 'absolutely not' featured heavily in his responses. In latter times his response became much more open to the possibility of his recollection being uncertain. The shift of stance occurred after the number of times his dogmatic certainty was shown to be unfounded.

I pointed out to him that he showed great pent up anger and bitterness when records contradicted his recollections; and that he then either dismissed the records as wrong or attacked those who had recorded them. He did acknowledge that he had experienced a number of occasions in his life where he had been overcome by his anger.

[437] Porter, Michael Laurence. *Interviews with author* (2012-2016).

[438] Ibid. Michael had never heard of such a place as a Labour Exchange and thought the term odd but memorable.

[439] Michael was 'absolutely' clear that the Sisters had nothing to do with him securing this placement, nor did he let them know where he had gone to. The Sisters referred to the farm failure in their recording of the Dargan work situation: 'Returned to Nazareth House–found the work did not suit him and went to Mr Dorgan (sic), Rosses Point, Sligo'.

[440] 1901 Census of Ireland. Living with mother and 3 sisters in Mullingar and working as a carpenter. Significantly for his later career advancement he was bilingual.

[441] Ibid.

[442] Hansard. House of Commons Debate. 7th March 1910. Vol. 14. pp. 1128-32.

[443] He played for Sligo Town and was also a member of the 1928 Connacht Cup winning team that beat Mayo in the final.

[444] Porter, Michael Laurence. *Interviews with author* (2012-2016).

[445] Laundry services were then common for men of Mr Dargan's class. His need to cut a reasonable figure because of his work position meant that he could hardly entrust this to an unskilled lad like Michael.

[446] From the Irish *gaimbín,* meaning 'monetary interest'.

[447] Joseph Campbell, Irish Poet (1978-1944).

[448] Porter, Michael Laurence. *Interviews with author* (2012-2016). He has no idea how he learned this technique or from whom.

[449] Small curly haired lad with a damaged leg driving a bony, dried up old beast must have been judged an insufficiently distinctive sight in Sligo market in the 1930's to ensure recognition by the jobber.

[450] It does not mean that they were unaware of it.

[451] Michael contrasted this crude play with the advice he was given later in life by a Newbiggin-by-the-sea golf professional, Tommy Fairburn. *Tommy didn't overburden you with technical matters. He said, 'Well Michael, don't let anybody ever interfere with your swing'.*

[452] Porter, Michael Laurence. *Interviews with author* (2012-2016).

[453] Porter, Michael Laurence. Nazareth House, Sligo. Care career records.

[454] This seems the most likely period when he may have briefly gone back to Nazareth House for three days, possibly in high dudgeon as he was understandably most aggrieved at his treatment.

[455] Porter, Michael Laurence. *Interviews with author* (2012-2016).

[456] Porter, Michael Laurence. Nazareth House, Sligo. *Care career records.*

[457] Porter, Michael Laurence. *Interviews with author* (2012-2016).

[458] As stated earlier he even wrongly believed that Mrs McGarrigle had not known that he had been at Nazareth House. In fact she was well known to the Sisters who had placed other 'Situation', boys with her. John (Sister of Nazareth, Sligo). Discussions with author, (2012-2016).

[459] Porter, Michael Laurence. *Interviews with author* (2012-2016).

[460] It was the last record the Sisters in Sligo had of him until I contacted them on his behalf early in 2012.

[461] Porter, Michael Laurence. *Interviews with author* (2012-2016).

[462] Ibid.

[463] 1. McGowan-Judge, Margaret. *Discussions with author re William McGowan.* 2. Fitzsimons, Imelda. *Discussions with author re William McGowan.*

[464] Fitzsimons, Imelda. *Discussions with author re William McGowan.*

[465] Porter, Michael Laurence. Nazareth House, Sligo, *Continuation record book (post-care events and contacts).*

At first Michael was 'absolutely certain' that the Sisters never knew that he was at Mrs McGarrigle's and that he had never visited Nazareth House when he lived in the hotel. After I managed to persuade him to the contrary, using the continuation record book log of his contacts with them, he then remembered visiting Nazareth House in an oversized 'borrowed' hotel resident's overcoat for Midnight Mass. As by this time Michael was in his late teens, and as he still has a first class memory for other matters, this denial of actuality is harder to understand. It does reveal, however, the oft-stated contention in this book that narrative can shape facts (just as more usually facts shape narrative).

[466] Porter, Michael Laurence. *Interviews with author* (2012-2016).

[467] Because Michael knew of the excursion I was able to work out the date through internet searches of match day, venue etc.

[468] Porter, Michael Laurence. *Interviews with author* (2012-2016).

[469] Michael was worried that he might be in trouble or lose his job if he did not return on time. He could not telephone to Mrs McGarrigle as he did not know how to make a telephone call, never having used a telephone previously.

[470] *Gray's Elegy:* 'They kept the noiseless tenor of their way'. line 76.

[471] Still passive; still hoping not to have to make a choice; still hoping to stick with what he knew and where he felt secure.

[472] Porter, Michael Laurence. *Interviews with author* (2012-2016).

[473] Porter, Michael Laurence. *Genealogical and family history documents.*

[474] Later renamed Portrane Hospital and then St. Ita's Hospital.

[475] 17 staff plus inmates worked in the laundry alone.

[476] 1. National Inventory of Architectural Heritage: website. 2. St. Ita's Hospital, Portrane: Wikipedia.

[477] 1. Porter, Michael Laurence. *Family photographs.* 2. Porter, Michael Laurence. *Interviews with author* (2012-2016). 3. Porter, Michael Laurence. *Genealogical and family history documents.*

[478] Brody, Hugh. (1974) *Inishkillane: Change and Decline in the West of Ireland.* London: Pelican Books. The cumulative impact of generations of emigration on the emotional and sometimes mental health of rural community members in the late 1960's was sensitively portrayed by Brody.

[479] When first we discussed Madge, Michael was very bitter towards her.

[480] His uncle Frank was 14 years older than Michael and 14 years younger than Michael's father.

[481] Porter, Michael Laurence. *Interviews with author* (2012-2016).

[482] Ibid.

[483] McGowan, William. Nazareth House, Sligo. *Care career records.*

[484] McGowan, William. *Irish Army Career records.*

[485] 1. McGowan, William. Nazareth House, Sligo. *Care career records.* 2. Fitzsimons, Imelda. *Discussions with author re William McGowan.* 3. McGowan-Judge, Margaret. *Discussions with author re William McGowan.*

[486] Baker, Patrick Joseph. (1994-1997) *Correspondence to William McGowan.*. (Paddy was actually 14 years old).

[487] Porter, Michael Laurence. *Interviews with author* (2012-2016).

[488] Baker, Patrick Joseph. (1994-1997) *Correspondence to William McGowan.*

[489] And by no means all of those fathers who did remarry did reclaim their sons. The views of the new step-mothers largely determined the outcome.

[490] Baker, Patrick Joseph. (1994-1997) *Correspondence to William McGowan.*

[491] 1. McGowan-Judge, Margaret. *Discussions with author re William McGowan.* 2. Fitzsimons, Imelda. *Discussions with author re William McGowan.*

[492] McGowan-Judge, Margaret. *Discussions with author re William McGowan.*

[493] Oursler, Fulton & Oursler, Will. (1949) *Father Flanagan of Boys Town.* New York: Doubleday and Company.

[494] Baker, Patrick Josesph. (1994-1997) *Correspondence to William McGowan.*

[495] Porter, Michael Laurence. *Interviews with author* (2012-2016).

[496] McGowan, William. Nazareth House, Sligo. *Care career records.*

[497] McGowan-Judge, Margaret. *Discussions with author re William McGowan.*

[498] (A summary of this is shown in chapter 1.2).

[499] The system did not mean absolute inheritance by only the one child, as other forms of financial or other arrangements were often made for the other children).

[500] 1. McGowan-Judge, Margaret. *Discussions with author re William McGowan.* 2. Fitzsimons, Imelda. *Discussions with author re William McGowan.*

[501] These tales of life abroad were not always reality based, or they were exaggerated by the migrant.

[502] My grandfather, Denis Murphy (1890-1952) who moved from the boglands of the Barony of Erris north west Mayo to the Northumberland coalfields told his daughter that she should be grateful to live in the smoke-blackened large coal mining town of Ashington rather than Erris for two reason: pavements and street lighting. (Information from Katy Byrne (nee Murphy).

[503] McGowan-Judge, Margaret. *Discussions with author re William McGowan.*

[504] McGowan, William. Nazareth House, Sligo. *Care career records; continuation book records (after-care contact).*

[505] Anthony Joseph (Sister of Nazareth, Mallow). *Correspondence to William McGowan.*

[506] John (Sister of Nazareth, Sligo). *Discussions with author* (2012-2016).

[507] 1. Anthony Joseph (Sister of Nazareth, Mallow). *Correspondence to William McGowan.* 2. Baker, Patrick Joseph. (1994-1997) *Correspondence to William McGowan.*

[508] McGowan, William. Nazareth House, Sligo. *Care career records; continuation book records (after-care contact).*

[509] Ibid.

[510] Walsh, William. Nazareth House, Sligo. *Care career record.*

[511] Walsh, William. Nazareth House, Sligo. *Continuation record book.*

[512] Ibid.

[513] See the chapter on Memory Mining in: *The Quartet: After-Care Lives of Irish Catholic Homeboys.* Paddy thought he was about 15 when he ran away, whereas he was probably about 13 to 14 years old. He had not run off in January 1936 when he sang for John McCormack at Nazareth House. It is probable that he ran off sometime later in 1936 when he would have been nearly 14 years old, as Michael Porter was still at Nazareth House then, and he also suffered the beating from Mahon.

Michael Porter had the benefit of nearly five years discussion and a raft of official documents and other records and someone to help him make sense of events. Although Paddy lacked much of this assistance his correspondence with Willie McGowan, regular visits to Nazareth House and especially his discussions with Josie Cummings provided him with some memory supplementation and correction.

[514] 1. Porter, Michael Laurence. *Interviews with author* (2012-2016). 2. Fitzsimons, Imelda. *Discussions with author re William McGowan.* 3. McGowan-Judge, Margaret. *Discussions with author re William McGowan.*

[515] Baker, Patrick Joseph. (1994-1997) *Correspondence to William McGowan.*

[516] Paddy mentions this but never seems, like Michael with Mrs McGarrigle, to wonder how the yardman knew her and connect this to Nazareth House.

[517] Again Paddy recorded this but never queried how he came to be have arrived at a place far distant from Sligo, deep in the countryside, that had been used by Nazareth House to place Situation boys there after care.

[518] *(It is not clear when this placement occurred in relation to the other three).* It proved very difficult to sequence the placements because: Paddy was so young when these occurred; his references to these occur in different part of his letter sheaf; he can suddenly leave the topic for another one; above all because he had no-one else to help him consolidate or correct them.

[519] Baker, Patrick Joseph. (1994-1997) *Correspondence to William McGowan.*

[520] The rural Irish would often refer to a farm as a 2 cow farm to indicate not the number of beasts they possessed but rather how many such animals the poor land could sustain.

[521] Freeman, T.W. (1969) *Ireland: A General & Regional Geography*. London: Methuen and Co. pp. 181-185.

[522] Ibid., 199.

[523] I was surprised to find that rush lights were used well into the 1970's in the west of Ireland, even when electricity had been laid on to the cabins. My cousin, Thomas Murphy, of Aughoos, Pullathomas, County Mayo remembers his father, Packie, making rushlights. The pervasive, land damaging rushes had to be removed to improve the land and were at least put to good use.

[524] As in the case of Michael Porter's farm placement.

[525] Baker, Patrick Joseph. (1994-1997) *Correspondence to William McGowan.*

[526] Somerville-Large, Peter. (1985) *Cappaghlass.* London: Hamish Hamilton. p. 342.

[527] Although in the case of Michael and Willie McGowan, perhaps also Paddy, consent from the living parent to such a placement might not have been forthcoming. Residential care can be less threatening than foster care to many parents who let their children go into care.

[528] Baker, Patrick Joseph. (1994-1997) *Correspondence to William McGowan.*

[529] John (Sister of Nazareth, Sligo). *Discussions with author* (2012-2016).

[530] Baker, Patrick Joseph. (1994-1997) *Correspondence to William McGowan.*

[531] Ibid.

[532] Ibid.

[533] Ibid.

[534] Ibid.

[535] Ibid.

[536] Organised by the Sisters with Paddy after Paddy was re-housed at Nazareth House.

[537] His own account, therefore, appears to contradict his own 4 placements. It is also contradicted by the Nazareth House records which have him leaving there in 1938 as recorded in: Nazareth House, Sligo. Details of cohort of boys who entered 1925-1932 and their destination and subsequent careers after discharge (Quartet's contemporaries). So this placement would have been in 1938, almost certainly making it his third placement. I don't think this means he was lying or even wrong about the placements; rather omitting some aspects that did not fit in with the story he was telling, and being confused about the order of his placements.

[538] Baker, Patrick Joseph. (1994-1997) *Correspondence to William McGowan.* This placement may have been the same one as Michael Porter experienced. The farm circumstances and location are certainly very similar.

[539] Ibid.

[540] Ibid.

[541] Ibid.

[542] Ibid.

[543] Ibid.

[544] So Paddy's whereabouts was well known to Nazareth House just as Michael Porter's 4 placements were tracked by the Sisters.

[545] It would be almost impossible to exaggerate how important security was to the Homeboys.

[546] Had Paddy ventured an answer it would in any case have been wrong. It would have exaggerated his age by up to 2 years because he did not know his date of birth (1923) and had taken his birth date from the Nazareth House foundation stone (1921). The request to know Paddys age would seem related to Jimmy planning a future in the Irish Army for his young brother. He would soon have realised that Paddy's youth would not make that plan a reality for some time.

[547] Baker, Patrick Joseph. (1994-1997) *Correspondence to William McGowan.*

[548] Ibid.

[549] As the unemployed miners, steelworkers and shipbuilders in Britain complained it took a war before government remembered them and did something to find them work; their enemy, Hitler, was the gatekeeper to work. Yet again crises force social changes rather than need being responded to at the time.

[550] Common, Jack. (1951): *Kiddar's Luck.* London: Turnstile Press. pp. 7-8.

[551] John (Sister of Nazareth, Sligo). *Discussions with author* (2012-2016).

[552] McCormack, William (Bill). (Undated). *An Angel Held My Hand.* Internet uploaded account of the author's experiences at Nazareth House, Sligo: 1943-1952.

[553] John (Sister of Nazareth, Sligo). *Discussions with author* (2012-2016). A number of the boys did become priests while others became religious Brothers.

[554] John (Sister of Nazareth, Sligo). Unpublished booklet: *Some Details from Records of Events in Nazareth House, Sligo. 1910-1941.*

[555] *The Sligo Champion.* Saturday April, 12th, 1934. p. 12.

[556] *People Like Us* (1997) London: The Stationery Office. p. 97.

[557] *Ibid.*, 99.

[558] Porter, Michael Laurence. (2012-2016) *Interviews with author.*

[559] At least at this period. Sister Attracta's successor was reported to be physically abusive. See: McCormack, William (Bill). (Undated). *An Angel Held My Hand.* Internet uploaded account of the author's experiences at Nazareth House, Sligo: 1943-1952.

Summerhill College was intensely disliked by Father Flanagan of Boys Town, Nebraska, a former student there, and by Willie McGowan. That Michael Porter had heard rumours of physical beatings and sexual interest in boys by priests there suggests significant concerns about the College at this period. Significant, too, because future priests would have been the subject of these activities.

No concerns were raised about sexual impropriety at the Marist Brother's school in the inter war period but several teachers, two of them Brothers, have been convicted of sexual abuse on boys there in the post-war period.

[560] Contrast this with a Local Authority in England which between 1970 and 1994 lost records on 400 of the 3000 children who had been in its care and did not know the leaving care whereabouts of 97 of these children. *Children's Safeguards Review* (1997) Edinburgh: Social Work Services Inspectorate for Scotland. p. 17.

[561] McCormack, William (Bill). (Undated). *An Angel Held My Hand.* Internet uploaded account of the author's experiences at Nazareth House, Sligo: 1943-1952. The testimony is all the more powerful because the author was not otherwise averse to criticising failures at Nazareth House in the 1950's.

[562] Kipling, Rudyard. (1943) *Rudyard Kipling's Verse: The Definitive Edition.* p. 443.

[563] John (Sister of Nazareth, Sligo). Unpublished booklet: *Some Details from Records of Events in Nazareth House, Sligo. 1910-1941.*

[564] See for example: McCarthy, Michael, J.F. (1914) *Priests and People in Ireland:* London: Simpkin, Marshall, Hamilton and Kent. p. ix. Also Ibid., 226-227 and Appendix, p. x.

[565] Swords, Liam. (2004) *A Dominant Church: The Diocese of* Achonry, *1818-1960.* Blackrock, Co. Dublin: The Columba Press.

[566] Ibid., 527.

[567] Siskind, A. B. (1986) Quoted in *Children's Safeguards Review* (1997). Edinburgh: Social Work Services Inspectorate for Scotland. p. 255.

[568] McAleese, Deborah. (2014) *BelfastTelegraph.co.uk.* 21.05.2014.

[569] Ibid., 15.

[570] Meynell, Alice. (1889) *The Poor Sisters of Nazareth, An Illustrated Record of Life At Nazareth House, Hammersmith.* London: Burns and Oates. p.40.

[571] Almost certainly after a recommendation from the Sisters at Nazareth House.

[572] Baker, Patrick Joseph. (1994-1997) *Correspondence to William McGowan.*

[573] 'Give me a dozen healthy infants , well-formed, and my own specified world to bring them up in and I'll guarantee to take any one at random and train him to become any type of specialist I might select.' Watson, John Broadhurst: *Behaviourism* (1945), p. 104. Quoted in Bartlett's Familiar Quotations, p. 949.

[574] O'Crohan, Tomas. (1967) *The Islandman.* Oxford: University Press. p. 242

Made in the USA
Charleston, SC
23 September 2016